AF660951

WORLD TRADE AND DEVELOPMENT

Economic Integration, Regional Blocs and Non-Members

Edited by

RAJ KUMAR SEN
KARTIK C. ROY
CLEMENT A. TISDELL

ATLANTIC PUBLISHERS AND DISTRIBUTORS
in collaboration with
INTERNATIONAL INSTITUTE FOR DEVELOPMENT STUDIES (IIDS)

Published by
ATLANTIC PUBLISHERS AND DISTRIBUTORS
B-2, Vishal Enclave, New Delhi-110 027
Phones 5413460, 5429987

Sales Office
4346/4C, Ansari Road, Darya Ganj,
New Delhi-110 002
Phones 3273880, 3285873, 3280451
Fax 91-11-3285873
E-mail:gupta.atlantc@axcess.net.in

Copyright © The IIDS, 1997

ISBN 81-7156-734-7

No part of this book may be reproduced in any form without permission from the publisher except for the quotation of brief passages in criticism

Typeset at
APD Computer Graphics, Delhi
Printed in India at
Mehra Offset Press, Delhi

Preface

The World Trade Organisation (WTO) which has replaced the GATT as the apex organisation of the World Trading System has come into being at a time when the World Trading System is being increasingly subdivided into many regional trading blocs. While the GATT was formed to apply and uphold the principle of multilateralism and non-discrimination in world trade, the supranational trade organisation also allowed the creation and existence of regional trading blocs under its clause XXIV.

As a result, different regional blocs have been formed with the European Union being the most formidable one.

While the net welfare effect of such regional blocs is uncertain they certainly can improve the welfare of their members at the expense of that of non-members. This is where the problem lies.

A large country such as India which needs to achieve and maintain high growth rates to provide a minimum standard of living to its burgeoning population will be at a disadvantage in trade negotiations with powerful trading blocs. Many other countries are in a similar situation. Although India is a member of South Asian Association for Regional Co-operation (SAARC), this organisation since its formation has achieved very little on any regional issue or global issue.

Therefore, it is quite important to initiate an informed debate on the issue of regional trading blocs and non-members in the World Trading System. It is with this intention that the present Volume has been published. A large number of articles have been devoted to the discussion of the implications of European integration for India and other Asia Pacific economies. Since the APEC has the potential to be in a position to exercise strong influence on world trade in the foreseeable future, a chapter has been devoted to the discussion of APEC and its implications.

Also, it seems that the Indian Ocean grouping may also become a reality. Hence a note on this issue has also been included.

Since China's emergence as a super economic power has significant implications for world trade, a chapter has been devoted to China.

Finally, how the small island economies can fare in such an international economic environment has also been discussed with reference to a case study of Fiji. It is hoped that this Volume will generate sufficient discussion and debate on these issues which would be of considerable benefit to policy-makers in different countries whether belonging or not to any trading bloc.

Quite a few of the articles included in this Volume were presented in the IIDS 1st International Seminar on Issues of European Economic Integration and Small Island Economies. The Appendix of this Volume includes a report from the Rapporteur on these papers.

The IIDS wishes to express its sincere appreciation to the Faculty Members of Department of Economics, University of Queensland and specially to Professor C.A. Tisdell, Head of the Department, for taking the initiative in matter of publication of this Volume and also for their contribution for this purpose.

The editors are thankful to Dr. K.R. Gupta of M/s Atlantic Publishers and Distributors, New Delhi for agreeing to publish this Volume.

The editors also wish to thank all others who have been associated in one way or another with the publication of this Volume.

September, 1997
Calcutta and Brisbane

RAJ KUMAR SEN
KARTIK C. ROY
CLEMENT A. TISDELL

Contents

List of Contributors

1. Dr. Raj Kumar Sen, Dept. of Economics, Rabindra Bharati University, Calcutta.
2. Dr. Kartik C. Roy, Dept. of Economics, University of Queensland, Brisbane.
3. Dr. Clement A. Tisdell, Professor of Economics, University of Queensland, Brisbane.
4. Dr. Joseph C.H. Chai, Dept. of Economics, University of Queensland, Brisbane.
5. Dr. K.P. Kalirajan, Australia South Asia Research Centre, Research School of Pacific and Asian Studies, ANU, Canberra.
6. Dr. R.T. Shand, Australia South Asia Research Centre, Research School of Pacific and Asian Studies, ANU, Canberra.
7. Dr. J.C. Debnath, Professor of Economics, North Bengal University, Raja Rammohanpur, West Bengal.
8. Dr. S.N. Guha Thakurata, International Institute for Development Studies, Calcutta.
9. Mr. Debesh Bhowmik, Pritinagar, West Bengal.
10. Mr. Supriyo Bhattacharya, Dept. of Economics, Kalyani University, West Bengal.
11. Dr. Santikumar Ghosh, Professor of Economics (*Retd.*), Rabindra Bharati University, Calcutta.
12. Mr. Bipul Malakar, Dept. of Economics, Jadavpur University, Calcutta.
13. Mr. Haripada Bhattacharya, Dept. of Marketing, Dhaka University, Dhaka.
14. Mr. Zhicun Gao, Dept. of Economics, University of Queensland, Brisbane.
15. Mr. Biman C. Prasad, Dept. of Economics, University of Queensland, Brisbane.
16. Dr. Sujit Kumar Ghosh, Dept. of Economics, R.K. Vidyamandir, Belur Math, West Bengal.

1

Economic Integration, Regional Blocs and Non-Members in World Trade and Development : Issues and Implications

K.C. ROY and C.A. TISDELL

Introduction

In recent years serious challenges to the GATT principles of multilateralism and non-discrimination appeared on the world trading scene in such forms as managed trade, aggressive unilateralism and regionalism. The growth of such forces may certainly have been contributed to by a sense of insecurity felt by big players such as the United States in the world trading system due to the performance of countries like Japan and by the resultant feeling that the current multilateral trading system is now unable to handle issues such as unfair trade policies followed by member countries. While the growth of protectionism after the second rise in oil prices in the early 1980s and the consequent world recession may have provided the reasons for the United States to make allegations of unfair international trade practices, the most important factor, as Bhagwati (*1991*) suggests, has been the relative decline of the United States within the world economy, as the super economic power leading to, what he called, "the diminished giant syndrome". Similarly, diminished giant syndrome occurred in Britain at the end of the nineteenth century, when Germany and the United States were the rising economic powers on the world scene.

However it is quite apparent that this unfair trade allegation is systematically used by the big players like the United States to rationalise their actions to extract concessions from others like Japan by a threat of tariff retaliation under a policy of aggressive unilateralism. Similar set of factors along with the frustration with the slow pace of negotiation with the Uruguay Round negotiations also are at work to strengthen the forces of regionalism in world trade.

Since the formation of the European Common Market in the late 1950s, while a number of important actual or nascent trading blocs such as ASEAN, APEC, SAARC, Gulf Co-operation Council (GCC) have been formed, the European Union has also become bigger by the inclusion of more and more countries. It is important to note that the formation of regional trading blocs is in conformity with article XXIV of the GATT which allows the creation and existence of free trade areas and customs unions.

Theoretical Basis and Motivation for Regional Trading Blocs

No definite conclusion can be drawn from economic theory as to whether such trading blocs can improve the welfare of their members or the world as a whole. Viner (*1950*) mentioned that the difference between trade creating and trade diverting unions of countries that maintained external tariffs would lie in the fact that the trade creating unions would create trade among its member countries at the expense of inefficient industries in its member countries. On the other hand, trade diverting unions would do so at the expense of more efficient industries in the non-member countries. While Viner's seminal work sought to disprove the common belief that any preferential move towards a total free trade was necessarily welfare improving, Bhagwati (*1992*) sought to prove that preferential moves can indeed be welfare improving depending on the parameters. Overall, the trading blocs can be said to be beneficial for its members if trade creation exceeds trade diversion, other things being equal (*Shiells 1995*). According to the theory, however, trade creation and trade diversion tend to focus exclusively on production costs although the benefits to consumers from lower prices should also be taken into account in estimating the welfare implications of a trading bloc for a region. Lower price of imports from a member country will encourage consumers to substitute partner imports for both domestic substitutes and non-partner imports whereas gains to consumers from lower prices will tend to increase the welfare of member countries. Moreover, the rationalisation of the industry structure resulting in the closing down of inefficient plants and improvements in the operational efficiency of others will also contribute to welfare gains.

However, the most significant dynamic gains that can accrue from the formation of a customs union is the increased competition that results, when trade barriers among member nations are dismantled, producers in each member nation will be forced to become more efficient to meet the competition of other producers within the union or go out of business. The enlarged market will allow even a small number to enjoy greater economies of scale. In addition, foreign direct investment is likely to be stimulated, leading to capital accumulation and higher economic growth. The massive investment in the European union in the mid-1950s and mid-1980s to set up the so called "tariff factories" bears testimony to this fact. Gains to the member countries could also arise from the reduction in long run average cost resulting from learning by doing, improved product quality and greater product varieties (*Salvatore 1995*). Apart from these, trading blocs by acting as a single unit in international trade, monetary, and even political negotiations would have much more bargaining power than all of its members separately. This certainly is true in the case of the EU.

While the factors noted above will provide strong incentives for countries to form trading blocs, the motivation may vary from region to region and from country to country. Nevertheless, as Shiells (*1995*) suggests, the following motivations seem to play a key role in the formation of trading blocs.

(i) To obtain economic benefits from achieving a more efficient production structure by exploiting economies of scale through spreading fixed costs over larger regional markets, increased economic growth from foreign direct investment, learning from experience etc.

(ii) To pursue non-economic objectives such as strengthening political ties and managing migration flows.

(iii) To ensure increased security of market access for smaller countries by forming regional trading blocs with larger countries.

(iv) To improve members' bargaining strength in multilateral trade negotiations or to protest against the slow pace of trade negotiations.

(v) To promote regional infant industries which cannot be viable without a protected regional market.

(vi) Finally, to prevent further damage to their trading strength due to further trade diversion from third countries.

As new trading blocs are formed and existing ones are enlarged, the diversion of trade from third countries by making the exporters' interests stronger than those of import competing firms, may strengthen the forces of political factors in third countries in favour of joining the blocs.

It has to be noted, however, that political factors may also prevent countries from forming a bloc or existing members from making it a well integrated community. This is true of South Asian countries despite the diversion of trade from these countries to member countries in many trading blocs around the world.

Regional Bloc and European Union as Trading Blocs

During the early 1990s efforts were made to achieve greater integration among countries in Africa, Middle East, South Asia, East Asia and America. While ASEAN has been in existence for many years, and the members signed a pact called ASEAN Free Trade Agreement (AFTA), the progress towards well integrated trading blocs has been very slow in Africa and South Asia. The recent devaluation of CFA Franc led the Economic and Customs Unions of Central African States to make progress towards reforming their tariff structures and gradual abolition of intrabloc duties. The South Asian Association for Regional Cooperation (SAARC) has been in existence in name only during the ten years of its existence. All it has managed to secure is an agreement among members to draft a preferential trading arrangement. However, two recent most significant and potentially very powerful regional blocs that have come into existence are Asia Pacific Economic Co-operation Form (APEC) and North Atlantic Free Trade Association (NAFTA). APEC is working on an agenda to significantly reduce tariffs on imports from other member countries, whereas NAFTA may become the most powerful rival of the EU by virtue of its members being also powerful members of APEC.

The European Union

The performance of powerful blocs such as EU has significant implications for member and non-member countries. If a trading bloc performs well, the welfare of member countries increases but at the same time, the welfare of non-member countries may diminish. This is more so for a very large and powerful union like EU as

(a) a small percentage decline in its total imports from non-members may mean a large decline in exports to EU of individual non-members; and

(b) a substantial increase to EU in export of one non-member due to special arrangements or political factors may occur at the expense of export of another non-member even when the share of import from non-members in total EU imports does not decline.

Since the EU satisfies the World Trade Organisation (WTO) rules, and has introduced some trade liberalisation measures on an MFN (most favoured nation) basis, one can say that the EU has not damaged the export trade of non-members and, so far, it may also appear that the rapid expansion of intraregional trade has not been at the expense of non-members although it is possible that non-members' trade with EU might have grown even faster in the absence of the Union.

The European Union passed through three distinct phases in its move towards greater European integration:

Phase I : 1958-69 : During this phase, the original six members set up a common external tariff at the average of 1957 tariffs of six members, eliminated internal tariffs and other quantitative restrictions and established a Common Agricultural Policy (CAP).

Phase II : 1970s and early 1980s : Restrictions on free movement of labour and capital were reduced, the European Council assumed prominence and the membership increased to 12 by 1986.

Phase III: Since mid-1980s : The Union cooperated with neighbouring non-members more closely and implemented the Single Market program. From January 1, 1993, it removed all remaining restrictions on the free flow of goods, services and resources including labour among its members thereby becoming a single unified market (*Salvatore 1995*). The inclusion of Finland, Sweden and Austria, makes it the largest trading bloc in the world.

Table 1 presents a comparative economic profile of EU, NAFTA and Japan. The first three rows of the table show the position of each country in respect of each indicator in 1991. While NAFTA's population and GDP are slightly lower than those of EU, its per capita income is about $605 less than that of EU and its export, import and total trade values are far below those of EU. The last two columns show the position of EU vis-a-vis those of NAFTA and Japan in respect of these indicators. The value of EU's exports, imports and total trade are about 255 percent, 234 percent and 244 percent of those of exports, imports and total trade of NAFTA. Furthermore, EU's export, import and total trade values account for about 575.5 percent, 669 percent and 618 percent of those of Japan. These are indicative of the massive trade creating and trade diverting powers of the EU.

TABLE 1

Economic Profile of EU, NAFTA and Japan, 1991

(value in US dollars)

Item	Population (millions)	GDP (billions)	Per Capita GDP ($)	Exports (billions)	Imports (billions)	Total Trade (billions)
EU	367.35	6633.40	18059.10	1999.81	1912.86	3912.67
NAFTA	363.30	6404.10	17454.00	782.20	818.50	1600.70
Japan	123.50	3362.30	26930	347.50	286.00	633.50
Total EU as % of						
(a) Total NAFTA	111.11	103.58	103.45	255.66	233.70	244.43
(b) Total Japan	297.44	197.28	67.05	575.48	668.83	617.62

Source: IMF (1993) : *International Financial Statistics Year Book*, Washington D.C.

EU and Member Countries

Several studies have been undertaken to estimate the overall impact of the EU on welfare of its members. One study concluded that the trade creation effects for industrial products totalled $6.2 billion and trade diversion effect amounted to $2.2 billion during 1965-67 and trade diversion was pronounced in agricultural commodities and raw materials (*Carbaugh 1991*). Recent studies show that the real income gains to the EU of somewhere between 2.4 and 3.4 percent of GDP is below the European Commission's estimate of somewhere between 4.3 and 6.5 percent (*Shiells 1995*). On the other hand Cecchini's 1988 study showed that the increase in employment due to the removal of customs formalities, opening of public procurement, liberalisation of financial services and supply side effects would be about 1.9 million.

EU and Non-members

Some indication of how non-members have done, however, can be obtained by examining trends of non-member imports into the EU. If appropriately scaled import volumes do not fall, gains to members have most likely not come at the expense of third parties. The term non-member needs to be defined clearly. A non-EU member may be a member of another powerful trade bloc. In this case, the damaging effect of EU's trade diversion on this non-member may be outweighed by the favourable trade creation effect of its own bloc. But if another non-member does not belong to any trade bloc or belongs to a very weak trade bloc, then the trade diverting effect of EU on this non-member would be quite severe. There are many countries which belong to the second category of non-members.

For these countries, in agriculture and raw materials, the CAP has led to significant trade diversion and welfare losses due to price effects. In manufacturing, pockets of discrimination continue to persist, although import restrictions on industrial goods from third countries were removed. The CAP, however, was reformed substantially in 1992 to make producers more responsive to demand conditions.

The Case of India

India as a non-EU member and a non-member of any powerful trading bloc is expected to suffer from the trade diversion effects of the European Union.

One way of examining the effects of trade diversion on India would be to look at (i) the share of imports from India in EU's total imports from the world; and (ii) the hypothetical increase in income from exports to EU, if 1970 share of India in EU's total import had been maintained.

TABLE 2

The EU's Total Import from the World and from India

Item	1970	1980	1985	1990	% increase between 1970 and 1990
1. Eu's total world import (US $ million)	110,378	829,645	823,432	2,361,127	+2239.12
2. Import from India (US $ million)	376	1,840	1,560	5,114	+1260
3. 2 as % of 1	0.34	0.22	0.18	0.31	

Sources : (a) Government of India (1995) : *Economic Survey 1994-95*, New Delhi.

(b) IMF (1993): *International Financial Statistics Year Book*, Washington D.C.

Tables 2 and 3 present some interesting results. Table 2 shows that the Community's total import from the world increased from 110.4 billion US dollars in 1970 to 2361.12 billion US dollars in 1990. This represents an increase of 2239.12 percent. Import of the Community from India during the same period increased from 376 million US dollars to 5.11 billion US dollars thus recording a rise of only 1260 percent. The last row of the table shows that India's share in EU's

TABLE 3

Hypothetical Increase in India's Earning if 1970 Share in EU's Total Imports had been Maintained (US$ million)

	1980	1985	1990	Total
India's actual earning from export to EU	1840	1560	5114	8514
Hypothetical earning	2820	2799	8028	13647
Increase/decrease in earning	+982	+1239	+2914	+5133

Source : Prepared from Table 2.

import continued to decline from 0.34 percent in 1970 to 0.18 percent in 1985. Although by 1990 it recovered significantly, it never reached the 0.34 percent as in 1970.

Table 3 shows what extra income India could have earned if the same 1970s market share had been retained by India in EU's total import in subsequent years. It shows some startling results. EU's total import from India in 1980, 1985 and 1990 could have been 13647 million US dollars instead of the actual amount of 8514 million US dollars. Hence India would have obtained an extra income of 5.13 billion US dollars.

This analysis would, therefore, indicate very roughly that India appears to have suffered considerably from the trade diverting effect of the European Community. Hence while a trading bloc may be beneficial for its members since its trade creation effects exceed trade diversion effects, it may not necessarily mean that it improves overall world welfare in Pareto's sense. Countries like India which do not belong to any powerful economic union are placed in a difficult situation.

On the one hand, they need to negotiate with the powerful trading blocs to gain some trade concessions and at the same time they need to improve their economic performance at home considerably so that their goods and services remain competitive in the world market. Gaining concessions is not so easy when the non-member's bargaining position is weak and does not belong to a powerful trading bloc. Therefore, on the one hand, non-members need to implement appropriate economic policies and development programmes to improve the performance of their economies and to open up their markets, and on the other hand, to try to form or be a member of a regional bloc. India has precisely been doing all these things. The opening up of India's markets will increase the export and investment opportunity of larger trading blocs. They, then, in return might hopefully grant greater concessions to India. A similar trend is already being noticed in China and EU trade relationship.

Removing Difficulties to Global Free Trade

Since the current rise of regionalism is likely to endure and gain strength because of the facts that (i) the United States, which was a pro-GATT player in the post-War period, changed its attitude on article XXIV and (ii) the Congress feels that the GATT is inadequate and the "regional card" should be played as a threat to those who will not move fast enough to change the GATT to suit America's desires and interests (*Bhagwati 1991*), it is necessary to comment on how the regional trading blocs can be designed so as to promote global free trade not just the welfare of members.

The GATT specifies in article XXIV that a free trade area should eliminate barriers to most trade among members. The article ought to be adhered to — to comply with WTO requirement. If MFN tariffs are lowered as trade between members is freed, the risk of trade diversion may be reduced. Also if liberal rules are applied for accession of members to the bloc, then liberalisation would also spread to the new members. Pressure for protection through anti-dumping measures against members and non-members should not be acceded to. It may be difficult to implement all these measures. Nonetheless, the coverage of most trade policies should be to remove most restrictions on global free trade. In this respect, the powerful trading blocs will have to take the lead.

The end of 1992 was the deadline for the completion of a single market which would include the removal of border controls on intra-EU goods shipments and the movement of people, harmonisation of indirect taxes, establishment of minimum product standards, removal of domestic regulatory barriers to cross-border provision of services, elimination of public procurement practices favouring national producers, and EU-wide competition policy to help assure free movement of goods between EU member states (*Shiells 1995*).

However, much work still remains to be done in some areas like the implications of the EU for India's future trade and development.

On the other hand, Australia, having been outside the powerful trading bloc, understood quite well the disadvantages of being left alone in a world of regional trading blocs. Therefore, it successfully took the initiative to form the Asia Pacific Economic Cooperation grouping (APEC). It includes all powerful Asia-Pacific countries and members of ASEAN and in time, it could provide a strong challenge to the EU. The combined economic strength of APEC and NAFTA would be awesome and its political implications would be far reaching. Economic performance of some of the smaller non-member countries and their difficulties in a trading world of regional blocs is also worth noting. At the other end of the spectrum of the sizes of nations, China's increasing integration with the world economy has far reaching implications for the global trading environment. Because of many similarities between the Chinese and Indian economies, China provides an interesting competitor. It is therefore important to consider the current trends and institutional variations in world trading arrangements and economic development. Since the current trends and changes in the global trading system are going to persist for some time, each nation should study these carefully and consider their consequences for future policy.

REFERENCES

Bhagwati, J. (1991) : *The World Trading System at Risk*, Princeton: Princeton University Press.

Carbaugh, R. (1991) : *International Economics*, Belmont: Wadsworth.

Cecchini, P. (1988) : *The European Challenge* : 1992, Brookfield, vt: Gower.

Government of India (1995) : *Economic Survey 1994-95*, New Delhi: Government of India.

IMF (1993) : *International Financial Statistics Year Book*, Washington D.C.: IMF.

Salvatore, D. (1995) : *International Economics*, New Jersey: Prentice Hall.

Shiells, C. (1995) : ''Regional Trading Blocs: Trade Creating or Diverting'', *Finance and Development*, 32(1).

Viner, J. (1950) : *The Customs Union Issue*, New York: Carnegie Endowment for International Peace.

2

Economic Transformation and Integration in Europe — Consequences for Asian-Pacific Countries

CLEM TISDELL

Introduction

We live in a dynamic and interdependent economic world which is generating considerable uncertainty about the economic future for Asian-Pacific countries, not the least India. Developments in Europe and in North America are fraught with consequences for the international trade of countries in the Asian-Pacific region for the flow of foreign aid to LDCs in the region and for foreign direct investment in countries in the Asian-Pacific area. These concerns arise from: (1) the likely impact of the single European Market for EC members, and the possible extension of this to other countries in Europe in the future; (2) uncertainty about the economic and political future of countries formerly a part of or associated with the Soviet Union and (3) the future consequences of the North American Free Trade Association (NAFTA). Asian-Pacific countries are afraid of reduced trade possibilities as a result of these developments, less foreign direct investment in them and less foreign aid. Most of the *final* export markets for exports from Asia and the Pacific are in Europe and North America. Although Japan is the main destination of Australia's exports, many of these are primary and intermediate inputs for goods exported by Japan to North America and Europe, markets on which Japan still heavily relies for its exports even if less so than in the past.

The EC was supposed to become a single Market in 1992 for commodities with the EC adopting uniform policies in relation to foreign trade. Also in that year it was planned that the Maastricht Treaty would be ratified by the 12 members of the EC. The long-term objective of this Treaty was complete monetary union by the end of 1999 and political union by the end of 2010. But the Danes rejected the Treaty, and the British expressed disquiet about it. Modifications to the Treaty are likely. "While union is still the most likely outcome in Europe, the timetable and final form of that union remains unclear", (Commonwealth Bank, *Economic Newsletter*, Sydney, Nov., 1992, p. 3). The Maastricht Treaty raises many problems for liberalism and creates some difficulties for Germany in its adoption of policies favourable towards Eastern Europe which it particularly wants to adopt to reduce the flow of Eastern European migrants to Germany (*Schmieding, 1992*).

Economic Developments in Europe and Impact on the Asia-Pacific Region

The establishment of a single European Market for EC members means that trade within the EC becomes truly unrestricted. This should mean that substantial economies of scale and specialisation should be obtained thereby making it more difficult for imports to the EC to compete and lowering the price at which industrial commodities can be exported from the EC. It has been said that "The concept of a Single Market is founded on the belief that the Community must make a quantum leap in productivity and competitiveness if it is to compete effectively with United States, Japan and the NICs, but this also means an improvement in competitiveness *vis-a-vis* the other Third World exporters. Other things being equal, this would mean a further redirection of trade away from traditional suppliers and towards partner EC members, analogous to the redirection that occurred after the initial elimination of internal tariffs. This is the trade diversion or price effect of 1992" (*Davenport, 1990,* p. 182). However, a free market and labour movements can also result in social disruption such as now appears to be occurring in Germany and which could arise elsewhere given existing levels of unemployment.

A particular fear of non-European countries is the possibility of a 'fortress Europe' — a Europe looking inward with relatively free internal markets protected from the outside world. Furthermore, there are fears that barriers to imports to the EC might be raised if the EC feels threatened by NAFTA or Japan. Even though the European Commission has not given an assurance that Europe will not be a 'fortress Europe' but a 'partnership Europe', developing countries still remain concerned because the Commission's assurances are general in nature. The formation of a single European internal market has been undertaken primarily to benefit Europeans and to compete more strongly with other economic groupings perceived to pose an economic threat. One writer has said, "Europe has an interest and an obligation to compete with the United States of America, or rather with NAFTA — the North American Free Trade Area — and with Japan, or rather with what the Japanese economists call the 'flying wild geese' — the formidable regional economic bloc in the making, composed of Japan as the leading goose, followed by the NICs, and in turn, by the ASEAN countries" (*Emmerij, 1990,* p. 224).

Economic theoreticians have predicted that apart from a trade diversion effect, a trade creation effect will occur because of rising incomes in Europe as a result of the single market in the EC. The net economic impact on the exports of non-EC countries such as India will depend on the balance of these effects. The European Commission has argued that on balance the import effect is likely to be positive. But it is difficult to generalise and one also has to take into account the impact of the single market on macroeconomic stability and employment. If for instance, the single market makes it more difficult to maintain employment in Europe the positive macroeconomic income effect mentioned by the Commission may be negligible or non-existent. In the case of India, it might be argued that the trade diversion effect could be small because most of India's exports to Europe consist of goods in which economies of scale and/or high technology as a component are small, e.g. clothing, shoes and leather goods. In addition, the trade creation effect may very well be minor.

While the European Commission predicted a 4.5 to 7 percent boost in the GDP of the EC as a result of the Single Market and because of multiplier effects and income elasticities a 10-20 percent increase in the imports of the EC, this does not mean that India's exports to the EC will increase by 10-20 percent. Given that the income elasticity of demand for India's exports to the EC are low, very little increase in India's exports can be expected from the income effect. Taking both trade diversion and income effects together, very little impact on India's exports to the EC seem likely as a result of current EC development. But as far as the trade of the EC with Eastern Europe and the longer term possibility for closer association of a number of East European countries with the EC are concerned, India could experience considerable 'trade diversion'. Many of the exports or potential exports of Eastern Europe are similar to those of India and so a displacement effect is likely.

As far as India is concerned external assistance (grants and concessional loans) constitute a most important component of its capital inflow (*Government of India, 1992,* p. 164). But its grant component has been falling and concessional terms for loans are now less available to India. This trend is likely to continue and even accelerate as a result of changes in Eastern Europe. EC members are likely to favour aid and loan concessions for assisting, stabilising and reconstructing Eastern Europe economically at the expense of countries like India. Furthermore, with the end of the Cold War India is not in position to play one superpower off against another to increase its aid support. A considerable reduction in foreign aid for India is to be anticipated. In addition, given the proximity of Africa to Europe and humanitarian considerations, there may be a tendency for European aid to concentrate on LDCs in Africa in the future.

India has not pursued an 'open-door' policy in relation to foreign investment in India. Foreign direct investment in India has been small and as recently pointed out:

> "Foreign investment has played a very limited role so far in the Indian economy...resulting from a relatively restrictive foreign investment regime followed by the Government till recently. Foreign technology was allowed generally in the areas of hi-tech, sophisticated technologies and substantial exports. The normal ceiling for foreign investment was 40 percent of the total equity capital, but a higher percentage of foreign equity, was considered in priority industries if the technology was sophisticated and not available in the country, or if the venture was largely export-oriented" (*Government of India, 1992,* p. 77).

However, the Indian Government has recently adopted a more liberal foreign investment policy and is cautiously moving towards the structural economic adjustment policies of a free trade nature as favoured by the IMF. Nevertheless, India is considered unlikely to adopt doctrinaire free market policies (*Gupta, 1992*).

One of the impacts of developments in the EC is likely to be to divert foreign direct investment away from other regions. Multinational companies based in Japan and the United States may prefer to invest in the EC rather than in third countries so as to take advantages of economies of scale and to be sure of being behind possible foreign trade walls. Thus a diversion of private investment funds from third countries, such as India, is possible. However, since private investment in India is small, this effect on India would also be small.

It should be noted that the effect of political disruption and uncertainty in the former USSR and in Eastern Europe has been extremely unfavourable to India. In 1989-90 just under 20 percent of India's exports went to this area. This trade has now been reduced and disrupted and remains uncertain because of political uncertainties in or near the Confederation of Independent States (*Government of India, 1992*, p. 70). The situation in this part of the world is of direct economic concern to India as well as considerable political significance to it.

The likely overall economic impact on India of Europe developments could well be as summarised in Table 1. This suggests the economic effect on India of the establishment of the Single Market

TABLE 1

Qualitative Impacts on India's External Economic Situation of European Developments

Impact	Sign and Size for India
Single Market for EC	
Trade Diversion	≃ 0. Small or zero reduction in India's exports to EC
Income Effect	≃ 0. Slight increase in India's exports to EC
Foreign Direct Investment	≃ 0. Zero or slight redirection of FDI away from India
Increased Competitiveness of EC Industries	Zero or slight increase in manufactured imports to India from EC
Net Expected EC Effect	Slightly **negative** or zero
Changed Status of Eastern Europe	
Trade	Significant losses for India
Aid and Finance on Concessionary Terms	Significant losses
Political and Economic Uncertainty	Significant losses
Net Eastern Europe Effect	Significantly negative

in the EC is likely to be small but that the economic effects on India of political/economic change in Eastern Europe could be considerable. Eastern European changes could have a significant adverse economic effect on India via trade diversion by the EC to East European countries away from India, aid diversion, and to a lesser extent, by redirection of foreign direct investment in favour of Eastern Europe. Further, economic disruption of some East European countries due to political upheavals and uncertainties will have adverse consequences and trade agreements are likely to be increasingly based on economic rather than political considerations, a factor which may be to India's disadvantage compared to the past.

It might be argued that since India's foreign trade as a proportion of its GDP is relatively small, its foreign trade dependence is small and that therefore some loss in its foreign trade would not seriously disrupt its economy. In 1989, for example, India's exports amounted to less than 6.2 percent of its GDP and its imports to 8.4 percent of its GDP. However, a closer look at the composition of India's exports suggests that its economy has become quite trade dependent and that any substantial fall in its imports could greatly affect the operation of its economy. One of the main reasons for this is the heavy dependence of India on energy imports which are essential to the operation of the 'modern' component of its economy.

Table 2 sets out the top five imports of India as a percentage of its total import bill for 1990-91. Petroleum, oils and lubricants head the list followed by capital goods, pearls and precious stones, chemicals and fertiliser. All of these seem relatively essential to the operation of the Indian economy in its present form. While pearls and precious stones may not seem essential, they are the basis of a very important export industry for India. Having already followed a parsimonious import policy, it would be difficult for India to prune its imports further.

Small Indo-Pacific Island Economies and European Developments

Many small Indo-Pacific countries have a particular interest in European economic developments because they are beneficiaries from the Lome Convention e.g. Mauritius and Fiji. The Fourth Lome Convention was signed in December, 1989 and will run for ten years. It provides an umbrella for EC aid to developing countries in African, the Caribbean and the Pacific and for agreements providing preferential

TABLE 2

India's Main Imports as a Percentage of its Value of Total Imports 1990-91

	Commodities	%
1.	Petroleum, oils and lubricants	25
2.	Capital Goods	24.2
3.	Pearls and precious stones	8.7
4.	Chemicals	7.4
5.	Fertilisers	4.1
	TOTAL	69.4

Source: Government of India, *Economic Survey* 1991-92, p. 68, New Delhi.

trade access for these countries to the EC. It has been said that the Lome Convention is intended "to create an unbreakable set of interrelations between Europe and the developing countries, with African a particular priority" (*Lister, 1991,* p. 21). In addition, France still has overseas territories in the Indo-Pacific e.g. Reunion, New Caledonia and French Polynesia, and these are directly affected by European developments.

Most of island economies in the Indo-Pacific are heavily dependent upon foreign aid to maintain their levels of per capita income and have a high degree of reliance on exports of primary products e.g. in the case of Mauritius and Fiji, sugar exports and in the case of the Maldives, tuna exports (*McKee and Tisdell, 1990*). In recent times, however, light manufacturing has developed in some of these island states, e.g. clothing manufacture in the Maldives and in Fiji, and there has been considerable development in service industries, particularly tourism, involving international exchange (*Cole, 1992; Elek, 1992*). This has been facilitated by significant improvements in international transport and communications. International tourism is, for example, important for the Maldives, Mauritius, Reunion and the Seychelles in the Indian Ocean and for Fiji, Guam and Hawaii in the Pacific.

Tourists from Europe are the main source of tourism from Indian Ocean islands, whereas in Pacific Islands, Japan and the United States are the most important sources of overseas tourists with Australia and New Zealand being an important source for these South Pacific islands in their proximity, e.g., Fiji and the Cook Islands.

European economic influence in the Pacific Island has shown a relative decline (*Cole, 1992; Elek, 1992*) and has been to an increasing extent replaced by Japanese influence, e.g. in the Solomons. However, the economic influence of the United States in the Pacific islands still remains strong by territorial necessity. Hawaii is a State of the United States and several territories are integrally connected to the United States, e.g. Guam, American Samoa, the Marshall Islands, the Federated States of Micronesia. The only European power to maintain its influence in the Pacific has been France. While this was threatened in the 1980s by a secessionist movement in New Caledonia, the political situation there now appears to be stable. At the present time, there is little indication of any change in the political and economic position of France in the Pacific but the influence of Britain has been much reduced.

With the possible exception of French territories in the Pacific, it seems likely that most Pacific islands will drift towards closer economic relations with East Asia. This has happened even in the case of United States associated territories. Japanese tourists, for example, account for the majority of tourism in Guam and in Saipan. On the other hand, Indian Ocean islands are likely to continue to have close economic connections with Europe and up to a point with India because of ethnic connections and proximity. European tourism can, for example, be expected to remain the mainstay of foreign tourism to the islands of the Indian Ocean because of their relative proximity of Europe and the higher per capita income on average of Europeans than Africans and South Asians. Tourism, especially foreign tourism, displays a relatively income elastic demand.

One suspects that as a result of developments in Europe, Indian Ocean islands will not be disadvantaged economically — they may even gain if European incomes rise, and the EC may recognize the special economic dependence of these islands on Europe. In the case of the Pacific islands, it might be anticipated that, except for French territories, European foreign aid and trade concessions will continue to be reduced and so developments in Europe will be to their disadvantage.

Possible International Responses of India to European Developments

India has in the past followed a 'non-aligned' policy in international relations. In the past this has enabled it to obtain economic advantage from the rivalry of major powers, to obtain foreign aid more easily and to build up trade with both Western and Eastern Europe. Furthermore, the development of political tensions between the former Soviet Union and China tended to be to in India's favour because to some extent China is a potential export competitor for India and a rival for political influence in Asia, e.g. in Burma and Indo-China. Now, however, the international economic situation has changed completely and new alignments and political arrangements do not appear to have had time to solidify. As a result India's past international economic and political policy would be of little advantage of it in the current situation.

How will India respond? Will India try to strengthen SAARC (the South Asian Association for Regional Co-operation), try to form a new trading bloc, join an emerging trading block, take some other special economic actions or attempt to respond on a broad front?

Prospects for strengthening SAARC do not seem strong possibly to a large extent because the exports of the countries concerned tend to be competitive. It has been suggested that alternatively India might try to link up with Asia-Pacific basin countries, an area which shows considerable economic growth, e.g. become a member of the Association for Pacific Economic Co-operation (APEC). However, India has relatively slight economic links with East Asia as we have already seen. International economic links would need to be developed further before this area be of prime interest to India. India is unlikely to become more closely integrated with East Asia in the near future.

The situation of India in this regard has been well summarised by S.P. Gupta as follows :

> "The South Asian economies under SAARC are attempting to work out a Preferential Trade Agreement between the member countries. But for many political reasons the economic integration under the SAARC aegis is seen to be rather slow. It is therefore commended that rather than on regional basis the individual member countries of this region should try to come closer with the South East Asian blocs on bilateral basis. In this context it should be remembered that India has already a special relation with ASEAN as 'dialogue partner' but unfortunately no member countries of SAARC unlike China or Vietnam has formally approached to be a member of APEC" (*Gupta, 1992*, p. 14).

One of the main aims of APEC has been to try to counteract international tendencies towards restrictions on international trade.

This is one of the reasons why it has been of particular interest to Australia (*Elek, 1992 a,b*). The Australian Government believes that it is in Australia's interest to support free trade policies because Australia is not a member of a major trading bloc. India has not in the past adopted free trade policies and there is little evidence that it is about to do so. However, in 1991 India introduced a number of structural reforms designed to make for a more market-oriented economy. However, as Gupta (*1992*) points out, implementation of these reforms has been sluggish and difficult for democratic and bureaucratic reasons, "There is a fear from time to time that unless the governments of this region [South Asia] can meet the social cost of adjustment specially among the large majority of poor and maintain the infrastructure development of the country, the reform process may get reversed." (*Gupta, 1992,* p.5). Given the social structure of India, full fledged free market policies seem unlikely to survive politically.

In the light of the above, it seems likely that India's response to European and other international developments will be on a broad front. India is likely to press for continuing favourable conditions under the Commercial and Economic Co-Operation Agreement between the EC and India, an agreement first entered into in 1981 and designed to develop measures to bridge India's trade deficit (*Sangwan, 1991*). Trade agreements with the newly emerging (emerged) East European Central Asian countries will also be pursued but the results here will be more uncertain than in the past. Apart from this, one might expect India to take an opportunistic stance in relation to other areas of the world, including East Asia, especially Southeast Asia. Overall India's international economic policies are likely to be more reactive than proactive in the foreseeable future, with China maintaining a lead over India in terms of economic growth. Consequently, India and South Asia as a whole face a more difficult international economic climate than that which has confronted them in recent decades.

REFERENCES

Cole, R.V. (1992) : "External Economic Relations of Pacific Island States". A paper presented at APDC Conference on "The Future of Asia-Pacific Economies: Pacific Islands at the Crossroads" held at Griffith University, Brisbane, November 1992.

Davenport, M.W.S. (1990) : "The External Policy of the Community and its Effects upon the Manufactured Exports of Developing Countries", *Journal of Common Market Studies*, Vol. 29, pp. 181-200.

Elek, A. (1992) : "The South Pacific Economies in a Changing International Environment". *Op. cit.* Cole (1992).

Elek, A. (1992a) : "Trade Policy Options for the Asia-Pacific Region in the 1990s" : The Potential of Open Regionalism," *The American Economic Review*, Vol. 82, No. 2, pp. 74-78.

—— (1992b) : "Pacific Economic Co-operation : Policy Choices for the 1990s," *Asian-Pacific Economic Literature*, Vol. 6, No. 1, pp. 1-55.

Emmerij, L.J. (1990) : "Europe 1992 and the Developing Countries : Conclusions", *Journal of Common Market Studies*, Vol. 29, p. 243-253.

Gupta, S.P. (1992) : "Global Economic Development and the Asia Pacific Economies — The South Asian Outlook". *Op. cit.* Cole (1992).

Government of India (1992) : *Economic Survey 1991-92*, New Delhi.

Lister, M.R.R. (1991) : "Rebalancing Lome : Human Rights, South Africa and the Future", *Journal of World Trade*, Vol. 25, No. 5, pp. 21-35.

Mckee, D. and C. Tisdell (1990) : *Developmental Issues in Small Island Economies*, Praeger, New York.

Sangwan, S. (1991) : "The European Community and the Non-Associated Countries : The Trade Agreement between the EEC and India", *Journal of World Trade*, Vol. 25, No. 3, pp. 33.

Schmieding, H. (1992) : *Maastricht : A Dead End of European Integration*?, Institut fur Weltwirtschaft, (Kiel, Discussion Papers, No. 192).

3

APEC and Its Implications

JOSEPH C.H. CHAI, KARTIK ROY and CLEM TISDELL

I

Origin of APEC

The idea of a Pacific economic community can be traced back to Kojima's proposed PAFTA (Pacific Free Trade Area) at an international conference in 1965 in Tokyo (*Rieger, 1989,* p. 21 and *Soesastro, 1994,* p. 80). Similar to the formation of ASEAN, PAFTA is a defensive move in response to the establishment of EEC in 1957. Kojima's PAFTA envisaged the formation of a free trade area (FTA) among 5 advanced Pacific nations (Australia, Canada, Japan, New Zealand and the U.S.) with associate memberships being offered to developing Asian and Latin American countries who wish to join (*Kojima, 1971*).

The immediate response of Pacific rim countries to Kojima's proposal had been far from enthusiastic for various reasons. One of the reasons has been the fear of Japanese domination of the economic gains of PAFTA. According to Kojima's original estimate based on trade statistics in 1965, Japan would benefit most through "the cheaper imports of raw materials and other primary products (and) the expansion of her exports of light manufactures" (*Kojima, 1977,* pp. 175 and 177) under PAFTA. Her trade balance would improve substantially as her exports would rise by 56 per cent and her imports by only 15 per cent. On the other hand, while the U.S.'s trade balance would remain more or less unaltered, imports were estimated to rise more rapidly than exports for Australia, New Zealand and Canada leading to a severe worsening of their trade balance which was mainly caused by the uncompetitiveness of their manufacturing industry. For the developing nations in the Pacific rim, the estimated increase of their exports generated by their increased access to advanced Pacific rim countries has been modest.

Another reason has been the lack of interest of developing Asian countries in Kojima's proposal. This is partly due to the historical animosity of Asian countries against Japan for the concept of a Pacific community led by Japan resembles that of the infamous Great East Asian Co-Prosperity Sphere established by the Japanese occupation forces during the Second World War. It is also partly due to the inward-looking trade strategy of import substitution adopted by these countries at that time which made them reluctant to open their domestic markets for foreign countries' exports.

And yet another reason has been the lack of interest of developed Pacific countries in the proposal. On the one hand, the U.S. was still committed to a multi-lateral trading system at that time and hence opposed to any new geographically discriminatory trade arrangement. On the other hand, Australia and New Zealand were still very much committed to protecting their own manufactured industries and hence were very unlikely to tolerate Japanese imports to wipe out a significant proportion of their manufactured industries (*Arndt, 1967*).

In view of the above, for the next decade (1966-1975), little progress had been made in Asia-Pacific economic cooperation with the exception of the formation of PBEC (Pacific Basin Economic Council) in 1967. PBEC is a private organisation established by business groups with 5 national committees (Australia, Canada, Japan, New Zealand and the U.S.). Its objective is to promote the study and discussion of issues of Asia-Pacific economic cooperation (*Soesastro, 1994,* p. 80).

In the late 1970s, however, there had been a change of wind which led to the revival of interest in the concept of a Pacific economic community. This time, Australia had taken over from Japan and became the main promoter of the idea. Two factors appear to have contributed to this new development. One is the increased popularity of Kahn's thesis that the centre of world economy is shifting from the North Atlantic to the Pacific (*Kahn, 1979*) because of the rapid growth of Japan in the 1950s and 1960s which was followed by that of the Asian NICs in the 1970s. Another factor is the increased integration of the Australian economy into the Asian and especially the Northeast Asian economy.

To translate the idea into reality, an Australian academic, John Crawford, and his Japanese counterpart, Saburo Okita, proposed the setting-up of some kind of OECD in the Asia-Pacific region under the name of OPTAD (Organisation for Pacific Trade and Development).

This proposal attracted the interest of the U.S. and subsequently, Peter Drysdale and Hugh Patrick had been commissioned to carry out the feasibility study of such an organisation in 1978 (*Soesastro, 1994,* p. 82). Further action at the government level occurred in 1980 when Prime Minister Fraser of Australia and Prime Minister Ohira of Japan convened a Pacific Community Seminar at ANU (Australian National University) which led to a series of tripartite conferences known as PECC (Pacific Economic Cooperation Conferences) involving government officials, businessmen and academics to discuss the issues of Asia-Pacific economic cooperation (*Rieger, 1989,* p. 22). Finally, in 1989 Prime Minister Hawke of Australia proposed to institutionalise a loose inter-government consultation at ministerial level on economic issues of common interest among the Asia-Pacific countries which led to the formation of a 12-nation forum known as APEC.

Entering the 1990s, the APEC integration process accelerated amidst a rapidly changing international political and economic environment after the collapse of communism. The signing of the Maastricht Treaty in 1993 which committed Europe to an economic union and the expectation that most of the former Eastern European countries are likely to join the EU in the 1990s renewed the fear of Asia-Pacific countries of being excluded from the European market and generated pressure for them to step up their regional integration effort. At the same time, the U.S.'s increased disillusion with the GATT progress in achieving the goal of multi-lateral free trade and the elimination of "unfair" trade practice as well as her increased displeasure with EU's inward-looking policy has transformed the U.S.'s position from opposing to supporting a regional trade arrangement (*Lloyd, 1992,* p. 30). As a result, the U.S. had launched her own trade bloc, the NAFTA (The North American Free Trade Area) in the early 1990s with an initial membership of Canada, Mexico and the U.S. and at the same time she endorsed the formation of APEC. Finally, not least, the changing trade strategy of the developing Asian countries also contributed significantly to the acceleration of the APEC integration process. The spread of export-oriented trade strategy from the Asian NICs to the ASEAN countries and China together with the increased competitiveness of their manufactured industries led to an increased liberalisation of their import regime and heightened their interest in an APEC free trade area.

The acceleration of the APEC integration process occurred in 1993 in the Seattle meeting when a regular annual summit among their political leaders was agreed upon. In the summit meeting in the following year in Bogor in Indonesia, member countries committed themselves to form an APEC free trade area and hence APEC was transformed from a loose consultative forum into a regional trade arrangement. A two-tier deadline was agreed upon with developed APEC members to fully liberalise their trade and investment by 2010 and the developing APEC members by 2020. By 1995, APEC membership has expanded to 18 (Australia, Brunei, Canada, Chile, China, Hong Kong, Indonesia, Japan, Malaysia, Mexico, New Zealand, Papua New Guinea, the Philippines, South Korea, Singapore, Taiwan, Thailand and the U.S.).

Nature of APEC

The precise nature of APEC regionalism is still very much undefined and hence the confusion it created. For instance, in a recent paper on the implication of APEC, the authors mistakenly assumed that the APEC FTA proposed in Bogor declaration is the same as the conventional FTA (*Lewis et al., 1995*). In fact, the kind of regionalism underlying APEC is open regionalism which is in sharp contrast to the conventional discriminatory regionalism. Under discriminatory regionalism, a region group reduces trade barriers between themselves without extending them to imports from non-member countries. Under open regionalism, in contrast, regional groups agree to reduce trade barriers among themselves and extend the reduction to non-member countries on an unconditional MFN basis as well (*Garnaut and Drysdale, 1994* p. 2).

Open regionalism, being non-discriminatory, has the economic merit of avoiding the trade diversion effects of the discriminatory regionalism. However, a difficulty with this kind of regionalism is the free rider problem i.e. non-member countries like EU and India would benefit from APEC's trade barrier reduction without being required to reduce their own barriers.

To deal with the free rider problem, several proposals have been advanced. One proposed by the American members of APEC is to extend the benefits of trade liberalisation to non-member countries on conditional MFN basis i.e. trade barrier reduction is extended to those non-member countries that reciprocate (*Bergsten, 1994,* p. 222). This approach is opposed by most of the non-American APEC members especially Australia for it represents a retreat from open regionalism. Another approach which is proposed by Australia and some other

TABLE 1

General Equilibrium Research on Impacts of APEC

Studies and Policy Change	Effects			
	Welfare		Distribution of Welfare Gain	Structural Change
	Member	Non-member		
1	2	3	4	5
1. Murtough *et al.* (*1994*) Policy Change: Eliminate all distortions on an MFN basis (a) of all APEC countries (b) of advanced APEC countries only Data base: 1988 Sector/market: 7/15 Model: GTAP	Real income change (a) 1.8 (b) 1.2	(a) -0.7 to -1.4 (b) -0.7 to -1.2	(a) China: 9.8 Malaysia: 9.2 Indonesia: 3.1 Philippines: 8.6 Thailand: 3.3 Taiwan: 2.2 Australia 3.4 Japan: 1.3 U.S.: 1.1	(a) Substantial adjustment pressure, e.g. Australia large decline of manufacturing output (-21.4 to -42.1%) and large increase of agricultural and resource-based output (6-38%).
2. Dee and Wash (*1994*) Policy Change: Removal of distortion (a) in manufacturing sector on discriminatory basis (b) in manufacture on discriminatory and agriculture on MFN basis Data base: 1988 Sector/market: 37/16 Model: Salter	(a) -0.7 (Australia) (b) 0.4 (Australia)	NA NA	NA NA	(b) Moderate adjustment pressure in Australia manufacturing output fell by 0.04% and agricultural and resource output rise by 10-11%.

(*Contd.*)

TABLE 1 (Contd.)

1	2	3	4	5
3. World Bank (*1994*) Policy Change : 50% reduction off tariff plus liberalisation of FDI in (a) East Asia on MFN basis (b) East Asia on discriminatory basis Data base: 2000 Sector/market: 7/19 Model: Unknown	(a) 2.1 (b) 1.2	(a) 0.1 (EU) (b) -0.1 (EU)	(a) China: 4.0 ASEAN: 5.0 NICs: 1.4 Japan & U.S.: 0.1 -0.2	(a) Considerable adjustment pressure for developing APEC. China: imports rose by 21% and exports rose only 15%. ASEAN: imports rose by 8% and exports rose by only 4%
4. Lewis *et. al.* (*1995*) Policy Change: Eliminate both TBs and NTBs on preferential basis Data base: 1992 Sector/market: 10/6 Model: GTAP	Real GDP growth (a) Static effect 0.0 -2.6% (b) dynamic effect 0.2 - 4.2%	(a) 0.0 (b) 0.0	(b) ASEAN: 4.7 NICs: 3.2 China: 2.2 Japan: 1.4 U.S. 0.2	(b) Considerable adjustment pressure; output of grain fell by 20% in Japan and 17% in Asian NICs with massive relocation of labour and capital out of grain and agriculture to manufacture in these countries.

Note: Percentage difference between observed real income in the model base year and that which would have been recorded with the relevant policy change in place.

Source: BIE (*1995*) and Lewis *et al.* 1995.

These studies also suggest that adjustment cost associated with APEC trade and investment liberalisation could be substantial for some countries. If this cost is taken into account, the net welfare gain for some member countries would be further reduced. Another neglected area in these studies is the environmental cost of APEC trade and investment liberalisation.

As for non-member countries, the cost of APEC liberalisation appears to be inconsequential as both TD and free ride effect appear to be modest. Thus the debate on the desirability of open vs discriminatory regionalism centering around the issue of how to minimise the free ride problem appears to be barking at the wrong tree.

II

APEC and India

The implications of APEC for India would depend on how APEC finally takes shape. If it becomes a formal organisation for negotiations on trade policies which Australia and the U.S. want rather than a forum for discussion which East Asian economies particularly Korea, China, Japan and Malaysia want, then, of course, it would have considerable implications for India. India would then have to deal with 3 giant trading blocs in three continents — EU, NAFTA and APEC. If the dominance of APEC reaches such a stage that it significantly diminishes the importance of ASEAN, then India would have to negotiate separately with APEC for trade concessions.

While at the present time trade diversion under APEC may appear to be smaller, it could become quite considerable in future if trade in agricultural products is liberalised. Such liberalisations would help immensely Australia, United States and Canada but could adversely affect non-member countries such as India as imports from such countries could be replaced by imports from APEC countries.

The World Bank, OECD and the GATT Secretariat estimated that the income effects of the implementation of the Uruguay Round Package will add between 213 and 274 billion U.S. dollars annually to world income (*Government of India, 1995*). The GATT Secretariat further estimated that while the total merchandise trade will increase by 745 billion U.S. dollars by the year 2005, the largest increases will be in the areas of clothing (60%), agriculture, forestry and fishery products (20%) and processed food and beverages (19%). Since India's existing and potential export competitiveness lie in these product groups, India expects to obtain large gains in these sectors provided the more important package relating to market access in textiles, garments and agriculture are implemented. Hence India would be benefiting from agricultural trade liberalisation measures under APEC provided these are extended to regional non-members on the basis of open-regionalism. But this seems unlikely at the present time as Australia, which opposes any retreat from open regionalism along with a few other APEC countries, wants to pursue trade negotiations on products where APEC countries are predominant suppliers. Such a move, if successful, would confine the benefits of trade liberalisation to the member countries.

As mentioned in chapter one, one way of minimising the adverse impacts of a trading bloc is to formulate and apply liberal rules for accession of non-members to the bloc allowing the liberalisation to spread to the new members. While one would have expected that the continuation of outward-oriented economic reform in India would have enabled it to become a member of APEC, upon its application for membership, it would seem that the rules for accession of non-members to the group are not liberal.

Being a non-member, India entered into bilateral trade negotiations with individual members of ASEAN and other non-ASEAN countries in East Asia in the same way as it did negotiate with individual members of the EU. Since the economic reform process began in India, India's merchandise trade with Malaysia, Singapore, Thailand and Indonesia has been rising. Among other East Asian countries, significant increases have been recorded in India's trade with Hong Kong, Taiwan and South Korea as Table 2 illustrates.

Row 1 of the table shows that India's exports to four ASEAN members increased significantly up to 1993, then declined in 1994. But its exports to Hong Kong, Taiwan and South Korea continued to rise even after 1993. The total exports to the two regions as a proportion of India's total export reached 14.73 percent in 1993 from 8.06 percent in 1988 (row 5). Furthermore, as row 9 illustrates, India's total trade with both regions rose continuously from 8.58 percent of its total world trade in 1988 to 11.85 percent of total world trade in 1994.

India would like to see that the shares of these countries in India's total export trade and merchandise trade do not decline as a result of APEC's retreat into old-style discriminatory regionalism. At the present time, India has maintained a reasonable surplus in its invisible trade account, but with the gradual opening up of the economy larger

TABLE 2

India's Merchandise Trade with South East and North East Asia

(Percent of total world trade)

		1988	1990	1991	1992	1993	1994
	India's exports to:						
1.	ASEAN members (Indonesia, Malaysia, Singapore, Thailand)	3.09	4.04	5.28	6.20	7.28	5.97
2.	North East Asia (Hong Kong, Taiwan, South Korea)	5.01	4.61	5.96	6.62	7.44	8.09
	India's imports from:						
3.	ASEAN members (Indonesia, Malaysia, Singapore, Thailand)	5.88	6.21	4.00	5.78	4.22	4.61
4.	North East Asia (Hong Kong, Taiwan, South Korea)	3.07	3.82	3.50	3.65	3.07	5.16
5.	Total export to two regions	8.06	8.66	11.24	11.84	14.73	14.07
6.	Total import from two regions	8.95	10.04	7.61	9.43	7.30	9.77
7.	Total trade with ASEAN members (4 countries only)	4.73	5.27	4.63	5.97	5.71	5.27
8.	Total trade with North East Asia (3 countries only)	3.85	4.16	4.67	4.54	5.20	6.58
9.	Total trade with both regions (7+8)	8.58	9.44	9.30	10.52	10.91	11.85

Source: IMF (1995) *Direction of Trade Statistics Year Book*, Washington D.C.

payments on transportation and investment income could create deficit on invisible trade account.

Hence relaxation of restrictions by APEC members on services trade would be beneficial to India as private transfer alone accounts for a substantial proportion of total receipts in services trade in India's current account balance of payment. In 1991, this item accounted for nearly 40 percent of total receipts in services trade.

Thus, it would appear that India's interests would be best served if the rules of accession of non-members to the group are relaxed and India joints the grouping as a member.

Otherwise India's interest would be better served if the group is not converted into a customs union.

III

APEC: Some General Considerations and Environmental Questions

The prospects for APEC are at this time (1995) still unclear. In particular it is uncertain how quickly and whether APEC countries will comply with the Bogor declaration that industrialised countries should remove all obstacles to free trade by 2010, with developing countries doing likewise by 2020. While the Osaka Action Plan drawn up in 1995 seems to exclude no sector from trade liberalisation the phrasing of the plan is reported (*The Courier Mail, 17 November, 1995,* p. 1) to be such that it allows some scope for flexibility or manoeuvre. Just how much scope is uncertain but Prime Minister Dr. Mahathir of Malaysia has emphasised that adherence to APEC resolutions is voluntary.

The time period required for the establishment of the APEC free trade region is relatively long from a *political* viewpoint. Political climates can change considerably in a decade or two. Furthermore, the non-attendance of the U.S. President at the Osaka Summit due to the budget crisis at home (because the President faces a hostile Republican-dominated Senate) has been interpreted by some to indicate that the U.S. does not give a high priority to APEC and may be keeping its options open about the nature of its development. On the other hand, Australia remains a leading proponent of the proposal for this open regional trading bloc.

Arguments in favour of such free trade arrangements are usually made on the basis of economic efficiency considerations. The situation, however, from a socio-economic point of view is liable to be much more complex than this. For example, free trade may in some circumstances fail to promote economic production and welfare to the maximum extent, may be to the disadvantage of particular countries, and have unwelcome income distribution and environmental impacts. It is dangerous to consider free trade as a cut-and-dried issue (*Tisdell, 1982,* Ch. 18).

The free trade argument does not, for example, accommodate the theories of List (*1983*). While one must be careful of a selective industry approach to economic development, its appropriate use could improve the development prospect of peripheral or backward economies. China would, for example, become restricted by APEC in its scope for using such policies which according to Nolan (*1993*) have played an important role in the development of other East Asian economies. This may be one reason why China's involvement in APEC has been cautious. Even in Australia, differences of opinion exist about whether a free trade industrial policy should be pursued or whether key infant industries should be encouraged by government support and concerted action.

The income impacts of APEC raise some issues. Free trade arrangements suggest that the positive income-effects of APEC could be considerable. But in dynamic world, involving external economies, learning phenomenon, barriers to entry and so on, it is far from clear that free trade always maximises the collective income of a group that engages in it. However, in any case, freer trade between APEC members is liable to have an impact on the distribution of income. In APEC *as a whole* relatively unskilled labour may be the most abundant factor. Free trade may result in the real wages for such labour being depressed in the more 'developed' APEC countries such as the USA and Australia. Freer trade conditions may already be impacting on this low-income group. On the other hand, if skilled capital-intensive labour is relatively scarce in APEC as a whole, such labour could gain in relative income terms by APEC's proposed policies, at least in the short to medium term.

In the longer term, it is probably naive to think that the currently more 'developed' APEC countries will retain their dominant position in relation to human capital. Investment in education has expanded greatly in East Asia and can be expected to do so even more. In the longer term, one must expect Asian countries to increase considerably their stock of human capital. The importance, for example, of India doing this has been recently stressed by Dhesi (*1993*).

In relation to the environment, a view has been propagated by some members of the World Bank that structural adjustment policies and freer trade are as a rule environmentally friendly (*e.g. Sebastian and Alicubusan, 1989*). If this were the case, APEC would be a step in the environmentally appropriate direction. However, there are also counter arguments to this which need to be considered and these are, for example, outlined in Tisdell (*1994*). To the extent that APEC increases demand on natural resources and total production, it is liable to place more demands on the natural environment, add to pollution and may accelerate loss of biodiversity. Problems for sustainable development may surface more quickly than expected, especially for a large country such as China (*cf. Tisdell, 1995*).

In addition under conditions of freer trade, individual countries may be less inclined to place restrictions on polluting or environmentally damaging industries for fear of losing international trade. On the other hand, higher incomes, if they occur, are liable to see greater value being placed on an improved natural environment because demand for environmental goods (many of which in economic terms are public goods) tends to rise with income. Now, for instance, that incomes are higher in Taiwan, there is increased demand for improved environmental quality there and this is reflected in increased budget allocations for this purpose. Unfortunately, however, some of the past environmental impacts of Taiwan's economic growth are only reversible at considerable cost or are irreversible. There is the further sobering possibility that economic growth in Asia could have adverse global environmental consequences, the impact of which can only be reduced or accommodated by more developed countries significantly lowering their global environmental loads. APEC members have not as yet squarely faced such issues.

IV

Concluding Comment

While considerable optimism exists in Australia about Australia's likely benefits from an APEC free trade zone, it has been suggested that no one really knows what the magnitude of these benefits will be (*Charlton, 1995*). The Prime Minister of Australia (*1995*), Mr. Keating, sees APEC as a suitable vehicle for Australia to benefit from economic growth in the Asia-Pacific. It is even suggested that APEC trade liberalisation could create an additional 500,000 jobs in Australia by 2010. However, it is difficult to say to what extent some of these claims are political 'hype'. Much is being made by Mr. Keating of the fact that Japan, Indonesia, and China have agreed to reduce trade barriers on a wide range of commodities (*The Courier Mail, 20 November, 1995*, p. 1). However, some of these changes may have already been in the pipeline and it is too early to judge the extent to which these are the first steps in the establishment of a free trade area.

Nevertheless, APEC remains a useful political forum and is improving political networking in the Asia-Pacific.

It is too early at this time to say how APEC will develop. A number of participating countries may still be keeping their options open by continuing their involvement in discussions. Certainly there are considerable disparities between countries (*Hirsh*, *1995*) which may make it difficult for APEC to keep to its free trade time table. Given the different stages of development of APEC countries, it may be very difficult to ensure a complete free trade area by 2020. Furthermore, APEC countries do not appear to have fully considered the income distribution, environmental and development consequences of the free trade proposal. The economic theory of customs unions that has been used to bolster support for the EU and NAFTA may need modification for APEC, even though a group of neoclassical Australian trade economists and policy-advisers (mainly at the Australian National University) appear to believe that traditional economic theory can be applied to APEC without modification for institutional differences and that it is safe to ignore the theories of List (*1983*) and those of Myrdal (*1956*). Such economic dogmatism (which is politically in Australia) needs to be counterbalanced by a dose of economic scepticism from a scholarly standpoint. Otherwise, there may be no debate, little enlightenment and the possibility of unwise policy choices by Australia and other nations. This is not, however, to deny that APEC is a useful forum for its participants.

REFERENCES

Arndt, H.W. (1967) : ''PAFTA : An Australian Assessment'', *Intereconomics*, No. 10, pp. 271-276.

Bergsten, C.F. (1994) : ''APEC and the World Economy: a force for worldwide liberalisation''. R. Garnaut and P. Drysdale, *Asia Pacific Regionalism*, Pymble: Harper Educational, pp. 218-224.

Bureau of Industry Economics (BIE) (1995) : *Potential Gains to Australia from APEC*, Canberra: AGPS, 1995.

Charlton, P. (1995) : ''Figures Falling on Level Playing Fleld'', *The Courier Mail*, 20 November, p. 6.

Dhesi, A.S. (1991) : ''The Emerging Trading System — some implications for LDCs'', *Development*, Vol. 1, pp. 54-57.

Elek, A. (1995) : ''APEC beyond Bogor : An Open Economic Association in the Asian Pacific region'', *Asian-Pacific Economic Literature*, Vol. 9, No. 1, 1995, pp. 1-15.

Garnaut, R. and Drysdale, P. (1994) : ''Asia Pacific Regionalism : the issues'', *Asia Pacific Regionalism*, op.cit., pp. 1-8.

Government of India (1995) : *Economic Survey 1994-95*, New Delhi.

Hirsh, M. (1995) : ''Which Asian Model?'' *The Bulletin*, November 21, pp. 52-56.

IMF (1995) : *Direction of Trade Statistics Year Book*, Washington D.C.: IMF.

Kahn, H. (1979) : *World Economic Development 1979 and Beyond*, London: Croom Helm.

Kojima, K. (1971) : *Japan and a Pacific Free Trade Area*, London: Macmillan.

—— (1977) : *Japan and a New World Economic Order*, London: Croom Helm.

Lewis, J.D. *et.al.* (1995) : Beyond the Uruguay Round : The Implications of an Asian Free Trade Area, *China Economic Review*, Vol. 6, No. 1, pp. 35-90.

List, F. (1983) : *The Natural System of Political Economy*, London : Frank Cass, First published in German, 1837.

Lloyd, P.J. (1992) : ''Regionalisation and World Trade'', *OECD Economic Studies*, No. 18, Spring, pp. 8-43.

Myrdal, G. (1956) : *On International Economy: Problems and Prospects*, London: Routledge and Kegan Paul.

Nolan, P. (1993) : *State and the Market in the Chinese Economy*, London: Macmillan.

Rieger, H.C. (1989) : ''Regional economic co-operation in the Asia-Pacific region'', *Asian-Pacific Economic Literature*, September, pp. 5-33.

Sebastian, I. and Alicubusan, A. (1989) : ''Sustainable development: issues in adjustment lending policies'', Environment Department Working Papers 1989-6, Washington D.C.: World Bank.

Singh, H. (1995); ''Exposing the hidden agenda of APEC'', *Third World Economics*, 16-31 January, pp. 11 - 15.

Soesastro, H. (1994) : ''Pacific economic cooperation: the history of an idea'', *Asia Pacific Regionalism*, op. cit., pp. 77-88.

Tisdell, C.A. (1982) : *Microeconomics of Markets*, Brisbane: Wiley.

—— (1994) : ''Conservation, protected areas and the global economic system: how debt, trade, exchange rates, inflation and macroeconomic policy affect biological diversity'', *Biodiversity and Conservation*, Vol. 3, pp. 419-436.

—— (1995) : ''Asian development and environmental dilemmas'', *Contemporary Economic Policy*, Vol. 13, pp. 38-49.

Wonnacott, P. (1995) : ''Merchandise trade in the AP region: is there a scope for liberalisation on MFN basis?'' *The World Economy* (Global Trade Policy), pp. 33-51.

—— and Wonnacott, R. (1992) : ''The Custom Union issue reopened'', *The Manchester School*, June, pp. 119-135.

4

Indian Ocean Grouping (IOG) : An Emerging Reality ?

K.P. KALIRAJAN and R.T. SHAND

Introduction

The primary objective of GATT (now WTO) has been to set non-discriminatory multilateral rules for trade in goods and services. However, this cannot be done in a static framework owing to the new emerging issues around the world which affect international transactions. For example, when GATT was formalised, its concern was only to set rules for trade in goods. But, later, the substantial increase in trade in services due to technological and communication developments led to its inclusion under the purview of GATT. The Uruguay Round contributed significantly to the achievement of this objective. While it took a long time to set rules for trade in services, their implementation would have a major impact. Under these circumstances, groups of economies which trade intensively with each other have felt the need to address emerging issues in smaller groups under the structure of economic co-operation. Political forces or in some cases market forces can initiate such co-operation. The cases of a single market for the EEC countries in 1992, and vouching for closer cooperation among the APEC nations in 1994 are respectively the most recent examples of this approach.[1] Market-driven economic co-operation which is the core of so-called 'open regionalism' discussed by Garnaut and Drysdale (*1994*), facilitates the process of 'globalisation' of nations to progress smoothly and steadily.

With the landmark economic reforms in South Asia and political changes in South Africa, several issues concerning trade and investment have emerged within the Indian Ocean region and internationally. Given the existing political frictions between some of the major IOG countries, initiatives for economic cooperation are less likely to be mooted by the political forces. The question investigated in this paper is whether market forces rather the governments could induce an Indian Ocean Grouping (IOG) structure to solve newly emerging development issues in the region. This paper is a part of a major research study titled 'the *Indian Ocean Trade and Investment Project* (INDOTIP) undertaken by the authors within the Australia South Asia Research Centre at the Australian National University. The study represents the first comprehensive attempt to document and analyse recent patterns and trends of trade among the Indian Ocean Rim countries.

The following section briefly discusses the process of internationalisation that has been taking place in some of the major Indian Ocean economies. The next section describes the method of analysis used in this paper. Results of the empirical analysis are discussed in the following section. Prospects and problems for economic co-operation are analysed in a final section.

Internationalisation of Key IOG Countries

There are some 47 littoral and land-locked countries in the Indian Ocean Rim (Table 1). A common feature in many of these IOG economies is that long term economic growth depends on economic transformation along a continuum, from initial reliance largely on primary sector production for export to the establishment of modern and efficient industrial sectors. Current and future rates of growth in IOG countries arguably are closely related to their ability and willingness to make investments in productive capacity and infrastructure. Whilst a majority of IOG countries remained closed and inward-looking, they lacked technical know-how and sufficient capital to modernise their industrial sectors.

The Uruguay Round of the GATT negotiations started in 1986 brought the developed and developing countries within the region together and initiated a productive dialogue on domestic policies affecting the free flow of trade, transfer of technology and even labour mobility between countries. At the forum, the GATT member countries, in principle, agreed to liberalise international trade in non-agricultural commodities and services. The promotion of trade in a multilateral context necessitated the member countries to reform their domestic policies to ensure free trade and mobility of capital, and transfer of technologies. The tariff and non-tariff barriers impeding the free flow of goods and mobility of factors of production, therefore, had to be removed. The beneficial effects of trade liberalization reached at the

GATT negotiations were reinforced by the marketisation in Eastern Europe and former Soviet Union. Thus, the post Uruguay Round talks of 1986, saw a period of outward orientation in many countries.

As in other parts of the world, IOG countries have made significant progress in outward orientation, though, they differ widely on the extent, pace and in the policy instruments. It is difficult to analyse the policy changes in individual IOG countries separately here. However, the common features of transformation include: ensuring macro economic stability through fiscal and monetary policies, currency devaluation to ensure realistic exchange rates, investor-friendly policies to attract flow of capital and technology, elimination of non-tariff barriers, general reduction in tariff rates and removal of exchange controls to gain outward orientation, and achieving greater efficiency in resource allocation through privatisation, deregulation of prices and marketing of industrial and agricultural products.

In the process of internationalisation, India introduced a first set of trade reforms in July-December 1991 which aimed to eliminate the subsidy scheme for exports and to reduce import licensing restrictions. In April 1992, additional reforms were introduced to eliminate virtually all licensing restrictions on imports of capital goods and intermediates. In March 1994, near full current account convertibility was established. The maximum tariff was reduced from 350 per cent in 1990-91 to 65 per cent since March 1994 with significant reductions also for tariffs below the maximum. The Union Budget for 1995-96 has further reduced the maximum tariff rate to 50 per cent. Import duties on machine tools have been reduced from 35 per cent to 25 per cent and tariffs on computers have been reduced from 65 per cent to 40 per cent. Export duty on finished leather has been completely abolished. Even after the reductions in import duties announced in the 1995-96 Budget, import tariffs continue to be slightly high and consumer goods imports are still restricted.

Evidence of the past decade indicates that structural adjustment in Australian manufacturing industries is being accomplished. The fact that export growth has been consistently strong since the mid eighties implies that the moderate rate of structural transformation taking place in the Australian economy is producing results. As a result of recent strong growth in manufactured exports, there has been a decline in the deficit on manufactures as a ratio of GDP after a long period of rises. This has occurred despite the increasing level of import penetration within the context of increasing international integration of the Australian economy. This in turn reflects Australia's commitment to reduce trade-inhibiting regulations and to allow competitive forces to shape trade flows.

South Africa's major structural weaknesses comprise of a highly protected manufacturing sector, a bloated public sector and slow growth. Apartheid and the effect of sanctions have left South African manufacturing largely unprepared to do away with inefficient industries and adjust to the non-protectionist post-Uruguay Round trade environment. South Africa's import control mechanism is still in place but it has not been used to limit imports for some years. However, within GATT limits, tariff protection is given to industries to counter dumping and against goods from countries with lower wages. Surcharges are applied at times to contain imports which reach high levels at times. In August 1988, the surcharge was raised as high as 60 per cent on some items in a bid to contain imports, but in May 1989 the surcharge on capital goods was eased from 20 per cent to 15 per cent. In the March 1990, the surcharge on general range of imports was cut by one-third and in 1991, further reductions were made, except on luxury consumer goods. Customs and excise duties were reduced in real terms in the 1992 budget.

Sri Lanka has also undergone a similar policy change to India, but the success of the strategy depends largely on the effectiveness of the policies to improve the investor confidence. Sri Lanka's policy reforms were spread over nearly two decades. Initially, an overvalued currency was devalued, tied to a basket of currencies and allowed to fluctuate according to demand and supply. At the same time, import controls and import licensing systems were largely removed and simplified. Public sector enterprises were transferred to the private sector or foreign companies. Public sector ownership is now confined to a few core areas such as aviation, telecommunication and plantations. The competition allowed in the two main State-owned commercial banks has improved their efficiency. The exchange rate liberalization has been implemented gradually and now the rupee is freely convertible on current account. Another area where considerable progress has been made is in privatization. Pakistan and Bangladesh also have implemented similar reforms, yet, they have a long way to go in achieving financial and trade liberalisation.

In August 1993, Bangladesh completed the third year of the IMF's Enhanced Structural Adjustment Facility (ESAF) under which it embarked on a broad program of structural reforms. VAT has been introduced which has broadened the tax base and raised revenues. Interest rates are now largely market determined. Liberalisation has advanced significantly to remove anti-export bias and anti-private sector bias. Measures have been taken to remove non-tariff trade restrictions, rationalise tariff rates and improve export incentives. Reforms need to go further. Policy changes are slow and often halting, especially in trade and industrial policy and in the banking and financial sectors.

ASEAN region began its policy reforms towards liberalizing trade and financial systems somewhat earlier than the South Asian countries. Even among the member countries of the ASEAN, the extent and the pace of liberalisation vary. For about three decades, liberalized trade was a critical component of the development strategy of Singapore and this became the 'model' for some other countries in the region as well. Most of the imports are not subject to tariffs. Domestic industries are not protected by tariff or non tariff measures. Singapore is an export-led economy dominated by the private sector with a fully convertible and a strong currency. In recent years, Singapore has been investing overseas, particularly in Indo-China.

During the 1980s, Indonesia transformed the structure of its economy; trade and investment deregulation, financial sector liberalisation, tax reform and substantial devaluation. Trade reforms have reduced the number of imports subject to non-tariff restrictions from 43 percent in 1986 to less than 5 per cent now. Foreign investment is now allowed in almost all sectors and land leasing restrictions have been relaxed. Complementary reforms have taken place in customs, ports and shipping operations. The financial sector had seen decontrol of interest rates, credit ceilings (1983), liberalisation of entry (1988), reduction in the volume of subsidised credit (1990) and promotion of capital market development. Deregulation has stimulated private and foreign investment and diversified the production and export base of the economy. Structural reforms unleashed private investment in the mid-1980s. They have transformed Indonesia from a protected primary-product-based economy to a more open diversified manufacturing economy that competes successfully on world markets.

Thailand has successfully integrated herself into the world economy by moving away from protectionism and import substituting industrialization policies followed in the past. The country has made significant policy changes to encourage free flow of capital. Some tariff and non tariff barriers still exist, but, they are confined to only a few sectors of the economy. Many quantity restrictions have been either replaced by tariffs or withdrawn, though tariff levels are relatively high and form a significant proportion of government revenue. Thailand also has a liberalised financial system and a flexible exchange rate regime. However, there are difficulties in the adoption of new technologies and perhaps, this has been a major factor hindering the competitiveness of Thailand's manufactures.

In Malaysia, although some state enterprises have been privatised, the public sector still plays an important role. Also, the policy of protecting infant industries is still important. Some small industries get protection for a limited period (5-years) and some key industries are protected for a longer period. At the same time, a number of exportable commodities are subjected to licensing and duties. Malaysia has encouraged foreign investments and, to a large extent, depends on the neighbouring countries for skilled labour which is in short supply. Malaysia is a strong supporter of the trade arrangements under the proposed CEPT and AFTA regional blocks. With diverse export-products (electronics, wood and steel products) Malaysia is in a better position to benefit further from such trade groupings. Similar diversification in exports has been achieved by Mauritius as well (from sugar to clothing and electronics).

In Africa, virtually every country has initiated reforms to liberalise trade policies, though the extent varies widely. Countries like Burundi, Malawi, and Madagascar began liberalization in the 1980s and have made considerable progress in integrating their economies with the world market. In these countries, in general, both tariff and non-tariff barriers have been reduced. In countries such as Zambia, liberalization is partial and some non-tariff barriers to imports have continued. Almost all the countries in Africa devalued their currencies to correct overvalued exchange rate to improve their trade deficits.

Liberalization policy in West Asia is somewhat complex. Egypt undertook policy reforms to transform the economy into a decentralised, market-based outward-oriented economy. To achieve this, Egypt has taken steps to restructure the exchange rate regime, remove restrictions on private economic activities and replaced non-tariff barriers with tariffs.

In summary, all IOG countries without exception have recently implemented or moving rapidly towards outward looking trade liberalisation and internationalisation of their economies. This has been the major thrust of the current economic policies in these countries. The process of transformation is not easy, but the process has been continuing.

Method of Analysis

Calculating the share of intra-industry trade in total trade between any two countries (Intra-industry trade (IIT) index) provides a methodological framework to examine whether an economic co-operation among the IOG countries can be induced by market forces[2]. Experiences of the existing regional groups suggest that economic grouping of countries with more or less similar factor endowments will be successful and sustainable because adjustment process following economic reforms, especially, liberalisation of trade policy within the grouping would be less disruptive, if adjustment process took place in the form of intra-industry trade[3] (*Balassa, 1962, Grubel and Lloyd, 1975, Krugman, 1981 and Tharakan and Kol, 1989*). It is argued in the literature that intra-industry adjustment is less disruptive in newly reforming countries because intra-industry adjustment requires re-allocation of resources mainly within firms in the same industry rather than across firms in different industries (*Fukasaku, 1992*). This means that adjustment costs in the former case are lower than in the latter.

The evolution of groupings with more or less similar factor endowments will be facilitated by the industrial characteristics comprising horizontal differentiation and increasing returns to scale. A question then arises as to whether vertical product differentiation would facilitate the growth of intra-industry trade among a group of countries. Studies by Falvey (*1981*), Schumacher (*1983*) and Tharakan (*1989*) indicate that countries with marked differences in factor endowments tend to produce different qualities which leads to intra-industry trade, given an 'overlap in demand'. Consequently, the number of models of IIT have proliferated. Briefly, IIT is invariably associated with imperfectly competitive product markets where consumers have diverse preferences (*Lancaster, 1980*), and the production function is subject to increasing returns (*Krugman, 1979*), and/or markets are segmented (*Helpman and Krugman, 1985*).

Whatever the causes for its emergence, IIT creates closer links between the countries by providing more positive gains to all the countries involved than inter-industry trade could provide. This proposition is valid in the context of reform and internationalisation of manufacturing activities, which enhance assembly production from imported parts and components in different countries (*Dixit and Grossman, 1982*). Under these circumstances, political opposition to such a market-driven economic co-operation would be minimal. Further, it is argued in the literature that changes in income distribution induced by trade liberalisation would be less alarming if structural adjustment in industries took the form of intra-industry rather than inter-industry characteristics (*Fukasaku, 1992*). Thus, the prospect for closer economic co-operation among a group of countries can be examined by analysing the status of intra-industry trade within the concerned group of countries[4].

It is hypothesised here that due to liberalisation and globalisation, the extent of intra-industry trade among some IOG countries will increase over time as an indicator of close co-operation in manufacturing activities. Examination of this proposition necessitates calculating the well known Grubel-Lloyd (*1975*) intra-industry index[5]. This is expressed as a ratio of the value of exports which is matched by imports to the total value of exports and imports of an industry.

$$\beta_j = \left[1 - \left(\sum_{k=1}^{m} |X_{kj} - M_{kj}| / \sum_{k=1}^{m} (X_{kj} + M_{kj})\right)\right] \times 100$$

Where β_j is the share of intra-industry trade in the jth country; X_{kj} and M_{kj} are respectively exports from and imports to country j in industry k. The measure should be, by definition, varying between 0 and 100 when expressed as an index. When exports exactly equal imports of an industry, $\beta_j = 100$, and where there are exports but no imports or vice versa, $\beta_j = 0$. In terms of the bilateral Grubel-Lloyd index of country i with country j,

$$\beta_{ij} = \left[1 - \left(\sum_{k=1}^{m} |X_k - M_k| / \sum_{k=1}^{m} (X_k + M_k)\right)\right] \times 100$$

$\beta_{ij} = 100$ indicates that all trade of country j with country i is intra-industry. When $\beta_{ij} = 0$, this means that all trade is inter-industry and that there is complete specialization in trade between two countries. The higher the ratio, the greater is the intra-industry trade and so, close co-operation in manufacturing activities of the countries concerned.

The following sequence is adopted for the analysis: IOG with other regional groupings and intra-IOG, particularly, Australia, India, and South Africa with other IOG countries. Analyses except the calculation of intra-industry trade indices are based on SITC 0-9 at 3-digit levels. Intra-industry trade indices are calculated for SITC 5-8 at

The IOG's share of India's total imports has increased from 19 per cent in 1989 to 25 per cent in 1992 (table 7). Imports from West Asia constituted about 16 per cent of India's total imports in 1992. From 1965, India's imports from other IOG countries have been dominated by West Asia. Imports from SEA and Australia shared about 5 per cent and 4 per cent of India's total imports respectively in 1992. Imports from other SAARC countries have been negligible.

Bilateral shares of South Africa's total exports to other IOG countries (table 8) show IOG's share of South Africa's total exports amounted to 8.49 per cent which were valued at only US $ 1.22 billion in 1992. North & East Africa's share of South Africa's total exports has been dominant within IOG at about 4 per cent in the nineties. The rest of the IOG countries had insignificant shares of South Africa's total exports until 1992. The IOG's share in South Africa's total imports has been increasing steadily from 2.82 per cent in 1990 to 6.91 per cent in 1992 (table 9). Imports from North & East Africa constituted about 2 per cent of South Africa's total imports. Recently import shares of Australia and SEA have been showing increasing trends.

The above analyses of direction of trade indicate that North Asia has been the most favoured destination for exports, and also the most important source of imports for IOG among regions outside IOG for several years. EEC-12 had been the second most important destination for IOG's exports until 1980, when North America replaced it. Among sources of imports for IOG, North Asia has been the most significant, followed by North America. The significance of the EEC-12 as a source of imports for IOG has been declining since 1985.

Trade movements within IOG countries are significant with the exception of South Africa. However, South Africa's position should be interpreted in the light of its years of apartheid policy and the trade embargo applied to her. Since these restrictions were lifted, South Africa has become an increasingly important destination for exports and source of imports for countries within IOG. Australia has been an important source of imports for several IOG countries, though it is an average destination for exports. Finally, results indicate that Indian Ocean Islands and West Asia are strategically well placed trade centres within IOG.

The above analysis also indicates that the volume of trade within IOG, though small in size, has been increasing steadily. With recent economic liberalisation and opening up of the economies in IOG, especially of India and South Africa, the possibility of increasing

Australia's exports to these countries cannot be taken lightly, as these countries embark on globalisation of their agriculture and industries. For example, Australia's expertise in dry-land farming, food processing and mining technology is world renowned, and the literature demonstrates that this has been acknowledged by the IOG countries. India's food processing technology is outdated and is in the process of being upgraded, which provides an opportunity for Australia to market its technology.

The Share of Intra-Industry Trade

The above analyses of the direction and the volume of trade provide information on the most favoured destinations of exports and important sources of imports for IOG countries. Next, it is imperative to examine the share of intra-industry trade in total trade that is taking place within IOG to focus on the possibility of a market-driven economic co-operation among the IOG countries.

First, the share of intra-industry trade in total trade between IOG and some of the major IOG countries was calculated in percentage terms (table 10). The share between IOG and Australia increased steadily from 14.96 in 1970 to 45.14 in 1990, which was the largest increase and highest value among intra-industry trade figures. With the recent accent on internationalisation in the IOG countries, and improving competitiveness of Australian manufacturing industries, this trend is expected to continue. While IITI between IOG and Australia declined to 39.42 in 1992, nevertheless, in 1992, the share of intra-industry trade in total trade between IOG and Australia was still more significant in terms of magnitude than for India and South Africa (table 10).

The share of intra-industry trade in total trade between IOG and South Africa increased from 28.49 in 1980 to 34.5 in 1985 and remained more or less at the same level until 1992. The share between IOG and India increased from a mere 8 in 1975 to 31.24 in 1990 and declined slightly to 29.1 in 1992. However, with the introduction of more trade and industry policy reforms aimed at globalising Indian agriculture and industries, the possibility of IITI between IOG and India increasing further appears highly likely. Examination of the trends of IIT between IOG and Australia, India and South Africa taken individually, suggests that there can be complementarity in production in relevant products between IOG and Australia, India and South Africa. A detailed study is necessary to identify the relevant products.

Next, the share of intra-industry trade in total trade was calculated bilaterally for countries within IOG. The analyses covered the periods 1970 to 1992. Table 11 gives IITI between Australia and other IOG countries and the world. Intra-industry trade between Australia and the World does not follow any pattern over the period of analysis. During the early seventies, the index increased but then declined from the late seventies until the mid eighties. It increased from 20 in 1986 to 30 in 1992. Among the IOG countries which had the largest share of intra-industry trade with Australia in 1992 in order of magnitude were Singapore (38), Thailand (24), Malaysia (24), South Africa (21), Mauritius (20), Indonesia (15) and India (11). IITI between Australia and South Africa has fluctuated around 27 in the eighties, but declined to 21 in 1992.

Shares of intra-industry trade in total trade between India and other IOG countries from 1980 to 1992, show India's intra-industry trade with Indonesia (36), Singapore (34), Thailand (25), Malaysia (20) and Australia (15) have been increasing significantly recently. For example, India's intra-industry trade with Indonesia increased sharply from 11 in 1990 to 36 in 1992. This may be interpreted as a sign of convergence of the industrial structures in these countries. With the rest of IOG, India appears to be reaping the advantages of complete specialisation in trade in manufactures.

Shares of intra-industry trade in total trade between South Africa and the other IOG countries (table 13) show that Australia and Mauritius are the only two countries which had some magnitude of trade in manufactures. In contrast, before apartheid in the early seventies, South Africa had significant amounts of intra-industry trade with IOG (table 13). This means that the potential for South Africa to increase its IIT within IOG is positive.

Given the variations in factor endowments and technological developments in the IOG countries, it is useful to examine the influence of industrial structure on intra-industry trade and on market-driven economic cooperation. One method of analysis in this context, is to regroup the trade data according to the 'factor-intensity' criterion to obtain a more technologically homogeneous group of products. The following four 'factor -intensity' groups were considered in this paper:

* *Capital intensive products*: SITC 5,62,64,672-679,71,722-726,729, 731-734,86,891,892,896 and 897.

* *Labour intensive products*: SITC 65, 664-666, 735, 81-85, 893-895, 899 and 951.
* *Mineral intensive products*: SITC 27,28,3,661-663,667,671 and 68.
* *Agricultural intensive products*: SITC 0,1,21-26,29 and 4 at 3-digit level.

Tables 14-17 show the share of intra-industry trade between Australia and other IOG countries in the above cited product groups from 1975 to 1992. The influence of product differentiation in terms of qualities on Australian trade with other IOG countries is evident in the case of capital intensive products, as Australia exports and also imports capital intensive products reasonably. Similar arguments appear to hold for intra-industry trade in labour intensive products. In both cases, Australia exports technologically high quality products to other IOG countries and imports lower quality products to meet local demands. The results also indicate the extent of links in terms of assembly and components production between Australian manufacturing and manufacturing in IOG countries. Australia has the highest share of intra-industry trade in mineral intensive products with ASEAN and bilaterally with Indonesia. Petroleum products (SITC 33) are the major contributors in this group. Australia does not have considerable intra-industry trade in agricultural intensive products with the IOG countries. Agricultural liberalisation in IOG, particularly in food processing is expected to create strong intra-industry trade between Australia and other IOG countries.

Tables 18-21 show the shares of intra-industry trade in India's trade in different product groups with other IOG countries. In 1992, half of India's trade in capital intensive products with ASEAN is intra-industry. Bilaterally, more than one-third of India's trade in capital intensive products with Australia and Indonesia is intra-industry. In the case of Indonesia, SITC 51 (Chemicals-elements and compounds) is a major two-way traded group. The share of intra-industry trade in India's trade in labour intensive products with ASEAN is about 30 per cent in 1992, while with the rest of IOG, it is not significant. The shares of intra-industry trade in India's both mineral intensive and agricultural intensive products trade with other IOG countries do not follow any pattern and are not significant.

The shares of intra-industry trade in South Africa's trade in different product groups with other IOG countries (tables 22-25) show that

South Africa has considerable two-way trade in capital intensive products with the region of Northeast Africa and Australia. South Africa's two-way trade with Australia in this group occurs in SITC 51 (Chemicals-elements and compounds) and 68 (Nonferrous metals). In other product groups, South Africa has significant intra-industry trade only with Northeast Africa. With on-going economic reforms in South Africa and its recent openness, the share of intra-industry trade in South Africa's trade with other IOG countries is expected to increase considerably.

Three explanations have been offered for varying growth rates in IIT among countries[6] (*Greenway and Milner, 1989*).

* country-specific variations which depend on the characteristics of the trading partners in terms of their level of economic development,
* industry-specific variations which depend on product/industry-specific demand and supply conditions, and
* policy-oriented variations which depend on existing political and institutional factors.

Our interest was to examine the variations in the growth of the share of intra-industry trade in total trade among the IOG countries with the following two policy-oriented hypotheses, namely, that IIT will be greater when tariffs and non-tariff barriers are low, and when economies are subject to some form of economic co-operation. The empirical results of our analysis above indicate that the amount of intra-industry trade taking place within IOG is at a low level, but, that the share of intra-industry trade in total trade between individual countries within IOG has been increasing recently.

The empirical results can partly be explained by the convergence of factor endowments. When the relative difference in capital stock per head between two countries is greater, then the share of intra-industry trade in total bilateral trade will be smaller. Next, an increase in intra-industry trade occurs when there is a simultaneous growth of economic size or a lowering of transaction costs among trading partners, whether from a relative decrease of prices for transport and communication services or by a removal of policy imposed trade barriers. Therefore, more liberalisation within IOG provides greater opportunities for IIT within the region which in turn, facilitates the formation and the sustaining of an IOG.

Problems and Prospects for IOG Co-operation

Discussion of prospects for economic co-operation within the Indian Ocean rim must take account of the broad changes taking place in the global arena concerning the rules for international trade and investment. The timing of this study is important because of the conclusion of the Uruguay Round and the creation of the World Trade Organisation. This is the setting in which judgments as to prospects for Indian Ocean development and cooperation must be made. Essentially it is a setting which is moving towards liberalisation of world trade and investment.

The broadest concept of the direction of national economic policies and their international relations is one based on a "liberal domestic economy". This is generally understood to be one where policy and legal distortions to the allocation of resources by the market are minimal. The government is entrusted with the responsibility of ensuring the proper functioning of markets. Thus the process of liberalisation can be equated with the elimination of governmental measures that are discriminatory or restrictive and which therefore distort the market.

Overall, the beneficial effects of the liberalisation process depend to a considerable extent on the presence, and where necessary, the strengthening of controls to ensure the proper functioning of the market and the promotion of broader economic and social priorities.

The early 1980s ushered in a sea change in attitudes towards economic liberalisation and globalisation of economic activities. Not only has there been a reversal of attitudes towards garnering the benefits of international trade, but this has been linked to radically new policies with regard to foreign direct investment. Developing countries are increasingly turning to foreign direct investment (FDI) as a source of capital, technology, access to markets and other resources that are vital for sustained and accelerated economic growth. This trend has become even more widespread in the 1990s as more developing economies and economies in transition have joined the process of liberalisation.

In 1993, further impetus was given to liberalisation efforts at international level. The number of bilateral treaties for the promotion and protection of foreign direct investment concluded by developing countries increased from 506 in January 1993 to 570 in January 1994. But more importantly, the Uruguay Round of Multilateral Negotiations was concluded.

The Uruguay Round negotiations were completed in December 1993 and the results were formally adopted in Marrakesh in April 1994. The crowning achievement was the creation of the World Trade Organisation. This comprised a range of agreements concerning trade in goods, trade in services and trade related aspects of intellectual property rights.

The Final Act of the Uruguay Round was centred on matters of trade. It contains a package of economic reforms that relate to key economic transactions within the global economy. Foreign investment was not explicitly negotiated in the Uruguay Round, but a number of issues discussed there has a notable investment dimension. The effect on FDI, albeit indirect, is substantial, with an overall strengthening of investors' confidence in the world trading system, a dynamic influence of freer trade on growth and consequently on FDI, and the impact of tariff reduction on trade and investment. Where the agreements deal specifically with FDI, the effect is direct.

Importantly for the Indian Ocean rim, the general strengthening of the trading system and the extensive liberalisation of market access negotiated in the Uruguay Round should open up new possibilities for productive and mutually beneficial foreign and domestic investments in tune with locational advantages of member countries.

The next important factor in projecting IOG development in economic cooperation is the direction of national economic policies. The most significant factor in favour of expanding economic ties within the region is the almost universal shift towards the concept of open economies, economic reform and liberalisation, away from past policies of economic autarchy. A major factor inhibiting the economies of the rim has been the inward-looking economic policies of member countries. The foregoing brief survey of national economic policies reveals a region-wide shift towards the open economy. Given the success of this approach in East and South East Asia, gains are inevitable. The same survey also reveals that many countries have a long way to go on this track.

Problems along this route will continue to be political instability which can be translated into insecurity for DFI and a slow passage towards fast economic growth in the region.

The IOG rim countries, unlike APEC contain far greater economic diversity and contain many of the world's least developed countries. It also contains a sub-region which is not only the most populous outside

China, but has enormous growth potential. Thus we need to take account of the diversity involved. To the East, there are the countries of South East Asia and Australia. These are already well on the road towards advanced development. They are relatively open and already have strong economic linkages with IOG countries. There will continue to be a major growth contribution form the eastern segment of the rim. In South Asia, especially India, growth potential has been under achieved in the past owing to autarchic policies. These are now being reversed and a major contribution can be expected from this region, even though may be years before intra-South Asia trade and investment takes off. But it can and will contribute none the less to the region's growth.

West Asia, small in population but fuel rich, will continue to be a source of energy and investment funds if the IOG proves attractive. Africa's contribution will continue to be dominated by that of South Africa and the question of whether political stability can be sustained to permit the development of its rich resources. Eastern Africa has resource potential but a record of political instability. It has suffered from the legacy of the Cold War and economic philosophies and policies which have not benefited these countries and have created deep divisions within and between countries. It may be that with the Cold War in the past, much greater stability will follow and economic potential can be realised. Thus, the concept of Indian Ocean Grouping has strong and significant potential to become a reality.

TABLE 1

Incidence of Bilateral Trade Between IOG Countries, 1990-92.

IOG Country	Trade with Other IOG Countries[a] (No.)	Importing Countries[b] (No.)	Export Destinations[c] (No.)
1	2	3	4
1. Australia	35	27	34
South East Asian:			
2. Brunei	5	5	4
3. Indonesia	30	25	27
4. Malaysia	33	27	30
5. Myanmar	11	6	11

(*Contd.*)

TABLE 1 (*Contd.*)

1	2	3	4
6. Philippines	24	24	21
7. Singapore	34	31	34
8. Thailand	36	30	36
SAARC:			
9. Bangladesh	26	21	23
10. Bhutan (included with India)			
11. India	38	31	38
12. Maldives (not separately reported)			
13. Nepal	13	12	6
14. Pakistan	36	31	33
15. Sri Lanka	26	24	22
West Asian:			
16. Afghanistan	11	10	10
17. Bahrain	18	12	17
18. Egypt	28	25	23
19. Iran	15	14	14
20. Iraq	16	15	11
21. Kuwait	17	13	16
22. Oman	22	18	15
23. Qatar	20	20	17
24. Saudi Arabia	26	26	21
25. U.A.E.	21	15	21
26. Yemen (unified)	15	15	1
North & East African:			
27. Burundi	5	5	2
28. Djibouti	(not separately given)		
29. Ethiopia	10	10	3
30. Kenya	32	23	31
31. Madagascar	20	17	8
32. Malawi	6	2	4

(*Contd.*)

TABLE 1 (*Contd.*)

1	2	3	4
33. Mozambique	12	12	10
34. Rwanda	6	5	3
35. Somalia	7	7	5
36. Sudan	15	15	6
37. Tanzania	14	14	14
38. Uganda	8	8	5
39. Zambia	12	11	12
40. Zimbabwe	27	15	27
South African Customs Union[d]:			
41. Botswana	(in SACU)		
42. Lesotho	(in SACU)		
43. South Africa	21	21	18
44. Swaziland	(in SACU)		
IO Islands:			
45. Comoros	6	6	0
46. Mauritius	25	21	14
47. Seychelles	12	12	1

Notes:

a. Numbers of countries with recorded imports or exports of over US$ 1 million with the country in any year between 1990 and 1992.

b. Where imports in any year during 1990 to 1992 were more than US$ 1 million

c. Where exports in any year during 1990 to 1992 were more than US$ 1 million

d. Includes Botswana, Lesotho and Swaziland.

TABLE 2

Total Export Values for All Commodities Between the Indian Ocean Group and Partner Regional Groups, 1965 to 1992

Year	Americas Developing	EEC-12	IO Group	North America	North Asia	World
1965	0.5	7.2	4.0	2.1	2.4	19.4
1966	0.3	6.8	3.5	2.2	2.7	18.5
1967	0.3	7.1	3.6	2.1	3.5	19.8
1968	0.3	7.2	3.8	2.2	3.9	21.0
1969	0.4	7.4	3.6	2.4	5.1	23.6
1970	0.5	8.4	4.4	2.5	6.2	27.5
1971	0.9	9.8	5.2	2.9	6.9	31.4
1972	1.2	11.4	5.6	3.7	8.8	37.6
1973	2.2	16.3	7.7	5.3	14.5	56.8
1974	5.3	37.7	14.9	9.3	27.2	128.4
1975	5.1	30.5	15.3	9.9	25.3	118.5
1976	6.1	37.2	17.4	12.9	31.4	141.9
1977	6.6	39.1	20.6	16.5	35.2	169.1
1978	5.2	48.7	24.4	24.6	42.0	173.1
1979	8.8	73.9	35.2	33.5	60.6	238.4
1980	12.7	98.5	51.0	40.7	86.4	341.2
1981	10.6	86.5	53.2	37.6	82.7	319.8
1982	9.7	65.4	50.8	24.0	74.4	268.4
1983	7.9	45.1	42.7	21 .9	59.9	227.9
1984	6.9	45.7	43.6	26.9	62.7	217.6
1985	3.4	35.2	31.9	22.0	41.7	188.9
1986	3.9	38.5	29.8	26.6	41.5	166.1
1987	5.7	47.9	38.7	33.8	60.7	217.8
1988	3.6	43.4	38.5	33.2	53.3	227.4
1989	4.2	5.05	47.6	39.1	64.8	269.9
1990	6.5	67.6	58.3	54.7	93.7	323.7
1991	5.7	71.9	71.5	54.8	93.8	340.3
1992	6.8	77.7	74.9	63.3	98.1	363.3

TABLE 2A

Exports of Crude Oil and Natural Gas from IOG Countries
(unit: US$ 1)

Year	South America	EEC-12 Countries	North America	North Asia	World
1965	0.21	2.49	0.34	0.54	4.87
1966	0.11	2.00	0.31	0.68	3.98
1967	0.13	2.54	0.28	0.97	4.93
1968	0.13	2.29	0.23	1.20	4.96
1969	0.16	2.26	0.19	1.77	5.89
1970	0.27	3.25	0.19	2.29	8.02
1971	0.59	4.90	0.39	2.93	11.14
1972	0.77	5.27	0.59	3.97	13.54
1973	1.64	7.31	1.O8	6.42	21.68
1974	4.25	26.73	4.04	15.84	78.82
1975	4.27	19.86	4.23	14.96	70.20
1976	5.07	23.39	6.37	18.34	85.26
1977	5.52	23.96	9.57	21.08	104.32
1978	4.44	31.85	14.99	26.68	101.37
1979	7.47	51.72	21.62	39.12	141.95
1980	11.23	73.24	27.44	62.37	212.77
1981	9.19	65.54	24.80	61.01	201.92
1982	8.44	44.77	12.34	53.10	154.12
1983	7.07	26.91	9.09	40.34	113.46
1984	5.90	21.90	8.57	39.71	101.81
1985	2.51	11.71	4.72	20.25	77.68
1986	2.74	13.36	6.61	17.34	51.80
1987	4.38	15.90	9.80	28.31	76.09
1988	1.98	7.28	3.92	15.43	55.29
1989	2.39	10.50	5.49	21.52	74.67
1990	3.59	17.39	15.76	29.30	83.65
1991	2.84	21.03	13.87	38.24	99.24
1992	2.99	18.91	12.26	38.97	97.1 0

TABLE 3

Total Import Values for All Commodities Between the Indian Ocean Group and Partner Regional Groups, 1965 to 1992 (US$ billion)

Year	Americas Developing	EEC-12	IO Group	North America	North Asia	World
1965	0.1	6.9	3.6	4.0	2.3	19.3
1966	0.1	6.7	3.8	4.4	2.3	19.8
1967	0.1	7.1	3.8	4.4	2.7	20.9
1968	0.1	7.4	3.9	4.4	3.0	21.8
1969	0.2	7.7	4.1	4.2	3.5	22.9
1970	0.2	8.5	4.1	4.9	4.3	25.6
1971	0.2	9.7	4.5	4.9	5.1	28.5
1972	0.3	9.8	5.5	4.9	5.8	30.4
1973	0.5	13.2	7.2	7.3	8.7	42.8
1974	0.8	20.2	13.7	14.9	13.9	71.3
1975	0.8	26.4	15.0	15.3	15.9	85.2
1976	0.7	28.5	17.9	17.4	18.2	93.8
1977	1.2	35.0	20.5	20.6	23.1	113.1
1978	1.2	44.7	22.7	24.4	28.3	134.8
1979	1.6	45.7	30.4	35.2	31.0	150.1
1980	3.3	57.8	44.9	51.0	42.2	207.3
1981	3.4	66.1	46.9	53.2	50.6	234.4
1982	3.3	69.6	47.7	50.8	52.0	240.1
1983	4.0	64.7	45.7	42.7	52.2	231.3
1984	4.1	60.4	45.3	43.6	50.3	220.1
1985	3.7	51.5	39.0	31.9	45.6	194.4
1986	3.1	51.7	33.4	29.8	45.2	186.8
1987	3.1	56.0	37.7	38.7	51.1	203.8
1988	4.4	64.6	44.1	38.5	64.1	245.5
1989	5.5	68.6	51.4	47.6	71.7	274.4
1990	6.1	79.3	62.9	58.3	82.4	316.7
1991	5.8	83.5	70.2	71.5	92.8	344.3
1992	5.9	91.4	72.8	74.9	96.8	364.0

TABLE 4

Bilateral Share of Total Australian Exports to Trading Partners within Indian Ocean Group and with World (%)

Year	India	IO Islands	N&E Africa	S Africa	SAARC	SE Asia	W Asia	Trade within IOG Countries	
								%	Value (US$ billion)
1965-69	1.56	0.13	0.61	1.22	2.66	5.63	1.66	13.47	0.45
1970-74	0.96	0.11	0.60	1.53	1.88	6.63	3.24	14.95	1.07
1975-79	0.95	0.14	0.31	0.65	1.93	7.16	5.60	16.74	2.35
1980-84	0.95	0.10	0.23	0.51	1.66	7.57	7.03	18.05	3.79
1985	1.21	0.08	0.20	0.23	2.25	6.45	7.11	17.53	3.81
1986	1.27	0.07	0.30	0.26	1.83	5.46	5.86	15.05	3.17
1987	1.16	0.09	0.12	0.24	1.55	6.04	4.57	13.77	3.33
1988	1.50	0.09	0.13	0.34	2.00	7.55	4.35	15.96	4.75
1989	1.25	0.08	0.09	0.34	2.06	8.57	4.83	17.22	5.72
1990	1.35	0.09	0.09	0.27	1.96	10.31	5.05	19.12	6.89
1991	1.37	0.11	0.10	0.41	2.03	10.48	3.23	17.73	6.70
1992	1.57	0.11	0.13	0.58	2.14	10.62	2.64	17.79	6.77

TABLE 4A

Australia's Exports: IOG (*$ Australian thousands*)

Year	1989	1990	1991	1992	1993	5 Year trend
United Arab Emirates	305,923	257,050	324,637	325,986	422,551	9.2
Bangladesh	95,538	64,090	95,012	77,788	78,111	-2.1
Bahrain	129,848	193,181	125,891	48,139	41,816	-30.6
Comoros	454	145	9	599	16	-41
Djibouti	76	137	272	293	144	22.6
Indonesia	941,355	1,355,120	1,427,764	1,728,523	1,812,643	16.8
India	523,682	641,615	662,625	840,233	921,600	15
Iran	370,723	633,729	353,905	236,098	435,948	-6.4
Kenya	9,717	7,013	11,046	6,918	6,448	-8
Kuwait	78,740	31,481	25,871	83,456	90,030	13.2
Sri Lanka	49,035	44,116	44,700	62,328	81,197	14.5
Madagascar	1,559	1,797	878	315	3,633	-0.5
Maldives	1,466	481	1,196	1,841	2,136	23 3
Mozambique	4,562	6,796	8,069	14,324	9,832	25.6
Mauritius	34,068	37,748	49,931	62,167	70,710	21.6
Malaysia	866,199	982,646	1,057,019	1,139,980	1,573,111	14.4
Oman	68,461	72,229	65,847	75,027	91,775	6.4
Pakistan	191,539	170,701	182,351	213,066	287,378	10.9
Qatar	21,667	24,832	24,244	38,216	41,132	18.7
South Africa	136,458	133,594	194,367	306,198	344,917	30.8
Saudi Arabia	210,389	286,818	274,173	313,185	303,515	8.6
Singapore	1,706,958	2,366,857	2,934,560	3,768,131	3,277,100	19.4
Somalia	31	57	30	1,913	321	126.8
Seychelles	2,245	3,211	2,034	2,622	3,082	4.4
Thailand	553,051	608,503	698,646	1,081,617	1,251,520	24.7
Tanzania	2,732	7,261	2,973	8,204	7,966	25.4
Yemen	114,264	128,727	67,983	71,160	60,919	-16.9
Total IOG	6,420,740	8,059,935	8,636,033	10,508,327	11,219,551	
World	47,004,306	50,892,330	53,717,352	58,399,502	62,780,971	7.4
IOG's share (%)	13.66	15.84	16.08	17.99	17.87	

Source: Information Supplied by The Department of Foreign Affairs and Trade, Commonwealth of Australia.

TABLE 5

Bilateral Share of Total Australian Imports to Trading Partners within Indian Ocean Group and with World (%)

Year	India	IO Islands	N&E Africa	S Africa	SAARC	SE Asia	W Asia	Trade within IOG Countries %	Trade within IOG Countries Value (US$ billion)
1965-69	1.09	0.00	0.42	0.59	2.07	3.69	4.97	11.74	4.20
1970-74	0.84	0.00	0.31	0.56	1.36	2.85	4.74	9.82	6.20
1975-79	0.72	0.01	0.22	0.56	1.04	4.61	7.36	13.80	17.51
1980-84	0.59	0.00	0.14	0.49	0.86	6.37	8.18	16.04	34.90
1985	0.51	0.01	0.12	0.46	0.76	4.94	3.93	10.22	23.60
1986	0.53	0.01	0.34	0.42	0.77	4.77	2.41	8.72	21.22
1987	0.52	0.01	0.98	0.35	0.80	5.73	2.19	10.06	26.99
1988	0.57	0.01	0.09	0.22	0.87	5.94	1.99	9.12	30.24
1989	0.53	0.01	0.07	0.22	0.77	6.20	2.62	9.89	39.43
1990	0.55	0.01	0.07	0.24	0.82	6.04	2.82	10.00	39.74
1991	0.59	0.01	0.08	0.19	0.89	7.58	2.53	11.28	44.51
1992	0.56	0.01	0.05	0.26	0.86	8.15	2.41	11.74	49.47

TABLE 5A

Australia's Imports : IOG (*$ Australian Thousands*)

Year	1989	1990	1991	1992	1993	5 Year trend
United Arab Emirates	515,569	476,824	406,099	592,716	738,679	9.8
Bangladesh	21,731	25,931	25,489	19,030	19,290	-5.3
Bahrain	22,140	13,332	13,826	5,539	12,610	-18.2
Comoros	10	9	3	3	6	-19 1
Djibouti	0	14	0	0	0	—
Indonesia	496,319	521,794	934,476	1,243,048	1,215,864	30.5
India	271,158	279,086	258,793	321,230	406,892	10
Iran	11,119	9,890	13,677	11,161	15,574	8.3
Kenya	7,580	6,222	8,425	8,349	9,807	8.4
Kuwait	105,562	104,804	9,359	47,716	64,022	-16 4
Sri Lanka	26,672	37,406	36,028	38,901	44,990	11.5
Madagascar	209	323	318	423	281	9
Maldives	2	159	9	1	75	24.4
Mozambique	1,482	1,361	977	89	12	-70.9
Mauritius	2,087	3,338	4,344	3,369	1,673	-4.2
Malaysia	747,662	653,903	775,521	966,418	1,036,107	11
Oman	12,097	52,515	31,707	752	8,492	-39.1
Pakistan	75,639	79,237	88,995	111,669	143,246	17.6
Qatar	46,221	17,716	2,015	3,983	84,309	-2.9
South Africa	110,132	118,158	94,617	148,322	230,229	18.6
Saudi Arabia	621,603	730,278	796,213	718,965	714,205	2.7
Singapore	1,272,223	1,183,904	1,349,407	1,329,030	1,602,768	5.9
Somalia	106	0	3	0	0	—
Seychelles	576	0	62	27	43	—
Thailand	480,311	479,804	583,411	715,843	766,783	14.3
Tanzania	1,012	1,007	726	951	842	-4.2
Yemen	14,312	30,724	58,723	0	26,965	—
Total IOG	4,863,534	4,827,739	5,493,223	6,287,535	7,143,764	
World	51,727,525	49,806,363	49,673,546	55,507,282	62,403,687	5
IOG's Share (%)	9.4	9.69	11.06	11.33	11.45	

Source : Information Supplied by The Department of Foreign Affairs and Trade, Commonwealth of Australia.

TABLE 6

Bilateral Share of Total Indian Exports to Trading Partners within Indian Ocean Group and with World (%)

Year	Australia	IO Islands	N&E Africa	S.Africa	SAARC	SE Asia	W.Asia	Trade within IOG Countries %	Trade within IOG Countries Value (US$ billion)
1965-69	2.09	0.10	2.82	0.01	3.69	3.03	7.64	19.38	0.33
1970-74	1.80	0.13	3.19	0.08	4.34	3.47	9.19	22.20	0.59
1975-79	1.43	0.25	2.60	0.04	3.38	4.10	14.07	26.77	1.54
1980-84	1.23	0.18	1.54	0.12	2.65	3.17	10.89	19.78	1.70
1985	1.13	0.14	0.99	0.05	3.03	2.33	9.43	17.10	1.53
1986	1.18	0.18	0.95	0.02	2.99	3.10	7.07	15.49	1.51
1987	1.15	0.22	0.77	0.02	2.60	2.96	7.21	14.93	1.80
1988	1.31	0.16	0.89	0.02	2.79	3.55	6.61	15.33	2.12
1989	1.21	0.16	0.87	0.02	2.52	3.99	7.51	16.28	2.77
1990	0.99	0.29	0.89	0.01	2.95	4.77	6.11	16.01	2.86
1991	1.14	0.32	1.03	0.03	3.48	5.61	8.64	20.25	3.62
1992	1.21	0.33	1.34	0.05	3.98	6.65	9.63	23.19	4.80

TABLE 7

Bilateral Share of Total Indian Imports from Trading Partners within Indian Ocean Group and from World (%)

Year	Australia	IO Islands	N&E Africa	S.Africa	SAARC	SE Asia	W.Asia	Trade within IOG Countries	
								%	Value (US$ billion)
1965-69	2.20	0.00	3.09	0.00	1.19	3.79	5.31	15.58	0.40
1970-74	1.97	0.00	4.72	0.03	0.81	1.05	3.63	12.21	0.37
1975-79	2.15	0.00	1.73	0.02	0.53	3.02	10.12	17.57	1.22
1980-84	1.44	0.00	0.77	0.02	0.56	5.22	22.32	30.33	4.26
1985	2.25	0.02	0.90	0.02	0.50	4.80	19.89	28.38	4.60
1986	2.02	0.00	0.76	0.00	0.53	5.13	10.57	19.01	2.99
1987	2.22	0.00	0.93	0.01	0.42	6.20	12.22	22.00	3.77
1988	2.49	0.00	1.08	0.01	0.50	6.21	11.58	21.87	4.23
1989	2.51	0.00	0.82	0.01	2.26	4.79	10.92	19.31	4.19
1990	3.15	0.00	0.67	0.01	0.42	4.91	13.56	22.72	5.41
1991	2.87	0.00	0.55	0.02	0.48	4.62	16.16	24.70	4.82
1992	3.85	0.00	0.66	0.01	0.79	4.46	15.50	25.27	6.12

TABLE 8

Bilateral Share of Total S. Africa's Exports to Trading Partners within the Indian Ocean Group and with World (%)

Year	Australia	India	IO Islands	N&E Africa	SAARC	SE Asia	W.Asia	Trade within IOG Countries %	Trade within IOG Countries Value (US$ billion)
1965-69	0.97	0.00	0.01	1.37	0.11	0.21	0.04	2.71	0.05
1970-74	0.93	0.00	0.03	0.22	0.08	0.02	0.07	1.35	0.04
1975-79	0.79	-	-	-	0.10	-	-	0.89	0.07
1980-84	0.46	0.00	0.02	0.36	0.09	0.01	0.07	1.01	0.19
1985	1.01	0.02	0.20	2.99	0.26	0.11	0.33	4.92	0.52
1986	0.89	0.00	0.12	2.96	0.53	1.23	0.17	5.90	0.68
1987	0.89	0.01	0.33	1.05	0.58	1.56	0.10	4.52	0.48
1988	0.57	0.02	1.00	1.09	0.56	0.36	0.47	4.07	0.51
1989	0.67	0.02	0.16	1.44	0.63	0.32	0.40	3.64	0.48
1990	0.68	0.02	1.25	3.31	0.64	0.36	0.39	6.65	0.93
1991	0.56	0.03	1.63	4.43	0.68	0.53	0.03	7.89	1.08
1992	0.78	0.01	1.81	4.08	0.53	1.23	0.05	8.49	1.22

TABLE 9

Bilateral Share of Total S. Africa's Imports from Trading Partners within Indian Ocean Group and from World (%)

Year	Australia	India	IO Islands	N&E Africa	SAARC	SE Asia	W.Asia	Trade within IOG Countries	
								%	Value (US$ billion)
1965-69	1.49	0.02	0.06	2.25	0.79	1.29	5.38	11.28	0.29
1970-74	2.24	0.06	0.05	0.50	0.37	0.21	0.80	4.23	0.20
1975-79	1.22	-	-	0.00	0.25	-	-	1.47	0.11
1980-84	0.89	0.01	0.00	0.32	0.17	0.00	0.00	1.39	0.23
1985	1.11	-	-	-	0.12	-	-	1.23	0.13
1986	0.67	0.02	0.00	2.28	0.17	1.64	0.02	4.80	0.43
1987	0.56	0.02	0.00	0.33	0.18	1.96	0.00	3.05	0.33
1988	0.81	0.02	0.04	0.25	0.14	0.03	0.00	1.29	0.17
1989	0.96	0.02	0.00	0.23	0.15	0.03	0.00	1.39	0.17
1990	0.79	0.02	0.05	1.77	0.17	0.02	0.00	2.82	0.36
1991	1.28	0.04	0.04	1.63	0.33	0.38	0.00	3.70	0.50
1992	1.16	0.20	0.03	2.06	0.38	2.99	0.09	6.91	1.27

TABLE 10

Intra-Industry Trade Index of Indian Ocean Grouping (IOG) with Other Regional Groups and Countries

Reporter Indian Ocean Countries
Commodity total - SITC 5 - 8 at 3 - digit level

Partner	1970	1975	1980	1985	1990	1992	Growth rate % (1970-1992)
America-Developing	24.19	25.07	25.08	28.25	23.03	31.93	32.00
Australia	14.96	19.22	26.57	34.65	45.14	39.42	163.50
Canada	10.25	15.28	19.42	26.79	28.78	32.19	214.05
India	6.89	8.06	12.85	28.19	31.24	29.10	322.35
USA	13.17	16.66	24.18	38.20	42.68	41.75	217.01
North America	14.28	16.82	24.34	38.11	42.26	41.69	191.95
EEC - 12	11.13	11.05	14.46	22.39	32.86	35.75	221.20
France	8.56	9.37	15.11	19.41	25.35	27.77	224.42
United Kingdom	10.97	10.67	13.73	29.44	34.81	39.92	263.90
Mauritius	9.17	17.84	15.11	9.87	16.97	21.57	135.22
North East Asia	6.79	7.57	9.21	12.55	27.70	31.36	361.86
S. Africa Customs Union	29.64	35.36	28.49	34.50	34.68	34.39	16.03
ASEAN	47.67	62.87	69.75	79.56	82.94	82.97	74.05

TABLE 11

Intra-Industry Trade Index of Australia with IOG

Reporter Australia, Commodity Total-SITC 5-8 at 3-Digit level,
Type Intra-Industry Trade (Aggregate), and Flow Exports

Partner	1970	1971	1972	1973	1974	1975	1976	1977	1978	1979	1980	1981
1	2	3	4	5	6	7	8	9	10	11	12	13
Afghanistan	0	0	0	0	0	0	0	0	0	0	0	0
United Arab Emirates	0	0	0	0	0	0	0	0	0	0	0	0.88
Bangladesh			0.08	0	0	0	0	0.11	0	0	0	0.09
Bahrain	0	0	0	0	0	0	0	0.82	0	0	0.09	0.02
Brunei	0	0.73	0	0	0	0	0.967	0.22	0	4.38	3.52	0.31
Myanmar/Burma	0	0	0	0	0	0	0	0	0	0.15	0.02	0
Egypt	0	0	0	4.08	0	0	0.53	0	0.04	0.06	0.01	0.06
Ethiopia	0	0	0	0.48	0	0	0	0.34	0	0	0	0
Indonesia	0.47	1.3	1.17	1	3.07	2.38	2.1	4.39	5.01	4.26	4.25	3.2
India	2.94	5.27	3.89	2.56	4.35	4.89	6.55	4.13	5.23	5.23	4.5	5.777
Iran	0.08	0.02	0.27	4.48	0.48	0.69	0.27	0.13	0.2	0.01	0.2	0.04
Iraq	0	0	0	0	0	0	0.05	0	0.18	0.02	0	0
Kenya	0.52	0.94	2.44	0.64	0.39	0.44	0.83	0.88	0.58	0.03	0.24	0.07
Kuwait	0	0	0	0	0.12	0	0	0.04	0	0	0.03	0.19
Sri Lanka	5.12	2.33	2.76	0.8	2.54	0.84	0.56	4.19	1.39	0.92	1.83	2.47
Madagascar	0	0	0	0	0	0	0	0	0	0	0	0
Maldives				0	0	0	0	0	0	0	0	0
Mozambique	1.53	0.44	0.13	0	0	0	0	0	0	0	0	0

(*Contd.*)

TABLE 11 (*Contd.*)

1	2	3	4	5	6	7	8	9	10	11	12	13
Mauritius	0.89	0.92	4.48	0.66	1.69	13.05	16.83	12.02	9.81	7.95	7.18	16.37
Malawi	0	0	0	0	0	0	0	0	0	0	0	4.08
Malaysia	2.94	3.31	3.42	5.99	14.43	17.37	21.59	27.85	19.87	21.7	25.45	27.1
Nepal	0	0	0	0	0	0.48	0	0	0	0.18	0.8	0
Oman	0	0	0	0	0	0	1.31	0	0	0	0	0
Pakistan	1.93	1.48	1.84	2.24	1.77	0.77	0.96	0.64	1.16	2.05	1.52	1.56
Qatar	0	0	0	0	0	0	0	0	0.54	0	0	4.31
Rwanda	0	0	0		0	0	0	0	0	0	0	0
S. Africa Customs Union	10.18	11.38	8	9.23	13.1	19.46	16.06	25.8	24.42	24.59	21.73	21.32
Saudi Arabia	0	0	0	0	0	0	0	0	0	0.02	0	0.01
Sudan	0	0	0	0	0	0	0	0	0	0	0	0
Singapore	8.15	13.92	14.95	17.79	39.21	16.52	22.54	32.01	22.27	38.79	34.32	41.28
Somalia	0	0	0	0	0	0	0	0	0	0	0	0
Seychelles	0	0	0	0	0	0	0	0	0	0	0	0
Thailand	5.36	4.13	8.85	11.91	11.65	12.4	10.44	13.47	11.21	11.04	13.33	19.63
Tanzania	0.57	3.06	0.18	0.55	0.22	0.07	0.14	0	0.07	0.11	0	0
Uganda	0	0	0	0	0	0	0	0	0	0	0	0
World	28.7	30.98	34.54	38.34	31.02	30.85	25.23	24.55	25.33	27.88	29.05	27.15
Zambia	0	0	0	0	0	0	0	0.37	0	0	0	4.35
Zimbabwe	0	0	0	0	0			0	0		0.37	0
SAARC	4.62	6.24	5.95	4.19	4.87	8.18	6.84	5.33	5.95	6.27	6.64	7.18
ASEAN	6.42	9.16	9.59	11.67	21.88	16	20.51	25.92	24.62	27.33	26.63	31.36
N-East Africa	1.25	1.67	1.16	2.48	3.21	0.86	0.92	2.34	0.56	0.18	0.68	0.63
West Asia	0.27	0.61	0.87	2.36	0.81	0.64	0.64	1.11	0.65	0.42	0.27	4.06

(*Contd.*)

TABLE 11 (*Contd.*)

Partner	1982	1983	1984	1985	1986	1987	1988	1989	1990	1991	1992
	14	15	16	17	18	19	20	21	22	23	24
Afghanistan	0	0	0	0	0	0	0	0	0	0.5	0
United Arab Emirates	11.39	3.51	1.44	0.48	0.35	1.47	2.17	4.25	3.28	2.95	2.38
Bangladesh	0.08	0.08	0.06	0.25	0.08	0.04	0.09	0.06	0.41	0.23	1.12
Bahrain	0	0.03	0.06	0.88	4.43	3.16	0.71	20.87	4.77	4.58	6.84
Brunei	1.24	2.41	0.25	0	0	10.22	0.74	0	0.6	0.44	0.61
Myanmar/Burma	0.46	0	0.1	0	0.25	0.26	0.19	0.5	0.12	0.14	0.25
Egypt	0.16	0.05	0.19	0.15	0.39	1.44	3.37	4.3	1.91	10.46	1.14
Ethiopia	0.81	0	0	0	0	0	0	0	0	0	0
Indonesia	3.45	2.7	5.63	4.94	7.75	8.34	9.43	10.15	9.96	11.03	14.94
India	5.43	7.73	7.86	6.25	7.02	7.53	9.44	7.14	8.89	8.78	1.23
Iran	0	0	0	0	0	0	0	0	0.02	0.02	0.09
Iraq	0	0	0	0	0	0	0	0	0	0	0
Kenya	0.09	3.87	2.22	1.71	1.31	0.28	0.38	4.43	2.66	1.21	2.87
Kuwait	0.12	0.28	0.37	0.33	1.89	0.95	1.18	0.2	0	0	0.01
Sri Lanka	5.02	6.42	6.86	6.01	5.51	9.45	3.03	11.7	7.11	7.73	7.12
Madagascar	0	0	0	0	0	0	0	0	0	0	1.98
Maldives	0	0	0	0	0	0	0	0	1.64	0	0
Mozambique	0	0	0	0	0	0	3.03	1.41	0	0.2	0
Mauritius	11.2	6.1	9	10.88	10.29	22.13	21.25	17.93	13.09	10.2	19.84
Malawi	0	0	0	0	0	0	0.7	0	0	0	0
Malaysia	28.41	24.68	22.92	20.06	17.61	16.99	18.63	19.95	24.02	30.22	23.57

(*Contd.*)

TABLE 11 (*Contd.*)

	14	15	16	17	18	19	20	21	22	23	24
Nepal	0.12	0.13	0	0.18	0	0.14	1.58	0.79	0.46	0.43	7.96
Oman	0	0	0	0	0	0	14	0	6.54	5.42	4.44
Pakistan	1.16	1.48	1.96	0.57	1.27	0.94	1.67	1.24	0.85	1.7	1.74
Qatar	1.01	5.71	1.43	1.18	1.1	1.12	0	0	0	0	0.3
Rwanda	0		0	0	0	0	0			0	
S.Africa Customs Union	27.2	24.97	25.78	27.24	27.34	24.28	29.33	28.29	28.42	29.59	21.18
Saudi Arabia	0.09	0.05	0	4.25	4.64	2.71	3.49	1.67	0.96	1.09	4.19
Sudan	0	0	0	0	0	0	0	0.74	0	0	0
Singapore	36.61	37.93	35.22	33.14	33.53	36.9	34.93	33.9	36.26	38.04	38.37
Somalia	0	0	0	0	0	0	0	0	0	0	0
Seychelles	0	2.15	2.74	0	0	0	0	0	0	0	0
Thailand	15.15	12.63	11.24	13.54	12.81	13.5	15.66	17.38	19.04	23.04	23.64
Tanzania	0	0	1.82	0	2.16	0	0	0.91	0.87	0	0
Uganda	0	0	0	0	0	0	0.94	0	0	0	0
World	23.32	23.99	21.7	19.83	20.28	24.86	23.72	22.16	26.28	30.09	30.07
Zambia	3.93	0	1.73	0	0.74	1.38	0	1.96	0	0	0
Zimbabwe	2.32	10.4	15.52	3.49	5.15	9.5	8.16	1.39	13.94	1.61	0.63
SAARC	8.78	8.95	8.78	7.67	7.15	8.29	8.23	8.07	10	10.33	11.08
Asean	33.01	28.45	29.66	27.81	28.84	32.58	31.41	32.23	33.35	33.66	32.91
N-East Africa	1.34	5.02	7.2	3.59	4.03	6.3	4.19	5.37	8.49	2.05	2.01
West Asia	3.11	1.68	3.78	5.39	3.67	3.87	3.2	5.79	2.77	4.59	4.73

TABLE 12

Intra-Industry Trade Index of India with IOG

Reporter India, Commodity Total SITC 5-8-Digit Level, Type Intra-Industry Trade (Aggregate), and Flow Exports

Partner	1970	1971	1972	1973	1974	1975	1976	1977	1978	1979	1980	1981
1	2	3	4	5	6	7	8	9	10	11	12	13
Afghanistan	0.12	0.92	0	0	0.29	0.02	0.14	0	0	0	0.23	0.08
United Arab Emirates	0.07	0.39	0.18	0.46	0.29	0.01	0.21	0.79	0.5	1.66	2.31	4.67
Australia	4.24	4.27	3.4	4.27	3.74	7.57	5.21	5.19	5.7	5.84	5.27	5.14
Burundi	0	0	0	0	0	0	0	0	0	0	0	0
Bangladesh			3.06	3.21	4.05	2.91	1.34	0.62	0.94	2.59	1.88	0.25
Bahrain	0.08	0.51	0.71	0.86	0.1	1.09	1.49	0.82	0.68	2.17	0.22	1.21
Brunei								0	0	0	0	0
Bhutan												
Myanmar/Burma	0.02	0.02	0.16	0.63	0.21	0.03	0.14	0	0	0.19	0	0
Comoros	0	0	0	0	0	0	0		0	0	0	0
Djibouti								0		0	0	0
Egypt	0.02	0.01	0.06	0.24	0.03	0.49	0.02	0	0.22	0.04	0.01	0.06
Ethiopia	0	0	0	0.43	0.09	0.05	0	0.09	0.02	3.42	0.95	0
Indonesia	0.13	2.33	0.03	0.33	0.05	0.07	0.03	0.81	1.42	2.23	0.36	0.24
Iran	0.1	0.17	0.98	0.8	0.66	0.73	0.55	0.96	0.96	2.61	2.06	0.11
Iraq	2.44	0	0	4.6	0.12	0.06	0	1.9	7.57	0.2	0.62	0
Kenya	0.21	2.35	1.49	1.84	0.94	0.61	1.42	0.73	3.03	2.35	1.97	3.36
Kuwait	0.09	0.5	0.65	0.71	0.24	0.22	0.54	0.19	1.92	0.76	1.57	1.36
Sri Lanka	0.75	0.16	0.26	0.55	0.3	0.41	0.51	0.12	0.21	0.9	2.11	1.38
Madagascar	2.17	0	0	0	0	0	0	0	0	0	0	0

(Contd.)

TABLE 12 (*Contd.*)

1	2	3	4	5	6	7	8	9	10	11	12	13
Maldives		0	0	0	0	0	0	0	0	0	0	0
Mozambique	0.51	0	0	0.34	0.78	0.4	0.69					
Mauritius	0	0	0	0.44	1.53	0.32	0	0.02	0.02	0	0.13	042
Malawi	0	0	0	0	0	0.08	0	0.06	0	0	0	0
Malaysia	5.38	0.4	0.63	0.86	0.69	1.11	1.28	5.34	3.4	2.47	1.14	1.89
Nepal	4.02	0.66	0.85	1.46	1.08	1.89	1.38	1.69	1.3	1.64	4.61	1.23
Oman	0	0	0	0.1	0.06	0.06	0.01	0.01	0.01	1.27	0.06	1.59
Pakistan	0					0	0	0.06	0.33	0	0	0.31
Qatar	0.43	0.14	0.34	0.11	0.05	9.08	0.86	0.3	0.16	0.23	0.03	0.36
Rwanda	0	0	0	0	0	0	0	0	0	0	0	0
S.Africa Customs Union	0.52	0.22	0.05	0	0	0	0	1.35	0	0.08	0	0.05
Saudi Arabia	0	0.02	0.07	1.04	0.04	0	0	0	0.01	0.21	0	0.32
Sudan	0	0	0	0.03	0	0	0.23	0	0.04	0.23	0.02	0.04
Singapore	1.79	13.99	14.3	8.79	11.72	7.65	23.62	11.87	21.28	21.8	21.75	24.28
Somalia	0	0	0	0	0	0	0	0	0	0	0	0
Seychelles			0	0	0.96	0	0	0	0	0	0	0.05
Thailand	2.86	2.82	2.41	5.08	4.44	2.1	1.66	1.37	1.97	5.05	5.05	4.9
Tanzania	0.17	0.35	0.04	0.03	0.15	0.17	0.09	0.24	0.98	1.72	0.27	0.18
Uganda	0.18	0.04	0	0	0	0	0	0.06	0.03	0.13	0.17	0.05
World	22.09	19.64	19.15	19.97	21.41	24.1	26.36	30.19	35.46	30.83	30.2	29.76
Yemen, unified												
Zambia	0	0	0	0	0.23	0.09	0.03	0.17	0	1.03	0	0.04
Zimbabwe											0	0

(*Contd.*)

TABLE 12 (*Contd.*)

Partner	1982	1983	1984	1985	1986	1987	1988	1989	1990	1991	1992
	14	15	16	17	18	19	20	21	22	23	24
Afghanistan	0	0	0	0.26	0.03	0	0	0.02	0	0	0
United Arab Emirates	15.47	5.15	1.5	5.24	8.04	4.52	5.06	7.95	6.55	5.44	10.62
Australia	6.48	8.28	9.46	6.9	8.82	9.81	14.33	13.47	12.46	13.66	15.38
Burundi	0	0	0	0	0	0	0	0	0	0	0
Bangladesh	4.8	1.62	1.12	0.45	0.34	0.86	1.2	7.79	0.5	1.54	0.52
Bahrain	5.79	0.8	0.11	0.82	0.25	0.59	26.85	13.44	0.77	1.11	1.74
Brunei	0	0	1.32	0	0	0	0	0	0	24.45	0
Bhuta									5.25	0	0.53
Myanmar/Burma	0	1.71	0.3	0	0.36	0.23	2.01	0		0.09	0
Comoros	0	0	0	0	0	0	0	0	0	0	0.78
Djibouti		0	0	0	0	0	0	0		0	0
Egypt	0.01	1.91	0.05	0.01	0.41	4.64	1.68	1.03	0.64	7.68	2.44
Ethiopia	0.42	0.03	0	1.49	0	0	0	0	0	0	0
Indonesia	0.82	4.46	1.29	0.77	1.42	3.98	21.77	9.53	11.08	35.97	36.17
Iran	0	0.3	0.08	0.55	0.26	0.33	0.59	0.03	0.75	1.93	5.23
Iraq	0	0	0	0	1.78	0.68	0.21	1.42	0	0	0
Kenya	0.76	4.8	1.82	1.36	2.68	2.12	0.04	0.62	0.16	0.3	2.26
Kuwait	15.48	1.04	0.42	2.05	3.39	1.06	0.5	0.32	1.13	0.1	0.41
Sri Lanka	6.44	4.19	2.28	3.01	4.17	2.8	3.65	4.35	2.16	3.7	2.26
Madagascar	0	0	0	10	0	0	0	0	0	0	0
Maldives	0	0	0	0	0	0	0	0	0	0	1.03
Mozambique		0.17	0	0				0	0	0.2	0
Mauritius	2.41	0.8	0.25	0	0.1	0.01	0.25	0.07	0.02	0	0.49

(*Contd.*)

TABLE 12 (*Contd.*)

	14	15	16	17	18	19	20	21	22	23	24
Malawi	0	0	0	0	0	0	0	0	0	0	0
Malaysia	4.17	2.58	4.81	8.85	5.02	9.56	12.94	16.13	11.8	16.54	20.37
Nepal	0	1	3.25	2.47	3.06	3.17	3.51	0	2.76	1.27	1.37
Oman	4.38	0.14	0.02	0.07	0.7	0.31	0.39	0.63	0.65	5.33	4.79
Pakistan	0.36	0.16	0.4	1.04	6.38	25.21	7.13	3.1	1.49	3.87	3.52
Qatar	0	0.02	0.04	0	0.16	0.1	0.17	0.77	0.7	0.21	0.46
Rwanda	0	0	0	0	0	0	0	0	0	0	0
S. Africa Customs Union	0	0.02	0	0	0	0	0	11.92	2.16	0.21	0.24
Saudi Arabia	1.93	0.75	0.14	0.44	2.29	0.95	6.29	1.34	2.5	2.33	2.5
Sudan	0	0.18	0	0	0	0	1.28	0.33	0	0	0
Singapore	19.96	14.43	22.25	19.69	22.95	27.29	25.25	29.9	30.48	30.38	33.52
Somalia	0	0	0	0	0	0	0	0	0	0	0
Seychelles	2.47	0	0	0	0	0	0	1.68	0	0	0
Thailand	6.65	4.02	11.66	12.83	8.03	7.23	6.97	10.32	15.37	19.5	25.01
Tanzania	0	0	0.31	0.07	0.06	0.79	0.23	0.2	0.08	0.19	0.41
Uganda	0	0	0	0	0.05	0	0	0	0	0	0
World	29.07	34.58	32.44	29.43	29.91	36.76	42.62	44.33	41.33	42.34	42.43
Yemen, unified									0	0	
Zambia	0	0.03	0.04	0.06	0	0.06	0	0.09	0.11	0.49	0
Zimbabwe	0	0	0.05	1.77	0	0.1	1.19	0.13	0.23	0.13	0.04

TABLE 13

Intra-Industry Trade Index of S. Africa Customs Union with IOG

Reporter S. Africa Cust UNI Commodity Total -SIC 5-8 at 3-Digit level,
Type Intra-Industry Trade (Aggregate and Flow Exports)

Partner	1970	1971	1972	1973	1974	1975	1976	1977	1978	1979	1980	1981
1	2	3	4	5	6	7	8	9	10	11	12	13
United Arab Emirates												
Australia	13.77	16.28	11.26	12.08	0	0	0	0	0	0	0	0
Bangladesh	.	.										.
Bahrain	.	.	0	16.39								.
Brunei												.
Myanmar/Burma	.	.	0	2.2								.
Egypt	.	.	0	0								.
Ethiopia												.
Indonesia	0	0		0								.
India	.	0	0.54	1.53								.
Iran	0	0	10.68	9.57								
Iraq	.	0	51.35	31.34								
Kenya	.	0	12.17	16.13								.
Kuwait	.	.	0	0								.

(Contd.)

TABLE 13 (*Contd.*)

1	2	3	4	5	6	7	8	9	10	11	12	13
Sri Lanka	7.7	10.05	4.65	19.03	0	0	0	0	0	0	0	0
Madagascar												.
Mozambique	.	0	0	0								
Mauritius	0	0	33.45	35.28								.
Malawi	0	0	50.09	32.38								.
Malaysia	.	0	0	0								.
Nepal												.
Oman												.
Pakistan	.	0	0.28	2.24								.
Qatar	.	0	.	.								.
Saudi Arabia	.	0	0.55	0.07								.
Singapore												
Seychelles												.
Thailand	0	0	11.59	24.3								.
Tanzania	.	0	26.09	.					0	.	.	.
Uganda	.	.	.	0					0	.	.	.
World	21.32	21.61	22.46	22.03	21.34	19.32	19	23.49	21.56	24.17	22.27	19.59
Zambia	0	0	25.15	14.67								
Zimbabwe												

(*Contd.*)

TABLE 13 (*Contd.*)

	14	15	16	17	18	19	20	21	22	23	24
Partner	1982	1983	1984	1985	1986	1987	1988	1989	1990	1991	1992
United Arab Emirates	.		0	0	.	.	0	.			
Australia	0	0	26.03	25.01	28.2	24.33	29.15	30.04	30.28	30.6	23.24
Bangladesh	.		0	0	0	0	0	0	0	0	0
Bahrain	.		0	0	.	0	.	0			
Brunei	.	.	0								
Myanmar/Burma											
Egypt	.		0	.	0	0	0	0	0	0	0
Ethiopia	.		0	0	0	0	0	0	0	0	.
Indonesia	.		0	0	0	0	0	0	0	0	0
India	.		0	0	0	0	0	11.92	2.16	0.21	0.24
Iran											
Iraq											
Kenya	.		1.8	0	19.7	17.17	17.99	.	5.8	0.95	.
Kuwait	.		0	.							
Sri Lanka	0	0	0.89	2.71	0.94	1.83	2	5.92	2.73	1.03	2.2
Madagascar	.	.	.	0	0	.	.	.	0	0.73	.
Mozambique											

(*Contd.*)

TABLE 13 (*Contd.*)

	14	15	16	17	18	19	20	21	22	23	24
Mauritius	.		0	0	.	0	.	.	7.88	4.8	9.72
Malawi	.		2.11	0	2.48	.	.	.			
Malaysia	.		0	0	0	0	0.63	0	1.8	8.94	.
Nepal	.		0	.	0	.	.	0	0	.	.
Oman	.		0	0	0	.	.	.	.	.	0
Pakistan	.		2.7	0	0.3	0.27	0.07	1.29	0	0	0
Qatar	.		.	0	.	.	0	0	.	0	.
Saudi Arabia	.		0	0	.	0	.	0	0	.	.
Singapore					1.28	2.29	1.52	0	0	0	2.79
Seychelles	.		0	0	0.38	1.13	0.99	0.63	0.23	0.08	.
Thailand	.		0	0	0	0.07	0.02	4.14	2.11	0.83	0
Tanzania											
Uganda											
World	21.24	19.66	14.82	21.77	21.31	17.54	17.1	18.21	23.09	24.61	24.99
Zambia											
Zimbabwe	.	.	32.15	0	28.21	.	.	.	27.32	20.46	.

TABLE 14

Australia vs. Other IOG Countries : IIT Indices for Capital Intensive Products

IOG countries	1975	1980	1985	1990	1992
ASEAN	15.85	32.1	37.12	45.26	42.9
SAARC	20.91	15.48	20.28	28.45	27.54
West Asia	0.2	0.23	8.45	3.09	6.29
Northeast Africa	0.44	0.37	3.59	8.95	6.31
India	18.86	12.11	17.35	24.62	24.03
Indonesia	2.19	3.5	7.85	12.4	20.63
South Africa	21.11	28.71	34.4	34.71	28.57

TABLE 15

Australia vs. Other IOG Countries : IIT Indices for Labour Intensive Products

IOG countries	1975	1980	1985	1990	1992
ASEAN	24.32	26.46	18.6	19.52	21
SAARC	1.11	1.74	1.88	1.83	1.85
West Asia	3.16	0.41	0.72	3.49	2.78
Northeast Africa	7.87	2.99	6.44	10.33	29.81
India	0.55	1.72	1.74	1.46	0.85
Indonesia	10.95	18.43	9.1	9.63	13.2
South Africa	25.95	17.95	23.75	33.78	32.84

TABLE 16

Australia vs. Other IOG Countries : IIT Indices for Mineral Intensive Products

IOG countries	1975	1980	1985	1990	1992
ASEAN	22.35	21.32	42.93	47.47	60.18
SAARC	4.78	9.2	5.16	5.35	4.68
West Asia	0.1	1.23	1.09	0.54	1.89
Northeast Africa	40.1	75.91	0.33	5.02	0.19
India	2.64	1	5.66	10.18	0.67
Indonesia	1.8	3.6	2.24	74	51.63
South Africa	12.03	3.89	9.87	7.76	10.77

TABLE 17

Australia vs. Other IOG Countries : IIT Indices for Agriculture Intensive Products.

IOG countries	1975	1980	1985	1990	1992
ASEAN	3.99	9.23	13.99	12.49	15.28
SAARC	2.14	3.26	2.57	4.05	5.51
West Asia	0.37	0.02	0.25	0.59	2.24
Northeast Africa	0.34	0.72	0.8	8.82	5.73
India	2.5	1.54	1.33	1.9	2.88
Indonesia	0.43	1.87	1.8	3.03	6.98
South Africa	12.63	19	12.05	13.26	4.71

TABLE 18

India vs. Other IOG Countries : IIT Indices for Capital Intensive Products.

IOG countries	1975	1980	1985	1990	1992
ASEAN	5.93	19.66	31.92	44.74	51.62
SAARC	3.12	3.27	6.77	4.52	3.27
West Asia	2.23	1.8	3.02	17.64	12.4
Northeast Africa	0.3	0.75	2.67	0.19	1.08
Australia	27.4	11.9	17.04	40.67	36.3
Indonesia	0.08	0.25	0.84	12.53	44.34
South Africa	0	0	0	0	0.64

TABLE 19

India vs. Other IOG Countries : IIT Indices for Labour Intensive Products.

IOG countries	1975	1980	1985	1990	1992
ASEAN	2	2.67	11.33	15.38	30.22
SAARC	4.51	2.81	12.29	10.88	4.69
West Asia	2.08	0.75	0.32	0.74	0.96
Northeast Africa	0.01	1.48	0.35	0	0
Australia	0.73	2.25	0.33	0.85	2.23
Indonesia	0	0	0	5.1	19.84
South Africa	0	0	0	0	0

TABLE 20

India vs. Other IOG Countries : IIT Indices for Mineral Intensive Products

IOG countries	1975	1980	1985	1990	1992
ASEAN	1.12	4.37	1.98	7.11	8.3
SAARC	1.33	6.34	8.73	11.18	2.85
West Asia	6.5	0.06	0.38	0.81	1.96
Northeast Africa	2.42	1.21	2.08	1.14	2.33
Australia	1.13	1.4	0.57	0.34	0.77
Indonesia	2.04	1.09	0	0.73	1.69
South Africa	0	0	0	0	0

TABLE 21

India vs. Other IOG Countries : IIT Indices for Agricultural Intensive Products.

IOG countries	1975	1980	1985	1990	1992
ASEAN	4.54	4.87	11.07	10.55	9.2
SAARC	8.94	32.16	25.12	18.98	14.92
West Asia	2.69	10.3	3.81	5.01	6.81
Northeast Africa	1.1	9.1	12.3	3.16	3.35
South Africa	0	0	0.58	0	1.57
Australia	1.89	1.57	1.02	1.69	1.04
Indonesia	6.58	8.73	7.67	4.8	8

TABLE 22

South Africa vs. Other IOG Countries : IIT Indices for Capital Intensive Products.

IOG Countries	1985	1990	1992
ASEAN	0	9.22	6.17
SAARC	2.58	3.78	8.6
West Asia	0	0	4.68
Northeast Africa	0	19.63	21.04
Australia	28.64	35.93	27.62
India	0	0	0.27
Indonesia	0	0	0

TABLE 23

South Africa vs. Other IOG Countries : IIT Indices for Labour Intensive Products.

IOG Countries	1985	1990	1992
ASEAN	0	5.15	0.93
SAARC	10.96	3.33	1.67
West Asia	0	0	1.04
Northeast Africa	0	43.63	30.75
Australia	25.96	41.02	33.3
India	0	0	0
Indonesia	0	0	0

TABLE 24

South Africa vs. Other IOG Countries : IIT Indices for Mineral Intensive Products.

IOG Countries	1985	1990	1992
ASEAN	0	0.37	13.28
SAARC	0	0.72	1.05
West Asia	0	0	0
Northeast Africa	0	26.96	33
Australia	9.37	7.97	9.32
India	0	4.76	6.72
Indonesia	0	0	0

TABLE 25

South Africa vs. Other IOG Countries : IIT Indices for Agricultural Intensive Products.

IOG Countries	1985	1990	1992
ASEAN	0	0.04	3.73
SAARC	1.52	0.59	5.08
West Asia	0	0	0.07
Northeast Africa	0	8.06	21.15
Indonesia	0	0	0
Australia	10.42	13.2	4.19
India	0	0	0.29

NOTES

1. APEC is set to evolve as an open economic co-operation avoiding unnecessary discrimination against the rest of the world, and emphasises consensus-building approach to decision-making [for a detailed discussion, see Elek (*1994*) and Garnaut (*1994*)].
2. IIT, as an undeniable fact of trade, is not a prediction of traditional trade theory.
3. Not only the relevance, but also the existence of IIT have been challenged in the literature [see, for example, Lipsey (*1976*)].
4. Although the growth of industrial activity in developing countries is likely to foster a pronounced intra-industry specialization in the production of manufactured products (*Linder 1961*), the possibility of agricultural products being a source of intra-industry trade (IIT) should not be overlooked (*Balassa 1962*).
5. Aquino (*1978*) criticised the Grubel-Lloyd index by saying that the index is a downward-biased measure of IIT in the presence of an imbalanced country's commodities trade. Aquino's suggested correction of the Grubel-Lloyd index was rejected by many researchers (see, for example, *Greenaway and Milner, 1981* and *Tharakan, 1984*). In fact, Aquino adopted Michaley's (1962) index which measures similarities in structures of exports and imports rather than IIT. In the literature, many researchers have effectively used the unadjusted Grubel-Lloyd index to measure IIT (see, for example, *Caves, 1981* and *Vona, 1991*).
6. Identification of the factors causing variations in IIT among countries will be attempted at a later stage.

REFERENCES

Aquino, A. (1978) : 'Intra-industry trade and inter-industry specialisation as concurrent sources of international trade in manufacture', *Weltwilrtschaftliches Archiv,* Vol. 114, pp. 275-295.

Balassa, B. (1962) : *The Theory of Economic Integration,* London : Allen & Unwin.

Caves, R.E. (1981) : 'Intra-industry trade and market structure in the industrial countires', *Oxford Economic Papers,* Vol. 33, pp. 203-223.

Dixit, A.K. and G.M. Grossman (1982) : 'Trade and prctection with multistage production', *Review of Economic Studies*, Vol. 49, pp. 583-594.

Elek, A. (1994) : 'An open economic association in the Asia Pacific', Australian, Indonesian and Japanese approaches to APEC, Australian National University Seminar Paper, September.

Fukasaku, K. (1992) : *Economic Regionalisation and Intra-industry Trade : Pacific-Asian Perspectives.* OECD Development Centre Technical Paper No. 53.

Garnaut, R.G. (1994) : 'Options for Asia Pacific trade liberalisation : A Pacific Free Trade Area?' *APEC : Challenges and Opportunities,* Institute of Southeast Asian Studies, Singapore.

Garnaut, R.G. and P. Drysdale (ed.) (1994) : *Asia Pacific Regionalism : Readings in International Economic Relations,* Pymble, Australia : Harper Educational Publishers.

Greenaway, D. and C. Milner (1981) : 'Trade imbalance effect and the measurement of intra-industry trade', *Weltwirtschaftliches Archiv,* Vol. 117, pp. 756-762.

Grubel, H. and P. J. Lloyd (1975) : *Intra-industry Trade : The Theory and Measurement of International Trade in Differentiated Products*, London : Macmillan.

Helpman, E. and P. Krugman (1985) : *Market Structure and Foreign Trade*, Boston : MIT Press.

Krugman, P. (1979) : 'Increasing returns, monopolistic competition and 'international trade', *Journal of International Economics*, Vol. 9, pp. 469-479.

Krugman, P. (1981): 'Intra-industry specialisation and the gains from trade', *Journal of Political Economy*, Vol. 89, pp. 959-973.

Lancaster, K. (1980) : 'Intra-industry trade under perfect monopolistic competition', *Journal of International Economics*, Vol. 10.

Linder, S. (1961) : *An Essay on Trade and Transformation*, New York : John Wiley and Sons.

Lipsey, R.E. (1976) : 'Review of Grubel and Lloyd (1975)', *Journal of International Economics*, Vol. 6, pp. 312-314.

Michaely, M. (1962) : Concentration in international trade, *Contribution to Economic Analysis*, Vol. 8, Amsterdam : North-Holland.

Tharakan, P.K.M. (1984) : 'Intra-industry trade between the industrial countries and the developing world', *European Economic Review*, Vol. 26, pp. 213-227.

Tharakan, P.K.M. and J. Kol (1989) : *Intra-industry Trade, Theory, Evidence and Extension*, Hong Kong : Macmillan.

Vona, S. (1991) : 'On the measurement of intra-industry trade : some further thoughts', *Weltwirtschaftliches Archiv*, Vol. 127, pp. 678-700.

APPENDIX

Key Economic Indicators of Major Indian Ocean Group Countries

INDIA

US $ Billions

Balance of Payments	1980	1989	1990	1991	1992	1993
Export of Goods & NFS	11.3	21.2	23.4	23.4	24.0	28.3
Import of Goods & NFS	17.4	27.9	32.1	24.9	27.9	28.8
Resource Balance	–6.1	–6.7	–8.7	–1.4	–3.9	–0.5
Curr. A/A Balance						
after Off. Transf.	–2.3	–7.3	–10.0	–2.5	–4.9	–0.3
LT Capital Inflow:	2.0	6.5	4.4	3.5	4.9	9.9
Direct Investment	–	0.4	0.2	0.1	0.4	4.1
LT Loans & Other	2.0	6.1	4.2	3.4	4.5	5.8
Change in Net Reserves	1.4	0.2	2.8	–2.6	–0.3	–8.4
As Share of GDP:						
Exports	6.6	7.8	7.9	9.3	9.9	11.3
Resource Balance	–3.5	–2.5	–2.9	–0.6	–1.6	–0.2
Interest Payments	0.4	1.3	1.3	1.5	1.4	1.7
Reserves incl. Gold	13.0	7.1	5.2	8.3	9.5	14.7

Official X-Rate (LCUs/US$)	7.9	16.7	18.0	24.5	30.0	31.6
GDP (Bn US $ current)	172.3	272.5	295.8	251.1	243.7	250.1

Shares of Gross Domestic Product

	1965	1973	1980	1991	1992	1993
Gross Domestic Product						
Agriculture	40.6	42.8	34.3	28.6	28.3	28.1
Industry	20.2	19.9	23.3	24.9	24.4	24.5
(Manufacturing)	14.3	14.3	15.9	15.7	15.6	15.5
Services	31.3	29.2	32.4	36.1	36.3	37.0

Growth Rates (% per annum)

	1965-73	1973-80	1980-93	1992	1993
Agriculture	3.3	1.8	3.0	5.0	2.3
Industry	3.9	5.2	6.2	2.2	3.3
(Manufacturing)	4.3	4.9	6.2	2.0	2.5
Services	4.1	4.9	6.4	4.5	5.2
Inflation Rates (Consumer Prices)	5.9	5.3	9.0	11.8	6.4
Population	2.3	2.3	2.1	–	–
GNI per capita	1.6	1.4	2.0	–	–

External Resource Flows

	1989	1990	1991	1992	1993
Total Debt (TD). US $ Bns	63.8	68.7	71.6	77.0	85.0
TD/GDP (as %)	23.4	23.2	28.5	31.6	34.0
TD/Exports (as %)	268.3	268.2	274.3	293.3	270.0
Total Debt Serv. (TDS) US $ Mns	–	–	7445	6637	8942
TDS/Exports (as %)	–	–	31.0	26.0	25.2
Off. Dev. Assist.. (ODA) US $ Mns	1874	1550	1657	2354	–
ODA/GDP (as %)	0.7	0.5	0.7	1.0	–
ODA/Exports (as %)	8.8	6.6	7.1	9.8	–

SOUTH AFRICA

US $ Billions

Balance of Payments	1980	1989	1990	1991	1992	1993
Export of Goods & NFS	29.1	22.4	23.3	23.4	23.2	27.3
Import of Goods & NFS	25.8	17.0	17.0	17.2	17.9	22.5
Resource Balance	3.4	5.4	6.3	6.2	5.3	4.8
Curr. A/A Balance after Off. Transf.	–	1.4	2.0	2.2	1.4	1.8

Direct Investment	–	–	–	–	–	–
Portfolio investment	–0.3	–0.1	–0.1	0.1	–1.5	–0.4
Other Capital	–0.3	–0.1	0.4	0.40	–1.3	–1.0
Change in Net Reserves	2.3	0.7	0.4	0.4	0.1	–
As Share of GDP:						
Exports	0.4	24.9	22.9	22.0	20.6	23.5
Resource Balance	0.0	6.0	6.2	5.8	4.7	4.1
Reserves incl. Gold	7.2	1.8	2.2	2.6	2.7	1.0
Official X-Rate (LCUs/US$)	0.8	2.6	2.6	2.8	2.9	3.3
GDP (Bn US $ current)	77.3	89.8	101.6	106.4	112.8	116.3

Shares of Gross Domestic Product

	1965	1973	1980	1991	1992
Gross Domestic Product					
Agriculture	9.5	7.5	7.5	4.4	3.5
Industry	27.9	27.0	30.1	24.9	25.2
(Manufacturing)	22.5	21.2	21.4	22.3	22.4
Services	45.6	47.7	41.0	47.4	48.9

Growth Rates (% per annum)

	1965-73	1973-80	1980-92	1992
Agriculture	9.6	12.9	4.7	-13.8
Industry	15.1	17.8	17.8	9.7
(Manufacturing)	14.8	19.7	7.4	7.2
Services	10.4	12.2	8.6	9.7
Inflation Rates (Consumer Prices)	–	14.6	14.7	15.3

	1989	1991	1992	
Population	2.5	2.4	2.3	–
GNP per capita	–0.1	–2.6	–4.3	–

AUSTRALIA

US $ Billions

Balance of Payments	1980	1989	1990	1991	1992	1993
Export of Goods & NFS	26.0	44.2	48.4	51.8	51.4	55.7
Import of Goods & NFS	29.7	51.2	51.3	50.6	52.2	57.2
Resource Balance	–3.7	–7.0	–2.0	1.2	–0.8	–1.5
Curr. A/A Balance after Off. Transf.	–	–17.7	–15.1	–10.3	–11.0	–10.8
Portfolio Investment:	1.6	0.4	2.1	4.3	–0.3	2.3
Direct Investment	1.3	4.5	6.0	2.3	5.4	2.0
Other Capital	1.1	11.2	3.4	7.0	5.0	5.1
Change in Net Reserves	1.3	0.2	2.3	–0.1	–5.5	0.4

As Share of GDP:						
Exports	25.4	16.1	16.6	17.6	18.1	18.7
Resource Balance	–3.6	–2.5	–1.0	0.4	–0.3	–0.5
Reserves incl. Gold	6.4	17.1	19.4	19.3	13.8	14.2
Official X-Rate						
(LCUs/US$)	1.2	1.3	1.3	1.3	1.4	1.4
GDP (Bn US$current)	102.3	275.3	291.2	294.5	283.6	298.6

Shares of Gross Domestic Product

	1965	1973	1980	1991	1992	1993
Gross Domestic Product						
Agriculture	9.3	8.0	5.3	3.0	2.8	3.0
Industry	35.2	25.5	32.0	31.1	31.1	29.9
(Manufacturing)	25.8	22.1	19.2	14.5	14.6	15.0
Services	51.2	55.5	58.1	65.8	66.1	67.1

Growth Rates (% per annum)

	1965-73	1973-80	1980-92	1992
Agriculture	15.5	14.1	2.5	1.7
Industry	13.4	11.6	12.3	–2.2
(Manufacturing)	16.9	12.9	4.5	1.1
Services	17.9	16.1	8.1	2.7
Inflation Rates				
(Consumer Prices)	4.7	11.6	7.0	1.0
Population	2.0	1.6	1.4	–
GNI per capita	3.5	1.8	1.1	–

Data Sources for all the above tables are:

1. Country Briefs (as on June 30, 1994), IBRD.
2. Human Development Report 1994, UNDP.
3. World Debt Tables (various issues), The World Bank.
4. International Financial Statistics (various issues), IMF.
5. Country Reports and Country Profiles, The Economic Intelligence Units, The Economist (various issues).

5

The Challenge of the Triad and the Indian Response : A Note

J.C. DEBNATH

International trade has undergone a sea-change during the last two hundred and a quarter years. In Adam Smith's time trade was complementary — a country sold a product to a country that could not produce it and vice versa. The English bought from India cotton they could not grow and sold mill-made cotton cloth that India could not — or was not allowed to — produce. From the middle of the nineteenth century trade became competitive when two or more countries competed with one another in the buying and selling of two or more commodities. Thus the Americans and Germans both sold chemicals and electrical machinery in the world market in competition with each other and also bought these commodities from each other. The emergence of Japan and other non-Western trading countries during the post-World War II period has ushered in the phenomenon of adversarial trade where a country tries to dominate an industry in a foreign country by pushing out or paralysing the competitors.

In the case of the Japanese, adversarial trade evolved out of protectionism. In the early 1960s when they had just recovered from the destruction of World War II they saw themselves quite backward compared to the Westerners. So they protected their home market from foreign competition and concentrated on export of some industrial goods where they had a slightly superior comparative advantage like automobiles, consumer electronics, photography, optics etc. Japan's ability to train and fully utilise low-wage workers along with the application of powerful management technology enabled the country to flood the U.S. and other markets with cheap Japanese products. The competitors soon realised that they could not produce those commodities at such low cost and hence they must retreat or perish. This was adversarial trade.

What is the answer to adversarial trade? Clearly protectionism is not the answer. It might have helped Japan in the early phase of this development due to some special reasons like Japan's ability to utilise low-wage labour. But in today's world protectionism is totally irrelevant and irrational.

Still there are vigorous protectionist lobbies—overt or covert—in almost all countries. Even the U.S which has repeatedly been eloquent in enunciating the case for free trade and against protection has adopted one protectionist measure after another — voluntary quotas on imports of Japanese cars, a prohibitive tariff on heavy motorcycles, subsidies on the sale of grain to Egypt and so on.

But as Milton Friedman and Rose Friedman have shown, these restrictive practices have not ultimately benefited the U.S. The U.S. in regarded as the "safest haven" for foreign capital because of its most extensive capital markets and the fewest barriers to the acquisition of assets. Foreign investors acquire dollars from their home markets that earn dollars mainly through exports to the U.S. If those exports decline due to restrictive practices, dollars become less available to investors who bid up the exchange rate of the dollar. This higher dollar value makes American goods dearer to foreigners and foreign goods cheaper to the Americans thereby reversing the process of restrictive trade practices.

The result has been that the U.S. has been experiencing a large deficit on current account. Moreover, in spite of the "safe haven" reason, the more expensive dollars might have made the U.S. a less attractive place to send capital thereby making capital inflow less than what it might have been. In this connection, it is to be remembered that capital inflow is as important as favourable balance of trade because both increase employment and income.

Thus protectionism does not ultimately benefit a nation, even when other countries do not retaliate. In practice, however, other countries are likely to retaliate and then world trade would decline even more and every nation would suffer. International trade can be compared with two men in a boat. If one man shoots a hole in the boat he jeopardises the lives of both, but if the second man retaliates by shooting another hole he jeopardises their lives still more.

Quite long ago in 1949 W. Arthur Lewis observed that free trade is prone to degenerate into protectionism and he gave a wise suggestion to remedy it:

> "We are left, therefore, with the conclusion that the level of obstacles to international trade will depend on whether or not measures are adopted to promote stability. If such measures are not taken, countries will insist on the right to control their currencies and their tariff policies, and to make bilateral arrangements." (*Economic survey 1919-39,* p. 175)

Thus the role of international agencies like the IMF and the World Bank in helping individual countries in times of balance of payments crisis is not only helpful for those countries but also for the preservation of free world trade.

Recently regionalisation has been emerging as an effective and practical answer to protectionism and adversarial trade. Regionalisation means formation of economic zones or blocs. The leading blocs in world trade are the so-called Triad countries comprising the European Economic Community (EEC), North American Free Trade Zone and the Japan-centred Pacific Rim region.

First of all regionalisation would give smaller economies the large regional market that they need for the critical amount of production and sales to be competitive. Secondly, regionalisation creates a unit that is capable of reciprocity that can work effectively against protectionism and adversarial trade. Under reciprocity each country's trade would have the the same degree of access to the other country's markets — no more or less. Reciprocity is the main feature of regionalisation.

As Drucker says, reciprocity is fast emerging as the new integrating principle of the world economy. It is going to be the main trade policy of the EEC as it offers a compromise between the traditional protectionists (the French and the Italians) and the traditional free traders (the British and the Germans).It is also becoming the policy of the U.S. in economic relations with Japan, Korea etc. Reciprocity is thus likely to become the vehicle for the integration of the international economy just as competitve trade was the vechicle for a similar integration during the last one hundred and fifty years.

But regionalisation is also likely to degenerate into protectionism or is extreme form—adversarial trade—if both the sides are not equally strong. This danger is not being well-articulated by the strong proponents of free trade or the architects of strong regional blocs, obviously because they do not want to lose their relatively better bargaining position by inducing others to take similar steps. The less developed countries, however, should not miss the point. They must reciprocate equally.

What would be the role of India in this age of reciprocity? Can she with her meagre economic strength reciprocate effectively with the economic giants like the U.S., Japan or the EEC? Certainly not. India should, therefore, form some economic zone in order to counter the pressure of the big giants. SAARC countries may form an economic zone, but in terms of economic strength it would be a dwarf in front of a giant. A more ambitious but more effective bloc may be formed with India, China and Russia. This would be a formidable bloc in terms of land mass, resources, population and economic power.

This Trio—India, China and Russia—can indeed be a matching competitor for the Triad. The Triad countries produce more food than they consume and practically all the industrial raw materials that they need. Moreover, they produce and consume two-thirds of the world's manufactured goods. If trade between the Trio and the Triad follows in terms of reciprocity, there is no reason to doubt that soon the Trio countries would match the Triad countries in material prosperity—they may even surpass the latter in the not so distant future.

Recent economic reforms are likely to boost the Indian economy thereby increasing India's exports and attracting foreign capital. However, this may not be sufficient in the context of increasing regionalisation in world trade. This is an age of globalisation via regionalisation — any country that pursues the path of globalisation without the latter is likely to feel the pinch sooner or later.

The U.S. and other multinationals and foreign investors are now entering Indian, Chinese and Russian economies at an unprecedented pace. This is good for these countries as per the doctrine of openness. But as more and more bilateral trade relations are established between the foreign agencies and these individual countries the prospect of forming an economic zone comprising these three Asian giants will become more difficult and remote. Therefore, any effort towards regionalisation among these countries must be pursued right now — before these individual countries are bogged down to binding trade relations with foreign powers.

We may conclude with a note of hope. If the diverse countries like Great Britain and Italy can come together under the banner of the EEC to protect and nourish their common economic wealth, why should the Asian giants lag behind?

REFERENCES

Bhagwati, Jagdish N., (1985): *Wealth and Poverty,* Vols. I & II, Oxford University Press, Delhi.

Drucker, Peter F. (1980): *The New Realities,* Asian Books Pvt. Ltd., Delhi.

Friedman, Milton & Friedman, Rose (1984): *Tyranny of the Status Quo.* Harcourt Brace Jovanovich, New York.

Lewis, W. Arthur (1949): *Economic Survey, 1919-39.* Allen & Unwin, London.

Union Budgets for 1991-92 & 1992-93, Government of India.

6

India's Export Possibilities of Capital Goods in the EEC

S.N. GUHA THAKURTA

The liberalisation policy and the relaxation of import restriction and partial convertibility of the rupee seem to follow a pattern of export-led growth of the Indian economy. This naturally raises question about our export potential. In the light of regional trade groupings like EC, NAFTA and a plan for Association of Free Trade Area (AFTA) etc., how big is our export potential?

The paper discusses the country's export possibilities in the European Community (EC) and more particularly of the capital goods. After giving a brief review of the post-war scenario in Europe and its recession hit economy in sec. I, we have discussed the country's changing structure of external trade and the import content of exports in sec. II. With this background information we have examined the growth of our capital goods industry and its export performance in sec. III. Sec. IV summarises the broad issues.

I

1.1 Post-Second World War Scenario in Europe : After the Second World War while the US took the leading role in providing international liquidity, and as a result thereof its BOP moved into deficit in the fifties and continued as such for many years, Europe's BOP improved considerably by the end of fifties. This helped boosting its foreign reserves. Most European countries declared their currencies convertible. Capital markets in Europe and in the US began to integrate with private capital flows becoming responsive to movements in interest rates. The period 1950-70 also witnessed progressive decolonization of the developing nations on the one hand and the official capital flows contributing to economic growth and trade expansion on the other. The institution of International Finance Corporation (IFC) in 1956, International Development Association (IDA) in 1960 and the Asian Development Bank (ADB) in 1966 (along with similar Institution for Africa) helped the growth process in the developing countries.

The period 1950-70 witnessed a higher growth in most of the countries in the EC; the annual average compound growth rate of Germany was 6.2 percent, France 4.8 percent, Belgium, Denmark and the Netherland around 4 percent. The growth rate of UK was much less (2.8 percent). In general, it may be said that till the end of the 1960s developed countries in Europe experienced a rapid growth in capital accumulation, employment, labour productivity and the GNP. But in the 1970s the decline was noticeable with a high rate of inflation (see tables 1 & 2).

1.2 Recession in the 1980s : Since the beginning of 1980 a deep recession had set in the industrial economies. In most of these countries budget deficit was so large that fiscal stimulus to escape recession could not help. Monetary control was used to tackle inflation.[1] The import was restricted. The developing countries, particularly the debtor countries, became the victim of increased protectionist pressure by the industrial economies. Their export was substantially reduced, and therefore, their capacity to import and service their debt. In the absence of substantial capital inflows, the debtor countries will have to raise sufficient export surpluses, and this in turn will require an increase in their domestic savings. Alternatively, such an unfavourable trade balance may also entail a much larger depreciation in the exchange rate which implies a higher social cost for adjustment.[2]

Cyclical fluctuation in so far as it is transmitted through foreign trade is expected to be mitigated in the EC countries when foreign trade among them takes place as internal trade. Besides, the Community's dependence on foreign trade outside the EC is also expected to be reduced substantially. These apart, economic integration is expected to facilitate economic growth by large scale economies of scale, absorption of technological change through trade and reduction in the uncertainty in intra-community trade.

TABLE 1

Phases of Productivity Growth (GDP) per man hour in some EC Countries 1870-1977

(Annual average compound growth rate)

	1870-1913	1913-50	1950-70	1970-77
Belgium	1.2	1.5	4.0	5.8
Denmark	1.9	1.7	4.1	3.2
France	1.8	1.7	4.8	5.1
Germany	1.9	1.2	6.2	4.7
Italy	1.2	1.8	5.4	5.0
Netherland	1.2	1.5	4.1	4.6
United Kingdom	1.1	1.5	2.8	2.4

Source : A. Maddison, Western Economic Performance in the 1970s : A Perspective and Assessment, Sept. 1980 quoted in Vijay L.Kelkar, Long-Term Growth Possibilities in OECD Economies in EPW XVII-4 (January 23, 1982)

TABLE 2

Average Annual Growth and Inflation Rate in E.C. (1965-83)

	Population 1983 (in millions)	GNP per capita US $ 1983	Av. annual growth rate % 1965-83	Av. annual growth rate % 1965-73	Av. annual growth rate % 1973-83
Belgium	9.9	9,150	3.1	4.4	6.4
Britain	56.3	9,200	1.7	6.2	14.3
Denmark	5.1	11,570	1.9	7.6	9.5
France	54.7	10,500	3.1	5.3	10.8
German Fed. Rep.	61.4	11,430	2.8	4.7	4.3
Greece	9.8	3,920	4.0	4.4	16.8
Ireland	3.5	5,000	2.3	8.5	14.5
Italy	56.8	6,400	2.8	5.1	17.4
Luxemberg		14,650	3.9	5.0	6.6
Netherland	14.4	9,890	2.3	6.4	6.2
Portugal					
Spain	38.2	4,780	3.0	7.0	16.7
India	733.2	260	1.5	6.3	7.7

Source : World Development Report, 1985.

II

During 1965-83 India's share of exports (in US $) to the industrial countries of Europe, USA and Canada fell only marginally from 58 to 55 percent with a corresponding increase in its share to developing countries from 23 to 26 per cent.[3] During the same period the share to the group of high income oil exporting countries (viz, Oman, Libya, Saudi Arabia, Kuwait, UAE) increased by more than three fold from 2 to 7 per cent.

2.1 Structure of India's Merchandise Trade: The structure of India's merchandise exports (see table 3) shows the familiar pattern of development : the share of primary products declined from about 51 to 40 percent and that of manufactures from 49 to 60 percent during 1965-82. Direction-wise 18-25 per cent of her exports is with the EC while the imports from the Community about 20-33 percent of her total import (all in value terms). Thus, in merchandise trade the country is in deficit in her trade balances. In the 1980s, particularly since 1983-84 the import-export gap has widened substantially. The gap which was of Rs. 2206 crores in that year almost doubled in 1988-89 (Rs. 4076 crores) (table 4). Overall and globally the country's trade deficit has gone up substantially from Rs. 100 crores in 1970-71 to Rs. 5800 crores in 1980-81 and to Rs. 7900 crores in 1988-89. It is necessary, therefore, to examine in depth our export policy not in isolation but in the context of economic growth.

2.2 Import Intensity of India's Exports: In an article in EPW Dholakia & others[4] have examined empirically the direct and indirect effects of a unit increase in demand for exports of 47 sectors of Indian economy and found, on the basis of the 1983-84 input-output table published by CSO, that there are 10 sectors (out of 47 commodity sectors) which show net exports (exports less imports) of more than one billion rupees. Items exported have varied amount of import content. The estimates of direct and indirect (D1) import content of inputs used

TABLE 3

Structure of India's Merchandise Exports (%)

Year	Fuels, Minerals & Metals	Other primary products	Textile & clothing	Machinery & Transport Equipments	Others & Manufactures	Total
1965	10	41	36	1	12	100
1982	7	33	24	7	29	100

Source : World Development Report, Table 10, pp. 192-93.

TABLE 4

Direction of Trade from India 1970-71 — 1988-89

Year	Exp./Imp.	Direction of Trade (% of Value)					
		OECD	OPEC	East Europe	Developing countries	Others	Total Rs. in crores
1970-71	Exp	50(18)	06	21	20	03	100 (1535)
	Imp	64(20)	08	13	15	neg	100
1980-81	Exp	47(22)	11	22	19	01	100 (6711)
	Imp	46(21)	28	10	16	neg	100 (12549)
1983-84	Exp	45(18)	09	16	16	14	100 (9771)
	Imp	52(25)	20	12	15	01	100 (15832)
1984-85	Exp	45(17)	08	19	12	16	100 (11744)
	Imp	49(25)	19	12	19	01	100 (17134)
1985-86	Exp	51(18)	08	21	13	07	100 (10895)
	Imp	54(27)	17	11	18	neg	100 (19658)
1986-87	Exp	56(22)	06	19	15	03	100 (12452)
	Imp	64(32)	10	08	18	neg	100 (20096)
1987-88	Exp	59(25)	06	16	14	04	100 (15741)
	Imp	60(33)	15	08	17	neg	100 (22399)
1988-89	Exp	58(24)	06	16	17	03	100 (20295)
	Imp	61(32)	13	07	19	neg	100 (28194)

Source : Economic Survey, GOI, 1989-90.

Note : Figures in parentheses under OECD refer to percentage of EC countries, and those under total column to absolute amount in Rs. Crores.

in manufacturing for the 10 major export oriented sectors are reproduced in table 5. The last two columns give two alternative measures of import intensity (defined as the ratio of total import of that sector to the corresponding sectoral output) namely (1) proportion of imported inputs in total inputs used in the export product and (2) imported inputs as proportion of the value of exports for a given sector. The table shows that import intensity measured as per alternative (1) varies from 6.9 percent in case of sugar to about 12 percent in case of cash crops. The weighted average of this ratio for all the ten export oriented sectors is 8 percent as against the corresponding national average of about 5 percent. According to alternative (2) which happens to be the conventional measure of import intensity, it is seen that the ratio varies from 0.6 percent in case of fishing to 5.48 percent in case of sugar. Both (1) and (2) alternative measures show a higher level of import intensity for export oriented sectors compared to the economy as a whole. It is also seen from the table that three of the ten sectors (viz, fishing, iron ore and other crops) show lower import intensity than the national average, and that import intensity for miscellaneous manufacturing industries is slightly less than 4 percent which stands above the national average as well as the weighted average of all the ten sectors. Higher intensity for exports may increase government's revenue (through customs duty etc.) but may not result in a net increase in domestic demand, output and employment. This also implies a lower linkage effects of the domestic economy. Emphasis on exports therefore has to be discriminatory between sectors and the trade-off carefully evaluated. The trade-off lies between revenue earnings, foreign exchange earnings and bridging the trade gap on the one hand, and generating net demand in the economy through increased income, on the other.

III

3.1 Growth in India's Capital Goods Industry: Measured by the net value added (NVA) time series data it has been estimated by Mundle and Mukhopadhyay that the growth of real NVA in capital goods sector has been 12.7 percent during mid-fifties to mid-sixties (henceforth period (1), and 7.4 percent during mid-seventies to the end of 1980s (henceforth period III)[5]. The interregnum decade from mid-1960 to mid-1970 (henceforth period II) was the period of "Structural retrogression' or stagnation in Indian economy during which the growth was considerably less (4.5 per cent). The output growth rate of electrical

TABLE 5

Estimates of Import Content and Import Intensity of Export Manufacturing for Major Export Oriented Sectors

Sector	Exp. (fob) value in Rs. lakhs	Inputs used in Exp. manuf. at factor cost Rs. in Lakhs	Direct & Indirect Im. content of inputs (cif) in value Rs. in lakhs	Imp. Intensity of Exp. Manufg.	
				% ratio of Imp. inputs to total	% ratio of imp. to total exports
Cash Crops	26434	5937	710	11.96	2.69
Other Crops	39873	7686	622	8.09	1.56
Fishing	27052	1906	161	8.44	0.60
Iron Ore	14599	2205	192	8.71	1.32
Sugar	23640	18714	1295	6.92	5.48
Cotton Textiles	29843	18451	1449	7.85	4.86
Jute Textiles	13940	9388	698	7.44	5.01
Textile products	102894	45308	3375	7.45	3.28
Leather & leather products	40988	25543	2138	8.37	5.22
Mis. manufg. industries	111706	53441	4367	8.17	3.91
Total of 10 Sectors	430969	188579	15007	7.96	3.48
All Sectors	1365360	600702	29968	4.99	1.19

Source : Dholakia & Others, *op. cit.*

machinery and of transport equipment was respectively 16 and 7.5 per cent during period I, 9 and 1 per cent during period II and around 7.8 and 8 per cent respectively during period III.[6]

Mundle & Mukhopadhyay's study also shows that for each category of capital goods the import share was quite high, although it is declining upto the early 1970s and stabilised thereafter. The import share for non-electrical machinery was stabilised at around 25-26 per cent, while for electrical machinery and transport equipment at around 10 percent (table 6). During period I (1955-65) capital goods production recorded the highest growth rate induced by a high growth rate of fixed investment and by import substitution policies. During the next period — period II — a sharp fall in the growth of fixed capital formation particularly in the public sector led to a significant fall in capital goods production; but for import substitution policy, the fall would have been sharper. In the recovery period — period III — the growth rate of GFCF and of the capital goods sector achieved almost period I level. But presumably the reinforcing impact of import substitution was much less in this period (period III), and hence the growth rate of domestic capital production (7.4 per cent) was much less than anticipated (table 7). According to Mundle and Mukhopadhyay, the extra growth achieved during period I from that of period III was due to the benefit of protection derived out of import substitution policy. This works out to be 16.7, 8.3 and 5.3 per cent respectively for non-electrical machinery, electrical machinery and all capital goods. Also, it is argued that the growth rate in capital goods industry would have been lower in the absence of import substitution policy.

Normally it is expected that 'extra' growth attributable to the import substitution policy should yield economies of scale which together with improvement in product technology should make the industry more competitive at the global level. Studies undertaken on this score show that the capital goods industry has gained in achieving a relatively better growth rate due mainly to the import substitution policy but failed to take advantage in scale economies for getting a foothold in international market[7]. This is, notwithstanding an increase in the concentration ratio in capital goods industry, unlike in consumer goods, during mid-and late 1980s compared to 1976 (table 8).

3.2 India's Export Performance in Capital Goods. India's performance in capital goods exports from 1961-62 is shown in table 8. It will be seen from the table that here has been a quantum jump in the export value of capital goods from the 1960s.

In three decades there has been more than hundredfold increase, but yet the country's share in export trade has virtually remained stagnant since 1970s. This implies that India's exports of capital goods did not keep pace with the rise in the world trade.

TABLE 6

Domestic Production, Exports & Imports of Capital Goods

(Rs. Crore at Current prices)

	Year	Domestic production	Exp.	Imp.	Net availability (col.2+4)	Import share (col. 4 as % of col. 5)
	1	2	3	4	5	6
1. Machinery machine tools & parts	1960-61 to 1962-63	158	3	230	385	59.8
	1965-66 to 1967-68	407	6	359	760	47.9
	1970-71 to 1972-73	816	28	276	1064	25.9
	1975-76 to 1977-78	1982	122	659	2519	26.1
2. Electrical machinery etc.	1960-61 to 1962-63	136	1	63	197	31.8
	1965-66 to 1967-68	367	5	93	456	20.4
	1970-71 to 1972-73	794	20	103	877	11.7
	1975-76 to 1977-78	1910	78	188	2019	9.3
	1985-86 to 1987-88	9439	214	1039	10264	10.1

(*Contd.*)

TABLE 6 (*Contd.*)

1		2	3	4	5	6
3. Transport Equipment & parts	1961-62 to 1962-63	347	2	70	415	16.8
	1965-66 to 1967-68	634	5	71	700	10.2
	1970-71 to 1972-73	989	35	87	1041	8.4
	1975-76 to 1977-78	1625	99	184	1710	10.8
	1985-86 to 1987-88	8745	216	711	9240	7.7
4. Total	1960-61 to 1962-63	641	6	363	997	36.4
	1965-66 to 1967-68	1408	16	524	1916	27.3
	1970-71 to 1972-73	2383	82	466	2767	16.8
	1975-76 to 1977-78	5517	300	1031	6248	16.5
	1985-86 to 1987-88	26773	851	4543	30465	14.9

TABLE 7

Exponential Growth of Real Net Value Added in Capital Goods Sector (Registered) during 1955-85 at 1970-71 price

Industry Group	1955-56 to 1964-65	1964-65 to 1975-76	1975-76 to 1984-85	Extra Growth during 1955-56 to 1964-65 as benefit of protection (Col. 2 — Col. 4)
1	2	3	4	5
Non-electrical machinery	22.5	4.7	5.8	16.7
Electrical machinery	16.1	9.3	7.8	8.3
Transport equipment	7.5	0.8	8.3	—
All Capital goods	12.7	4.5	7.4	5.3

Source : Mundle & Mukhopadhyay, *op. cit.*

TABLE 8

Changes in Concentration Ratio (%) 1976-1989

Industry	Four-firm concentration Ratio (%) 1976	1983-84	1988-89
Capital Goods Industry			
Commercial Vehicles	93	95	100
Cars	100	100	100
Boilers	80	88	100
Ball/Roller Bearings	76	74	75
Chemical/Pharm. Machinery	42	53	51
Agricultural Machinery	54	56	
Jeeps	100	100	100
3-Wheelers ...	96	93	100

Source : CMIE, Market and Market shares (different issues).

TABLE 9

India's Exports of Capital Goods

	Value of Exports (billion dollars)	Quantum Index of Capital Goods (1970-71=100)	Percentage Share in World Exports	Annual Growth Rate (Percentage)	
				Value of Exports	Quantum of Exports
1961-62	0.01	7.73	—	19.97	16.80
1962-63	0.01	10.19	—	10.82	31.68
1963-64	0.02	10.40	0.05	23.78	2.15
1964-65	0.02	13.97	0.06	16.03	24.28
1965-66	0.03	19.92	0.06	34.54	42.55
1966-67	0.02	25.39	0.04	12.02	27.43
1967-68	0.03	31.28	0.05	24.13	23.27
1968-69	0.05	53.92	0.08	85.03	72.36
1969-70	0.07	78.92	0.10	42.50	46.36
1970-71	0.10	100.00	0.11	36.02	26.71
1971-72	0.10	90.79	0.10	0.18	9.21
1972-73	0.11	95.78	0.09	11.87	5.49
1973-74	0.15	155.73	0.09	33.54	20.31
1974-75	0.27	235.05	0.13	79.56	103.99
1975-76	0.30	195.22	0.12	10.23	16.84
1976-77	0.33	224.31	0.12	11.85	14.90
1977-78	0.39	277.05	0.12	16.25	5.68
1978-79	0.49	291.80	0.13	23.14	23.10
1979-80	0.56	281.97	0.13	14.55	3.37
1980-81	0.67	377.34	0.13	19.90	33.81
1981-82	0.65	374.41	0.13	3.85	0.78
1982-83	0.61	320.29	0.12	12.11	14.45
1983-84	0.52	223.06			
1984-85	0.58	334.88	0.10	6.39	22.64
1985-86	0.57	385.25	0.10	3.05	15.04
1986-87	0.77	530.58	0.11	34.44	37.73
1987-88	1.10	784.09	0.13	42.86	47.78
1988-89	1.60	—	—	44.95	—

Source : Dilip Rath & Amarendra Sahoo, India's Exports of Capital Goods : An Evaluation in *EPW*, XXV 34 (Aug. 25, 1990).

When we look at India's performance in exporting capital goods destination-wise we find that her exports to the developed countries is moving up. But if we compare her performance vis-a-vis her competitors in developing countries, we see not a very encouraging picture.

Tables 10 through 13 capture the scenario. It will be evident from the tables that if one views in isolation the country's performance may look commendable, but when set against the performance of her competitors, it would not appear to be so. Exports of other developing countries to the German, UK and Italy's markets are moving up faster than India. For example, if in Germany and Italy, India could just hold on its share, her competitors have gained a larger ground in these markets.

TABLE 10

Destination of India's Export of Capital Goods (Percent of Total)

	North America	US	Europe	EEC	Centrally planned Economies	USSR	Asia Developing	Africa
1970	1.40	1.40	NA	7.70	NA	NA	NA	NA
1971	0.80	0.70	17.89	6.25	8.61	2.89	43.52	32.30
1972	1.61	1.35	15.85	4.27	10.50	5.85	49.60	25.45
1973	1.79	1.59	18.04	8.57	10.72	4.51	52.94	16.99
1974	1.91	1.63	14.62	10.43	7.11	4.85	53.08	16.20
1975	1.20	0.92	13.02	7.29	7.99	6.15	56.04	19.67
1976	1.95	1.56	12.22	8.95	10.07	8.04	52.18	22.05
1977	2.66	2.31	12.50	8.63	8.58	6.64	51.76	23.48
1979	4.46	3.89	11.07	8.55	7.08	4.83	48.82	26.79
1980	4.34	3.91	8.25	6.38	12.43	7.87	48.36	27.04
1983	2.30	2.30	NA	14.80	NA	NA	NA	NA
1984	4.39	4.12	9.32	6.82	29.71	26.02	34.38	21.81
1985	5.79	5.54	10.52	7.53	36.90	31.04	29.95	17.08

Source : Commodity Trade Statistics and Year Book of International Trade Statistics as quoted in D. Rath & A Sahoo. *Op. cit.*

TABLE 11

India and its Competitors in German Market
(Percentage share)

	India	Japan	Argentina	Brazil	China	Hong-kong	Korea (Rep.)
1966	0.02	2.08	0.04	0.06	0.01	0.04	0.03
1967	0.02	1.83	0.05	0.12	0.02	0.09	0.03
1968	0.03	2.17	0.01	0.10	0.05	0.15	0.01
1969	0.04	2.55	0.01	0.10	0.04	0.16	0.01
1970	0.06	2.95	0.02	0.16	0.09	0.15	0.01
1971	0.07	3.58	0.03	0.11	0.11	0.17	0.01
1972	0.04	4.33	0.02	0.10	0.00	0.25	0.05
1973	0.06	5.43	0.04	0.08	0.00	0.36	0.07
1974	0.10	4.95	0.02	0.20	0.00	0.42	0.18
1975	0.09	5.01	0.02	0.35	0.00	0.63	0.17
1976	0.08	6.34	0.01	0.33	0.00	0.70	0.26
1977	0.08	7.00	0.01	0.37	0.00	0.64	0.22
1978	0.08	7.27	0.01	0.42	0.00	0.49	0.32
1979	0.06	7.13	0.01	0.38	0.00	0.57	0.34
1980	0.05	10.19	0.00	0.30	0.01	0.56	0.36
1981	0.04	11.89	0.04	0.28	0.01	0.53	0.33
1982	0.04	11.05	0.05	0.33	0.02	0.64	0.29
1983	0.03	12.19	0.03	0.19	0.07	0.61	0.32
1984	0.04	13.96	0.03	0.23	0.11	0.74	0.37
1985	0.04	14.41	0.02	0.34	0.07	0.69	0.52

Source : International Year Book and Commodity Trade Statistics as quoted in D. Rath & A. Sahoo *op. cit.*

TABLE 12

India and Its Competitors in UK Market

(Percentage Share)

	India	Japan	Argentina	Brazil	China	Hong-kong	Korea (Rep.)
1966	0.26	1.84	0.02	0.10	—	0.60	0.00
1967	0.25	1.17	0.05	0.02	—	0.10	—
1968	0.04	2.11	0.02	0.04	0.01	0.47	—
1969	0.16	1.68	0.04	0.07	0.03	0.44	0.01
1970	0.16	2.49	0.11	0.05	0.06	0.51	0.01
1971	0.13	3.83	0.06	0.08	0.12	0.61	0.01
1972	0.11	6.83	0.05	0.16	0.01	0.69	0.02
1973	0.12	7.62	0.03	0.19	0.02	0.72	0.05
1074	0.11	7.59	0.03	0.14	0.03	0.63	0.08
1975	0.16	7.65	0.09	0.16	0.04	0.42	0.08
1976	0.11	7.48	0.07	0.20	0.14	0.48	0.15
1977	0.10	8.24	0.09	0.22	0.05	0.47	0.15
1978	0.08	7.83	0.08	0.33	0.05	0.53	0.14
1979	0.09	7.50	0.06	0.120	0.05	0.61	0.19
1980	0.10	8.68	0.06	0.10	0.02	0.75	0.22
1981	0.13	11.76	0.08	0.15	0.03	0.05	0.22
1982	0.37	11.70	0.02	0.13	0.03	0.78	0.29
1983	0.12	12.36	0.00	0.19	0.02	0.81	0.88
1984	0.33	11.59	—	0.21	0.03	1.30	0.49
1985	0.11	11.32	0.00	—	0.03	.89	0.62

Source : International Year Book and Commodity Trade Statistics as quoted in D. Rath & A. Sahoo *op. cit.*

Input price and tax differential apart, scale economies could not be achieved by the Indian capital goods industry due to some characterists of Indian domestic market. The Indian market for capital goods is not large and homogeneous enough due to high income differential and therefore of choice and preferences. Demand coming from upper income groups for high quality differentiated good is small which does not induce firms for gaining scale economies. Thus domestic market for capital goods gets fragmented and differentiated on the basis of income, taste and quality of products etc.[8]

TABLE 13

India and Its competitors in Italian Market
(Percentage share)

	India	Japan	Argentina	Brazil	China	Hong-kong	Korea (Rep)
1966	0.01	0.51	0.01	0.01	0.01	0.12	—
1967	0.01	0.49	0.03	0.06	0.01	0.06	—
1968	0.01	0.63	0.02	0.01	0.02	0.08	0.00
1969	—	0.84	0.01	0.00	0.04	0.10	0.00
1970	0.02	1.01	0.02	0.01	0.04	0.13	0.00
1971	0.01	1.09	0.01	0.05	0.07	0.11	0.01
1972	0.01	1.62	0.03	0.04	0.01	0.09	0.10
1973	0.01	2.42	0.02	0.03	0.01	0.13	0.05
1974	0.03	2.19	0.02	0.03	0.01	0.19	0.06
1975	0.03	2.34	0.02	0.05	0.01	0.17	0.07
1976	0.12	3.50	0.02	0.06	0.01	0.30	0.15
1977	0.21	2.94	0.02	0.36	0.01	0.36	0.22
1978	0.23	2.24	0.35	0.56	0.01	0.26	0.19
1979	0.10	2.17	0.13	0.66	0.01	0.33	0.27
1980	0.03	3.17	0.13	0.82	0.02	0.35	0.26
1981	0.02	3.89	0.19	1.46	0.02	0.36	0.28
1982	0.02	3.55	0.13	2.32	0.03	0.04	0.31
1983	0.01	4.26	0.17	1.99	0.04	0.32	2.24
1984	0.02	5.08	0.16	1.48	0.01	0.40	0.29
1985	0.01	1.85	0.03	0.66	0.01	0.14	0.12

Source : International Year Book and Commodity Trade Statistics as quoted in D. Rath & A. Sahoo. *Op. cit.*

IV

Summary and Conclusion: Following import liberalisation India's trade gap with EC, US and Japan is increasing. In some countries in EC although she still holds her position but her trade is not expanding as fast as some of her competitors in developing countries. If this continues the position will be very much vulnerable. So far the government seems to be concerned with finding temporary and ad-hoc solution to contain the adverse economic and political repercussions. Temporary measures like bilateral negotiation with US and multilateral talk with the members of the EC and seeking adjustment in FERA and MRTP Acts give an impression that government is falling in line with trade related investment measures (TRIM) or trade related intellectual property rights (TRIPS) within the framework of GATT.

The MRTP and FERA notwithstanding, Indian industries have by and large come to be dominated by oligopolistic characteristics[9] due mainly to entry barriers through licensing, regulation etc. rather than, as explained above, to the presence of scale economies. The formal integration of European economy poses a big challenge to India, as the former's dependence on markets outside EC will be relatively less.

More important is that the integration will offer vast scope for deriving benefit for large scale economies and for technological change.

Relatively high import content in India's exportable goods and input cost differential detrimental to her external trade interests, skewed income distribution and restricted domestic demand for quality goods etc. are some of the reasons for which the producers are believed to have been not able to derive full advantage of scale economies. Thus, the protection enjoyed by the Indian industries and the import substitution policies followed by government during the last four decades have resulted in a large industrial base of capital goods industry. But the industry, as we have seen, although remained protected could not exploit scale economies to take advantage in the export markets. In the context of export, therefore, it may be said that scale economies and technological innovation — the two plus factors on which monopoly and oligopolistic characteristics of Indian industry might be supported have not yielded desirable benefit.

NOTES AND REFERENCES

1. The World Bank (1985) : *World Development Report*, 1985, OUP.
2. *Ibid.*
3. *Ibid.*, Table 12 at p. 196.
4. Dholakia, Ravindra H., Dholakia, Bakul H., and Kumar, Ganesh (1992) : Issues in Strategy for Export Promotion — An Inter Industry Analysis, *EPW* XXVII-48 Nov. 28.
5. Mundle, Sudipto & Mukhopadhyay, Hiranya (1992) : Protection, Growth and Competitiveness : Study of Indian Capital Goods Industry, *EPW* XXVII-9, February 29.
6. *Ibid.*
7. *Ibid.*, Patibandla, Murali (1992) : Scale Economies and Export in an Import Substituting Regime — Some Observations for Indian Industry, *EPW* XXVII - 9, Feb. 29.
8. Two examples cited by Patibandla (*op. cit.*) are relevant. One is India's bicycle industry — supposed to be the largest in the world. But since the major part of the domestic demand is from low income strata for low price and low quality products, a substantial part of production is meant for catering to demand from this group while the demand from the developed countries is for high quality products. The other is the demand for diesel engines. About 70 per cent of its demand comes from small and medium farmers who demand low quality sturdy engines.
9. Bardhan, Pranab (1984) : *The Political Economy of Development in India*, Basil Blackwood, N.Y.

7

Problems and Prospects of Maastricht Treaty : Its Impact on India and other LIEs

DEBESH BHOWMIK

Introduction: The steps from Werner Plan to Maastricht Treaty of the European Union in the world economic space have produced a keen oligopolistic competition among the emerging world trading blocs and evolved knotty problems in the international monetary system. Politically too, it is an endless challenge to U.S.A. (or NAFTA) or to any big power whose economic and political supremacy have been emerged doubtful. In this paper, I shall endeavour to analyse the pros and cons of the Maastricht Treaty and its impact on India and LIEs.

Optimum Goal of E.U.: The Maastricht Treaty is an historic attempt in the world economic and political scene. Among the lobby groups in W.T.O., the relative strength for determination of political economy of trade policies were among the EU, NAFTA and Japan. A movement toward free trade area of the emerging trading blocs in the multilateral trading system and the domination of world trade and mode of payments can give birth to a single currency. Keynes's 'bancor' (*Keynes, 1943)* concept profounded the stability of the international monetary system and the survival of capitalism under free trade doctrine. This notion is ultimately required for currency dictatorship and the supremacy of world trade (*Preobrazhensky, E. 1954, Marx, K. 1954).*

Will the revival of free trade area and the introduction of single currency in EU under one parliament dominate world trade and mode of world payments mechanism when the international monetary system is in turmoil and unstable? Will the Europe or EU be the world's mightiest political power? These are easy to answer.

The EU (15 countries except Luxembourg) has captured 44.12 per cent of world exports and 43.44 per cent of world imports whereas America's exports and imports shares were 11.77 per cent and 14.55

per cent, NAFTA's shares were 16.21 per cent and 19.05 per cent. In comparison with Japan's exports and imports shares were 9.49 per cent and 6.10 per cent respectively in 1992 (*W.D.R. 1994*). More precisely France dominates Africa's trade and U.K. dominates Asia's trade. (*IMF, Direction of Trade Statistics, 1993).* Thus, the supremacy of the world trade is unquestionably in favour of EU.

But EU is still lagged behind in case of controlling world's payments' mechanism. 65 per cent of world trade is invoiced through U.S. dollar, 48 per cent by global bond; 70-80 per cent of international bank lending dominated in U.S. dollar in spite of continuous declining of U.S. dollar hegemony and a decline of half to a fifth of world GDP (at PPP exchange rate) during 1950-1993 of U.S. economy (*Persaud, A.D. 1994: 72).* Presently, currencies of 14 countries are pegged to French franc, 6 currencies are pegged to SDR and 4 currencies are pegged to ECU other than EU's freely convertibility to ECU with each other. (*I.M.F. 1992:6-7).* Continuous deteriorating of dollar value (*Persaud. A.D. 1994 : 79)* and the declining trend of nominal and real effective exchange rates of dollar since 1985 (*IMF 1992: 11, Piter Bofinger 1994: 44)* have created deceleration of dollar hegemony and have overvalued ECU and yen also. These have stabilised EMS more than before and emerged as an alternative standard of international exchange. The clear avenue of EU is that if single currency or ECU be realised within 2000 A.D. as an effect of Maastricht Treaty through ratification by each state in European Parliament, and, if ECU is regarded as a composite or basket currency in SDR in the offing, then the dream of Keynes's 'bancor' as an international currency will come true and the stability of international monetary system will be assured. However the theme is debatable; this reality may tend to political trade war among EU, NAFTA/USA, Japan and other super powers in the world money game. Now, if common/key currencies of regional trading blocs compete for each other to dominate world payments structure and for international trade shares, then the degree of protectionism and liberalisation in inter-trade and intra-trade diverge the trade policies as well as monetary policies in W.T.O. and in world monetary institutes where IMF and EMI may function as substitutes which may deter from the stability of the multilateral trading and world monetary systems. What political process does solve such diverging situation. The answer is nil.

A brief on convergence criteria : The Maastricht Treaty has formulated the following convergence criteria.

(1) The price stability or the inflation convergence is given the topmost priority for successful functioning of monetary union.

(2) The exchange rate stability where the wider or narrow margin of fluctuation of exchange rates produced debatable concept, is another tool of convergence criterion. The conflict between fixed or floating exchange rate lies in this criterion.

(3) The policy of identical interest rate structure for the union is another convergence policy of interest rate structure for the union. The behavior of nominal and real interest rates both in the short run and in the long run is to be critically verified.

(4) Fiscal convergence criterion assures a deficit consistently under 3 per cent of GDP, and debt level consistently 60 per cent of GDP.

For successful functioning and supervision of EMS and issuing of a single currency, the European Central Bank namely European Monetary Institute will be set up. To maintain the stability of ERM and the degree of monetary co-operation, the valuation of ECU and to look over the clearing window, EMI is the central authority to control EU's monetary policies.

A critique on convergence criteria : The inflation convergence criterion in the Maastricht Treaty requires countries to register a rate of consumer price inflation within 1.5 per cent of the average of the three best performing countries over the year prior to entry of EMU. The index is expressed in terms of CPI which should be common level accross the countries.

Some have argued that 2.3 per cent inflation rate can adjust the convergence criteria. However, there should be room instead of "convergence towards the best" because wage/price trends may not be equally competitive in less developed nations like Spain, Greece, Portugal etc. Moreover, low inflation at the expense of high unemployment will not be sustainable for the stability of EMS. It is hardly questioned how member nations adjust common monetary and price policies from a ECB to maintain structural flexibility. In the different saving investment potentialities of member countries, the inflexibilities will be the regular phenomenon due to variation of exchange rates in which autonomy has been given in a specified margin

(*Crockett, A. 1994: 180-181*). Recent turmoil of exchange rate variation hinder the inflation convergence. Nominal convergence becomes problematic if inflation rates start diverging and it would occur in a single currency in EMI when fixed exchange rate is applied. Thus nominal convergence is paradoxical to start a monetary union. (*Granwe and Tullo, 1994: 196*).

For exchange rate stability it is argued that EMI will be to progressively create a situation in which a narrow margin can prevail. It may do more harm than good because exchange rate stability need not necessarily be defined in terms of narrow ± 2.25 per cent margin. (*Crockett, A. 1994: 180*). A wider margin with stable price and interest rate can reproduce exchange rate stability and efficient management of the forex. The decision of ECOFIN Council to widen margin of ± 15 per cent could be seen normal margin and it is wise to intervene EMS currencies through EMI (*Thygesen, N. 1994: 215-216*). For the interest rate convergence, the treaty argued that long term interest rates have remained within two percentage points of the average rates prevailing in the three countries. But long term interest rate depends on global interest rate and currencies specific discount rate which depends on long term appreciation and depreciation of the currency.

If nominal convergence is desirable for monetary union, then equality of nominal interest rates becomes the more reliable convergence criterion. Positive interest differentials, approximating the expectations of exchange rate movements, indicate the two countries are not in monetary equilibrium, at least during the period of maturity of such interest rates (*Giovannini, A. 1994: 190*).

To establish the conditions for determining the ECU's interest and exchange rate, it should be noted that whilst interest rates converge asymtotically, the ECU exchange rate appreciation accelerates towards EMU as the ECU/basket interest spread widens. But Maastricht euphoria has lowered ECU interest rate whilst the exchange rate has not moved. Both together are inconsistent with a terminal exchange rate of unity (*Steinherr, A. 1994: 248-249*).

The fiscal convergence is the precondition for EMU. But then several issues arise: In the general situation what is the best measure of government deficit? Should the target deficit be adjusted to take account of cycle and should the criterion be different for countries at different stages of development? (*Crockett, A. 1994 : 178-179*). To answer the first question, it was observed that the Keynesian deficit financing was the general policy of EU to yield higher growth rates and employment which have proved uncorrelated with the deficit financing. In the behavior of last recessionary trends of most EU members the target deficits were not adjusted during anti-cyclical fiscal policies. For the last question, it can be readily said that the member nations of EU have evolved different growth paths with different sizes of deficits. Because the unequal capital — output ratios investment — saving ratios may produce heterogeneous growth rate even if same amount of deficits were chosen by members, even though the size of deficits is not the only macroeconomic tool to achieve a specified stage of development. The unique federal fiscal structure which can regulate the financial relationship among the members is required through strong political will.

On the text of Maastricht Treaty, the decision and judgement by leading economists are controversial and debatable. Sixty German economists with a text of memorandum argued that EC currency union is an acid test for Europe which is still not united economically, socially and in terms of political interest. Weaker members will fall into a greater pressure which may jeopardise the goal of integration and the decision of Maastricht will put Europe in the doldrums. On the other hand, 62 German economists leading by Alfred Steinherr, argued that the single currency will respond external shocks uniformly and obtain sizeable economic benefits that can not be through exchange rate stability. The democratic function through ECB can yield monetary union other than the precondition of political union for achieving convergence criteria.

For institution building to stabilise EMS, the setting up of the EMI as ECB is unique to issue ECU as the single currency and to smooth functioning of the ECU clearing system. It may play a role as the settlement agent in ECU banking market and can extend to BIS with limited lender-of-last-resort function.

One dilemma is that the ECU, as the 16th currency and as EMU currency, circulated along with 15 national currencies, may face strong asymmetrical shocks which will produce heterogeneous impact on national economies, e.g., changes of shares in ECU, disintegration of monetary policies and national objectives of development. In case of freely floating exchange rate mechanism, weaker currencies may hit hardly due to exchange rate fluctuations and the change of value of ECU. What will be the co-ordinating policy of EMI to regulate circulation of ECU and national currencies? What will be the ultimate standard of ECU, gold or dollar with fixed or flexible exchange rate? To answer these issues, EMI should find out the functions of ECU to stabilise the world monetary system and to work for a world currency. Long run visual concepts among Germans, French and Englishmen are differnt as their roles in international money game are competitive and not co-operative as European. National sovereignty appears to be vital objective to be a world power. It is doubtful that how far political union will realise to give birth to an optimum monetary integration to be EU as a world supreme power and not as an individual European state. But this possibility is however minimum to fail convergence criteria to pave the way of success for the above goal.

Again, the crucial and stumbling bloc is the maintenance of ECU value as unity with identical interest rate for all. Volatility of interest rates, two-speed-EMS, approach effect, and any fiscal divergence may destabilise the ECU value from unity (as have been seen from SDR value). It is hardly questioned whether the index of relative economic performance of 25 years using an average of seven indicators would be favourable for Maastricht Treaty because of its downturn since 1988. The decision is up to the politicians to act. (*Steinherr and Gros, 1994: 299*). So to speak clearly, political integration is thus the necessary and sufficient conditions of Maastricht Treaty that is ultimately required for an Eurofed with Common Foreign and Security Policy including co-operation of internal security issues (*Crowford. M. 1993:297-299*). On the other hand, according to R.N. Cooper (*1994:71*), the Maastricht Treaty would increase the democratic gap in the Community beyond the point of tolerability when persued the policies of convergence which are not politically independent.

Future Agenda for Maastricht Treaty ': The following are the agenda for Maastricht Treaty.

1. A perfect competition is required in the EU.
2. Perfect mobility of factors of production is the precondition for convergence.
3. ECU should not be the 16th currency/basket of currencies, on the contrary, it would be a new currency for EU.
4. ECU should be fully convertible to gold with fixed parity.
5. ECU must be convertible to all hard currencies with freely floating exchange rate mechanism.

6. ECU should be linked to either SDR or it should be circulated as an international money i.e. ECU should be as an intervention currency for multilateral clearing.
7. EMI should not be independent of European parliament.
8. To combat recession and unemployment, European parliament must fulfil Werner report which stated political integration is an addition to monetary and economic union.
9. The stability of value of ECU should be maintained through counteract policies of the destabilising factors.
10. For optimum economic integration, EU necessitates optimum currency area extending multicountry multicommodity framework by eleminating asymmetrical real shocks alongwith complete market and financial integration.
11. Elimination of hegemony of national currencies and national sovereignty are the preconditions for political integration.
12. EU should require common monetary and fiscal policies to activise identical interest rate.

Impact of Maastricht on India and LIEs : From the inception of the Indo-EU trade, India's B.O.T. has gone unfavourable to India and has increased cumulatively. The value of exportables increased from Rs. 14,470 crores in 1980-81 (22 per cent of India's total) to Rs. 89,3074 crores in 1990-91 (27 per cent of India's total) and further enhanced to Rs. 22708.27 crores in 1994-95 (27.9 per cent of India's total) after the establishment of SEM. The value of importables shot up from Rs. 26,390 crores in 1980-81 (21 per cent of India's total) to Rs. 1272.09 crores in 1990-91 (30 per cent of India's total) and again fell to Rs. 23004.36 crores in 1994-95 (25.56 per cent of India's total) in the EU market. Germany is the largest importer of Indian goods and services accounting for about 27 per cent followed by U.K. (26 per cent).

The impact of single EU market on India's exports depends on trade creation and trade diversion effects as a result of tariffs and non-tariffs barriers. It is argued that these will be no significant improvement of Indo-EU trade. According to C.A. Tisdell *(1993:4)*, the trade creation effect would be minor and trade diversion effect would be zero, thus net effect may be zero or negative and India may lose significantly due to changed political and economic situation in trade and foreign direct investment etc. This view is not unanimously true. But, Ceechini *(1988)* established from his model that Indo-EU exportables would decline by 2.19 per cent due to trade diversion and increase by 3.27 per cent due to trade creation, thus a net effect of increase of exportables would be 1.08 per cent during the prediction period 1993-1996. India's total exportables would improve by 0.225 per cent and the net percentage of trade deficit would become 2.94 per cent as a result of two effects where Ceechini assumed that EU would acquire GDP growth rate of 5.3 per cent and decline in price level of 6.1 per cent.

Again, Anderson (*1989*) concluded from his model that Indo-EU exportables would reduce by 1.59 per cent due to trade diversion effect and enhance by 2.69 per cent due to trade creation effect, thus a net effect of 1.10 per cent increase of India's gain. Again, India's total export would also increase by 0.22 per cent and percentage of trade deficit would rise by 2.98 per cent as a net effect where he assumed EU would grow by 6.5-7.5 per cent in GDP and price would decline by 4.5 per cent external balance during the predicted period 1993-96.

The above results surely nulify the hypothesis that the European Integration will adversely affect the India's trade to EU (*R. Mehata 1993:12*).

Moreover, the trend regression equations of both exportables and importables of India-EU trade during pre-integration period (1980-81 — 1989-90) and post-integration period (1991-92 — 1994-95) suggest that there exist upward drift and significant improvement but rise in negative trade balance.

The following are the pre-integration trend values of exportables, importables and B.O.T. (1980-81 = base year) of log linear regression which are fitted through OLS method.

$$\text{Log } X = 2.97 + 0.076\, t + u_t$$
$$(17.78)$$
$$u_t = 0.062\, u_{t-1} + \epsilon_t$$
$$D.W = 1.055$$
$$\text{Log } M = 3.33 + 0.069\, t + u_t$$
$$(43.36)$$
$$u_t = 0.022\, u_{t-1} + \epsilon_t$$
$$D.W. = 1.735$$
$$\text{Log } B.O.T = 4.63 - 0.16\, t + u_t$$
$$(-4.7)$$

$$u_t = -0.74\, u_{t-1} + \epsilon_t$$
$$D.W = 0.109$$

Again the following are trend values of exportables, importables and B.O.T. at the post European integration period.

$$\text{Log } X = 1.838 + 0.136\, t + u_t$$
$$(3.84)$$
$$u_t = 0.614\, u_{t-1} + \epsilon_t$$
$$D.W. = 0.097$$
$$\text{Log } M = 1.851 = 0.138\, t + u_t$$
$$(4.75)$$
$$u_t = 0.893\, u_{t-1} + \epsilon_t$$
$$D.W = 0.011$$
$$\text{Log } B.O.T = 1.375 + 0.105\, t + u_t$$
$$(3.911)$$
$$u_t = 0.462\, u_{t-1} + \epsilon_t$$
$$D.W = 0.642$$

All of the above findings have been satisfied through t, Durbin-Watson statistic and Dicky-Fuller test.

Lastly, the report of the Ambassadors' Committee on the Single European Market 1992 and India concluded that the integration will vary from one product to another, e.g., unfavourable for traditional products like garments, gems and jewellery, leather products, but favourable for rice, jute, drugs, dyes, insecticide, but unfavourable for chemical and engineering sector due to common standards. (*Sandip Waslekar, 1993:1-2*).

A significant impact of Single European Market on developing countries exports was observed. The percentage changes of net exports to EU as a result of trade creation minus trade diversion are positive. The net effects of changes in exports of Morocco 0.8 per cent, Tunisia 0.9 per cent, Kenya 1.2 per cent, Zimbabwe 1.3 per cent, Sri Lanka 2.0 per cent, Thailand 1.5 per cent and developing countries 2.7 per cent were calculated by Devenport and Page (*1991*).

The above impact of Maastricht to India and other developing countries was measured by OLS method without considering the effects of Uruguay Round, harmonisation of technical standards as imposed by EU, and second and higher order multiplier effect due to increased demand of EU markets in the world (*R. Mehta 1993 : 23, 13*).

On the signing in W.T.O. at Marrakash, India has got 22 per cent tariff reduction from EU as against 18 per cent from U.S.A., 38 per cent from Canada and 41 per cent from Japan. Thus India, according to International Textiles and Clothing Bureau, may increase from 176625 tons of clothing and textile in 1994 to 264304 tons in 2004 due to MFA with EU provided India will modernise its industry, improve quality and standardisation within 10 years transition period. (*Raghavan Chakraborty 1994 : 16, 19*).

Other developing countries may be benefited through cut of tariffs from EU after Uruguay Round. In case of all products, the developing countries will get 12 per cent additional duty free exportables to EU, e.g. 7 per cent additional duty free in industrial products, 3 per cent in natural resource based products, 11 per cent in other tropical products, 44 per cent in tropical agricultural products, and 2 per cent in non-tropical agricultural products etc. Again, EU have reduced 29.8 per cent tariff reduction in MFN tariff average and 30.3 per cent in GSP tariff average (trade weighted) in all imports from the developing countries which were more than U.S.A. and Japan but less than Canada (*T.D.R. 1994 : 140-142*).

Thus, developing countries including India can boost their exportables as a result of increase in net effect due to trade creation and trade diversion at the post Uruguay regime.

Maastricht may have an accelerating impact on free flow of FDI to India and other LIEs as a consequence of following the policies of liberalisation. Presently, EU dominated FDI flows to India and South Pacific, but it has placed third rank in SAARC and ASEAN (*Bhowmik D. and Sen, R.K. 1995*). There are ample scope for widening the regional domination in the Asia-Pacific Southern African region by EU through the ratification of Maastricht which may stimulate outward and export oriented growth in the LIEs in the era of globalisation.

Maastricht Treaty may produce a stable international monetary system with introducing a single currency in EU that could pave the way of success to dominate world's payments mechanism in the offing through its key currency. The hypotheses requires that EU might dominate world's trade by economic and political supremacy and secondly it might dominate international payment mechanism by its single currency.

Now, EU dominates India's and Africa's foreign trade. But it has third rank followed by Japan and U.S.A. in Asia. In the developing countries, EU's share were 22.6 per cent in exports and 16.7 per cent in imports in 1989 followed by Japan and U.S.A. which were enhanced from 22.1 per cent and 16.6 per cent respectively in 1993 where France dominated the largest share followed by Germany and U.K. (*Direction of International Trade Statistics, Yearbook 1990:179, 186, 399*).

Thus, trade domination in India and other developing countries is in favour of European Union. But payment mechanism is dominated in these regions by U.S.A. even to-day. Presently, 14 African countries are dominated through French franc. But, European Currency Unit might have ample scope to dominate managed floating and independently floating areas of 67 countries of the world including India and some of the SAARC, ASEAN, CEAO and ECOWAS countries (*IMF 1992:6-7*) if Maastricht can give birth a stable monetary system or at least evolve an alternative system against the present dollar/international monetary system.

Concluding Remarks : Maastricht Treaty needs optimum economic integration irrespective of structural convergence in the political process of EU. In case of world security, the common parliament of EU may bubble with diverging factors such as alignment, power hegemony, unequal exchange, military strength etc. On the basis of European history, the above concept lies in utopean democracy. However, I would like to say, the Treaty is an attempt to speed up capitalist economic integration in the race of the development of socialism and socialist economic integration. Above all, the Maastricht Treaty may (i) hinder unipolar world economy, (ii) challenge dollar hegemony, (iii) threat the defence power of the big giants, (iv) redound cold war and rivalry among super powers in the intra Community which can disturb world peace, (v) widen the distribution of income between the LDCs and DCs, (vi) evolve a new world monetary system with an international money, (vii) gear up European Economic Integration and EMS.

The fear is that the European integration from Werner Plan to Maastricht Treaty may be turned to political and economic sabotage as have been seen in Eastern Europe through Glasnost and Perestroika formulated by Gorbachov as a dream of single Europe via CMEA-2000.

TABLE 1

Basic indicators of Development of Japan, U.S.A. & E.E.C

	GNP Per Capita 1993, $.	GNP per Capita Growth Rate (%) 1980-93	Average Inflation (%) 1980-93	GDP Growth Rate (%) 1980-93	Industry Growth Rate (%) 1980-93	Growth of Export (%) 1980-93	Growth of Imports (%) 1980-93	B.O.P. $ ml (Current Account before official transfer)		International Reserve $ ml	
								1970	1993	1970	1993
E.E.C. (Average)	18644	2.13	6.67	2.56	2.76	5.66	5.09	+4452	+2634	+37779	455640
JAPAN	31490	3.4	1.5	4.0	5.0	4.2	6.3	+2170	+131510	+4876	+87828
U.S.A.	24740	1.7	7.5	2.7	2.9	5.1	6.0	+4680	−103925	+15237	+173094

Source : World Development Report, 1995.

TABLE 2

Indo — EU Trade (Rs. Million)

Year	Exports to EU	Percentage of Export to EU to Total Exports.	Imports from EU	Percentage of Import From EU to Total Indian Imports.
1970-71	2,820	18	3,200	19
1980-81	14,470	22	26,390	21
1981-82	14,170	18	33,340	25
1982-83	14,700	17	34,220	24
1983-84	17,560	18	39,620	25
1984-85	20,020	17	42,220	25
1985-86	19,290	18	52,340	27
1986-87	27,360	22	65,410	33
1987-88	39,570	25	74,410	33
1988-89	49,460	25	90,220	32
1990-91*	89,307	27	1,27,200	30
1991-92*	1,18,578	—	1,39,724	—
1992-93	1,52,820	28.64	1,66,230	26.41
1993-94	1,82,080	26.18	2,13,970	29.38
1994-95	2,27,080	27.98	2,35,040	25.56

Source: CMIE, Basic Statistics relating to Indian Economy, Vol-1, 1989

* DGCI & S, Calcutta.

REFERENCES

Bhowmik, D. (1992) : "Europa as international Money"? Seminar delivered in Kalyani University, April, 1992.

——. & Sen R.K. (1995) : Role of FDI in the Asia-Pacific Region — Third Conference paper, II DS July, (*forthcoming*).

——. (1994) : "Dimensions of Economic Integration in the theory and practice of international trade" — paper selected and Abstract published in 77th Indian Economic Association Conference, Mysore.

——. (1995) : "Maastricht Treaty and International Monetary System", *Arthik Prasanga*, Vol. 41, No. 2, 1995, pp. 89-96.

——. (1992) : "U.S.S.R. and the problem of Socialist Economic Integration in Perestroika". Paper selected in 10th World Congress of IEA, Moscow.

Cooper, R. (1994) : "Yes to European Monetary unification, but no to the Maastricht Treaty". A. Steinherr Ed. *30 Years of European Monetary Integration* Orient Longman, pp. 69-71.

Crawford, M. (1993) : *One Money for Europe?* Macmillan.

Crockett, A. (1994) : "The role of convergence in the process of EMU", A. Steinherr *op. cit.*, pp. 171-183.

Giovannini, A. (1994) : "The debate on nominal convergence before and after the 1992 crisis". A. Steinherr *op. cit.*, pp. 184-191.

Gross, D. and Steinherr, A. (1994) : "Alternatives to driffing along during Stage Two". A. Steinherr *op. cit.*, pp. 199-288.

Granwe, P.D. and Tullo, G. (1994) : "The exchange rate changes of 1992 and inflation convergence in the EMS". A. Steinherr *op. cit.*, pp. 192-202.

Habermeir, K & Ungerer, Horst (1992) : "A single currency for the European Community" *Southern Economist*, Vol. 31, No. 11, October 1, pp. 13-16.

IMF (1990-1993) : *Direction of International Trade Statistics.*

IMF (1992) : *Developments in International Exchange and Payments System,* New York.

Keynes, J.M. (1943) : "Proposals for an international clearing Union". Reprinted in Gruble H.G. (1963) Ed. "*International Monetary Reforms: Plans and Issues*, Stanford University Press & Oxford University Press.

Marx, K. (1954) : *Capital*, Vol-1 Progress Publishers, Moscow.

Mehta, R. (1993) : *Single European Market and India's Trade — A Macro-econometric Analyses,* RIS-New Delhi, O.P. No. 42.

Mitra, Soumya Kanti (1992) : "ERM crises, the need for a harder ECU", *Economic Times*, 20.9.1992.

Persaud, A.D. (1994) : "Will New Empires be Build from the Ashes of the Old? Dollar Decline and Emerging Markets" AMEX Bank Review Awards — *Finance and the International Economy*-8 Oxford, pp. 70-85.

Preobrazhensky, E. (1994) : *The New Economics,* Oxford University Press.

Raghavan, C. (1994) : Gains and Losses in Market Across under W.T.O. *Mainstream*, November 12, pp. 15-22.

Robertson, D. (1994) : ''New Burdens for trade Policy'' AMEX Bank Review Awards *op. cit.*, pp. 108-119.

Steinherr, A. (1994) : ''ECU interest and exchange rates: The key role of EMU''. A. Steinherr *op. cit.*, pp. 243-251.

Thygesen, N. (1994) : ''Reinforcing Stage Two in the EMU process''. A. Steinherr *op. cit.*, pp. 209-226.

Tisdell, C. (1993) : Economic Transformation and Integration in Europe — Consequences for Asian-Pacific countries, especially India, and including Small Economies, Paper presented in IIDS Seminar, Calcutta, 1993, pp. 1-12.

Ungerer, Horst (1990) : ''Europe — the quest for Monetary Integration'' *Finance and Development*, December.

UNESCO (1994) : *Trade and Development Report*, 1994.

U.N.O. (1994) : *Trade and Development Report*, 1994.

Waslekar, S. (1993) : *Response of Indian Firms to the Challenges of The Single European Market*, RIS, New Delhi, O.P. No. 38.

World Bank (1994) : *W.D.R.*, Oxford.

8

Transformation of Eastern Europe and the Problems and Prospects of Its Integration into the E.E.C

SUPRIYO BHATTACHARYA

Systemic Transformation in Eastern Europe — an Introduction

Commenting on the complexities of the systemic transformation going on in different countries of Eastern Europe, Vaclav Klaus had described the situation in the following words : ''I like to compare the transformation process with chess playing. When we want to play chess, we must know how to move various pieces on the chessboard. We must know the basic opening strategies. But it is not possible to know the situation on the chess board after the fifteenth or twenty-fifth move'' (*Fisher & Gelb, 1991*). As a matter of fact, the problem with the East European economies is not simply one of knowing the situation after the 'fifteenth or twenty-fifth move', but, more fundamentally, one of knowing 'how to move various pieces on the chess board' in a particular framework that for long suffered from the lack of cultivation of individual capabilities and freedom and the presence of various inhibitory socio-politico-economic practices.

In order to understand the broad features of and the basic problems associated with the current reforms in Eastern Europe, one has to separate these reforms out from the earlier reforms. The earlier reforms concentrated on steps like ''the decentralization of decision making, the scrapping of central planning, and the loosening of price controls'' (*Murrell 1991*). But these reforms did not quite deliver the goods. Murrell suggests why this could be so. He has argued that the better working of market economies as against centrally planned economies cannot be explained by naively holding up the 'invisible hand paradigm'of neo-classical economics. To provide a theoretical basis for economic reform in East Europe, argues Murrell, one should not get stuck with a characterization of capitalism merely in terms of decentralization within a price system, because simply relaxing constraints to create markets is not enough for fruitful reform; what is required is "positive effort at creation of institutions."

Thus, the most important lesson to be drawn from the earlier reforms can best be summed up in the words of Lin *(1990)* : "...the devolution of income rights, and even property right through greater enterprise autonomy, in the absence of fundamental changes in both the political and ownership system leads to a perverse form of the classic Soviet-type system...a system where the fundamentals of command planning are not disbanded but market processes are simply grafted on to existing structures. Moreover, cultural (broadly defined to encompass economic) attitudes, values and behaviour associated with the old system remain and thus distort the objectives of marketisation. For example, commenting on the flaws of the earlier reforms of Yugoslavia which relied heavily on workers self-management of enterprises, Estrin (*1991*) had this to say : "....the Yugoslavs never fully resolved two fundamental questions : the appropriate balance of managerial and employee prerogatives in the democratically run firm, and the decentralized capital market institutions to be associated with self-managed enterprises. In the former area, they initially relied excessively and then leaned excessively against management; in the latter, they placed control over the capital market in the hands of enterprises and political authorities, arguably the worst solution".

Perhaps, the most important area in the current spate of reforms, that needs close attention, as Svejner (*1991*), and many other experts on Eastern Europe rightly argues, is the tardy development of "well-functioning markets" in different spheres of the economy. The experts (*Estrin, Hare, Fischer and Gelb, 1991*) seem to agree on the complex of factors behind this phenomenon : the inability or slowness of governments to create a clear and consistent legal framework and well-defined property rights, competitive market institutions, infrastructure and essential practices in the sphere of financial services, real estate, domestic trade, transportation and telecommunication, accounting, auditing and other information systems.

It is universally accepted that the functioning of a market economy crucially depends on a simple legal framework. 'Legality' refers to rule by law as against the discretion of leaders. Recent research in economic history has underlined the importance of the legal (in place of discreationary) rule in the rapid economic growth of the western countries; the importance of the legal framework also explains the difference in wealth between the rich capitalist and underdeveloped countries (*Litwack, 1991*). For example, North and Weingast argue very cogently that rapid growth in England in the 17th century took place chiefly because of political changes that permitted the property-owning bourgeoisie to curtail the discretionary power of the Sovereign. Brief, Milgram and Weingast suggest a theory for explaining the appearance of merchant guilds between the eleventh and fifteenth centuries, that emphasizes the "creation of institutions to support multilateral response to deviant behaviour". North has drawn pointed attention to the "complex interaction of cultural, political and economic variables" behind this institutional development. Williamsom too stresses the importance of those institutions that "support the possibility of "hands-off" as opposed to "hands-on" governance".

Therefore, though the creation of suitable markets in various fields is one of the central tasks in the current reforms of Eastern Europe, the reform process has to take note of the fact that an effective market is one which works freely, but within a structure of norms and legal institutions. The fallacy in the view that individuals must be free to choose anything and government should not intervene has been clearly exposed by Basu (*1992*) : "...to start with, individuals could be thought of as having been free to choose anything. The institution of government then is a historical outcome of free individual decision and choice over hundreds and thousands of years. If whatever emerges from free individual choice is desirable, it follows that the activities of the government, including government intervention, is desirable. This contradiction exposes the fallacy."

In stressing the importance of a simple and consistent legal and institutional framework, we should not lose sight of another fundamental factor summarized by North : "Although formal rules may change overnight as the result of political and judicial decisions, informal constraints embodied in customs, traditions and code of conduct are much more impervious to deliberate policies." This is of especial importance in Eastern Europe where the so-called contracts were very often superseded by administrative orders or replaced by negotiations and bargaining between enterprises and the central authorities.

The Issue of Property Right in Systemic Transformaton in Eastern Europe

Another important feature of the current reforms is the uncertainty or lack of clarity about initial property right. The earlier reforms in the 1980s in most of the Eastern European economies aimed at decentralization of planning functions, increase of enterprise autonomy and the expansion of workers' role in enterprise decisions. Partly as a result of this, (particularly in Poland) the State treasury, the appropriate local government body and employees (including management) have claimed ownership right in a particular enterprise (*Vickers and Yarrow, 1991*). But this lack of clarity regarding property right is especially harmful for it may give rise to serious 'incentive failure'. For example, as Vickers and Yarrow point out, "managers and employees might begin to expropriate potentially productive capital. Moreover, uncertainty can lead rival claimants to devote their energies and resources to influencing the allocation of property rights, rather than to more socially productive activities." It was, therefore, essential for the government of Eastern Europe to reach an "acceptable property right settlement", failing which privatization in certain spheres could not be properly launched.

Indeed, the crucial variable determining the transition from a traditional command model to a full-fledged market, according to many Eastern European economists, is a change in property right. As Balcerowiecz of Poland has argued, a command management system involves centralisation of organisational rights and as such there is little scope for changes in rights which is crucial for bringing about a higher level or technological innovation (*Narayanswamy, 1990*). The prevalance of what is called the 'vertical links' in a command system rules out the "competitive threat" to suppliers. Though command systems try to provide organisational structures to facilitate innovation, Balcerowiecz doubts the capacity of 'Socialist Corporations' to replicate the innovation process of the capitalist systems, because in a command system the enterprise suffers from a lack of effective autonomy and competitive ambience and control over its functions by a stock market.

Balcerowiecz has made an incisive analysis of the above issue. His own words in this context merit close attention:

"The severity of these problems and the comparative disadvantages of central level decision-makers in the role of direct investors obviously varies depending on several factors. On an average, these problems tend to be less serious in infrastructural investment than in the area of actual production. Uncertainty related to technological change tends to be lower in the former. Also, the optimal scale of undertaking in the infrastructure is often larger than in production. Those problems become more acute in proportion to economic growth and the level of technological investment. At lower levels, it is relatively easier to pinpoint more pressing investment needs and solutions which can be used may be drawn from technical knowledge tested abroad. At higher levels, the choice of invesments is much less obvious and the technological complexity of alternative solution and inherent uncertainty much greater''.

The upshot of the above discussion is that reform-minded economists of Eastern Europe are now stressing the necessity for extending the market from products to factors, particularly land and capital markets. But most of the literature on Eastern European economies (upto 1991) point to the lack or imperfect nature of capitalist financial markets and institutions (like stock market, pension funds, private banks, mutual funds and so on) in these economies. The creation of these institutions is essential for the privatization (an eagerly sought measure) to take roots.

At this point, it is useful to pose some counter-arguments against the arguments of reform-minded economists mentioned above. The first question that may be raised is whether the institutions of western economies (particularly its legal, political and economic infrastructure) which had developed over a long period are all easily replicable in the Eastern European economies. Drawing upon certain features of the Japanese economy, Bardhan and Roemer (*1992*) have described a model of bank-centric organisation which may, it is hoped, partially straighten out an 'historical handicap' in capital market institutions. They draw our attention to an important fact in economic history : "it is important to realize that it was the underdevelopment of capital markets in late 19th century Germany that gave rise to its present system of heavy bank involvement in the financing and managment of industrial companies. Even in the case of Japan, as Horiuchi points out, the main bank system originated in the highly imperfect financial markets and economic uncertainties of the immediate post-war period''.

Modern large-scale enterprises under corporate capitalism are not immune from information or agency problems qualitatively similar to those in a traditional socialist economy. As a result of the separation between ownership and management in a capitalist enterprise, managers, instead of maximizing the share value of the firm, may reap their own gains or take decisions which give rise to wastes and mistakes. The individual investor is also neither able nor willing to monitor a particular problem. As Bardhan and Roemer further point out, a different kind of 'soft budget syndrome' (which was, as Kornai showed, so much prevalent in socialist countries) operates in corporate capitalism when one observes the 'astronomical salary raises' which the chief executive officers in American and British companies regularly give themselves with the aid of shareholders' money.

It is known that replicating the capital market without private ownership is very difficult. For in the usual socialist system there is no stock market that can arrange to evaluate managerial performance. The usual examples in corporate capitalism are the 'threats of corporate takeover (along with stock options in managerial compensation)'.

But recent research shows that financial discipline of corporate takeovers is actually a time-consuming affair and also gives rise to much waste. As Jensen has shown that in the U.S.A., ''takeover and leveraged buyout premiums average 50 per cent above market price, which illustrates how much value corporate managers can destroy before they face a serious threat of disturbance.'' Moreover, the takeover process entails what Bardhan and Roemer call 'a basic asymmetry of information', for outside buyers have little access to information about the source of a firm's problem than managers.

It must also not be forgotten that 'corporate raids' so typical of the U.S. — British experience, have not been essential for good performance of firms in some economies of continental Europe like France or Germany, nor in Japan. The East European countries should see whether they can take a leaf out of the book of the post-war Japanese system (at least upto the mid-70s) of ''mutual stock-holding of private companies within keiretsu, a corporate financial grouping often with a ''main bank'' as the nucleus, providing an alternative model of monitoring by involved parties''. Bardhan and Roemer have developed an interesting model along these lines, which can be viewed as an alternative financial system of monitoring. The present reformers of Eastern Europe must seriously ponder the feasibility of the model.

Aspects of the Privatization Drive in Eastern Europe

The wave of privatization of state-owned enterprises has swept over the entire Eastern Europe. Though the modalities of privatization differ across countries, two fundamental facts emerge : one is the distinction between the privatization of small firms and that of large firms; second is the debate that is raging around the question whether privatization should be a rapid or slow process.

The small firms have been privatized primarily through auctions and this seems to have been a smooth sailing in Czechoslovakia, Hungary and Poland. The statistics upto 1991 show (*Svejnar, 1991*) that more than 20000 outlets had been sold in Poland and most of the retail trade there is now in private hands; Hungary had planned to transfer about 10000 small-scale units to private hands in 1991 and Czechoslovakia (former) intended to auction 100000 small business in 1991-92. This 'small privatization' has been found to have positive effects on efficiency of resource use.

The privatization schemes of large firms have been of various kinds : for example, reliance on a combination of 'regulated spontaneous privatization' (where the management of an enterprise draw up a privatization scheme, possibly with a foreign partner), sale of property or shares to domestic or foreign buyers (as attempted in Hungary), distribution of some shares of the enterprise to employees (envisaged in most countries), distribution of shares mostly through vouchers or mutual fund shares to the general public (planned in Czechoslovakia (former), Poland and Romania).

One difficulty with the privatization of large scale companies is the paucity of assets required for buying a controlling number of shares in any particular enterprise. The choice that remains, as of now, is to allow large-scale foreign ownership (a proposition that faces some resistance except in Hungary) or to set up 'diluted shares ownership' by local individuals. If the latter course is followed, then one meets the well-known problem of seperation of ownership and control. As Svejnar shows, in Poland this problem is partially taken care of by distributing to all adult citizens bulk of the shares of 400 large enterprises (out of a total of about 5000 large and medium-sized farms) through shares in 20 or so mutual funds that will hold enterprise shares, exercise control over management of enterprise and will be administered by western experts. Czechoslovakia (former) has sought to follow an intermediate path permitting individual share ownership in most large and medium-sized firms both directly and through mutual funds. How far these schemes actually helped to improve efficiency of the enterprises is not however clear.

Coming to the debate centering around the desirable pace of

privatization, we find that there are conflicts between objectives e.g. between objectives of state revenue and the penchant for privatizing rapidly — so that the benefits of privatization may be reaped in no time and the whole affair does not get bogged down.

There are, however, some important considerations which may be urged against rapid privatization. There is, first of all, the danger that such rapid privatization may end up in huge failures and may call for renationalization, as it happened in Chile in the early 1980s. Another problem is that with such rapid privatization there may not be, in all probability, reasonably enough time for the provision of enduring 'incentive structures' for efficiency. For example, as Vickers and Yarrow (*1991*) have pointed out, in the absence of market liberalization, many state-owned enterprises would merely be converted into private monopolies, as was the case in Britain so far as large privatizations were concerned. The researches of Vickers and Yarrow (*1988, 1991*) and others (*Levy, 1981; Kay and Thampson, 1986*) show that competition rather than ownership is a most important factor making for enterprise efficiency. In Poland, however, the Solidarity government has adopted certain policies like liberalization of foreign trade and withdrawal of subsidies and most of the state-owned enterprises are such that they can be quickly exposed to competition with the aid of these policies.

Still another argument against rapid privatization is that, even if such privatization is not allowed to go the way of the Chilean privatization process ending up in 'highly leveraged enterprises', the stopping of subsidies and the exposing of markets to foreign competition may go so fast that efficient response may not be called forth; therefore, enterprises that could have been viable in the long run, may find the going too tough in the short run and as such wind up. According to this view, first of all competition should be promoted, more realistic price signals which the State can use to restructure enterprises should be set up and finally when all these steps are fully taken, privatization should be adopted (this is the sequence which the British Government pursued very successfully in the case of British Steel). This sounds rather like the 'infant industry argument' and it suffers from the well-known difficulty that the protection may never be withdrawn.

On balance, we can agree with the view that "if market failures are large relative to government failure in the new political situation, then State-owned enterprises might perform better relatively to privately-owned enterprises in the period of transition than when market failures are smaller and political agenda are less constrained.''

In fact, any form of ownership is imperfect, as this analysis has clearly shown : market failures may give rise to divergence between profit and welfare objectives in private firms; government failures give rise to divergence between political/bureaucratic and welfare objectives in state-owned enterprises; monitoring failure gives rise to divergence between the objectives of enterprise managers and their 'principals' whether the principals are 'private owners' or 'political superiors'. The outcome of ownership changes on welfare will hinge upon the 'relative magnitudes' of these imperfections. Privatization can be looked upon (as a first approximation) as a step towards lessening the impact of government failure, though this enhances the risk of market failures and of altering monitoring arrangements.

The reformers of Eastern European economies should not forget, in their zeal for privatization, that it would be wrong to consider privatization as a universal panacea for 'agency problems' in the public sector. This is so because of three particular factors cited by Vickers and Yarrow (*1991*) :

(a) In the spheres of significant market failure (and at times when they are not significant), government intervention persists after privatization with the consequence that the government will find enough opportunities for implementing its strategies/bureaucratic policies.

(b) Though privatization may make it pretty difficult for the government to intervene, the government, by being committed not to intervene, may lose credibility, particularly in monopolistic industries or other market failures. This may lead to inefficient underinvestment.

(c) Privatization is itself a government activity fraught with far-reaching distributional and political consequences. In the process of transfer of assets fresh opportunities may emerge for the political decision-makers to follow their own private policies.

Therefore, the effect of privatization in any given context will depend upon a host of factors : the wider market, regulatory and institutional setting in which privatization is undertaken. However, in future privatized firms in Eastern Europe are likely to suffer from much inefficiency owing to 'principal-agent problem'; as Ben-Ner and Michael Montias (*1991*) point out in the context of Romania, these problems are most likely to plague the privatized firms because of the "absence of widely diffused information, the narrowness of capital markets and the total absence of an effective market for corporate control". Moreover, for the privatization programme to succeed, as Hare (*1991*) points out in the context of Hungary, there should be simultaneous reforms of financial institutions. For as Stiglitz argues, banks and other financial institutions accumulate and redistribute funds in the economy, but also have an important task for choosing efficient and productive projects. In Hungary, for example, where banks have been utilized, prior to the reforms, largely as channels of centrally decided credit allocation, this selection function of the banks has remained undeveloped. Thus, along with the privatization programme, substantial restructuring of the banks will be vitally necessary.

One difficulty with the privatization process is the lack of domestic and foreign capital. However, much depends on the integration of the Eastern European economies with the European Economic Community which is, despite some hurdles, now converted to European Union.

Integration of Eastern/Central Europe into European Economic Community : Problems and Prospects

It is against this backdrop of difficulties associated with the systemic transformation in Eastern Europe, that we have to consider the fact that the East European countries particularly Poland, Czechoslovakia (former) and Hungary, where the reform process has been most advanced — have shown much eagerness to join the EC. These three countries want to be full members by 2000. They are pressing for membership primarily because of its value to them : first of all, as the three Central European countries see it, membership is the key to modernisation and the EC's free trade pact ensures the integration of its members into the world economy. This is warranted by the code of conduct set down by the EC, the observance of which may lead to the resolution of Central Europe's deep-rooted security problems and "keep lunatics from coming to power". And the East Europeans assert that their demand for membership is justified on the ground that they are now democratic countries and well on their way to market economies, whatever may have been the stresses and strains during the transitional phases. The EC on its part has not shown any reluctance. The signing of a Joint Declaration between the Community and Comecon in June 1988 can be looked upon as a breakthrough in relations between the EC and the East Europeans. This made possible official relation between the EC and Comecon and paved the way for trade cooperation agreements with each of the East European countries. In 1991 the EC signed "Europe Agreements" for giving the Central Europeans associate member status. At its summit meeting in Edinburgh in December 1992, the EC had made a commitment to the effect that the Central Europeans should be allowed to join as full memebrs in due course. Yet things are not so simple. Though the Central Europeans want a time table for membership, they have been refused. The suggestion of the EC Commission to invite the three countries, Poland, Hungary and (former) Czechoslovakia to some meetings on foreign policy has been brushed aside. The "Europe agreements" have yet to be ratified by all EC members.

Let us examine the reasons which the members of the EC have advanced as an explanation for the deliberate delay in granting full membership to the Central Europeans. An examination of these reasons (stated by "The Economist" in *1993*) would help us to judge the feasibility as also the desirability of the integration of Eastern/Central Europe into the EC.

There are broadly the following five reasons :

(a) *Migration.* As a result of the full implementation of the single European market, people, goods, services and money will be able to move around as freely as within one country. If free movement of people takes place between Poland and Germany, a polish worker might earn ten times more in Germany.

But the EC need not be much worried on this count, because the emigration rates from either Poland or Hungary have been low, except at times of war. Moreover, as an official publication of the Commission of the European Communities (*1992*) reveals, the underlying philosophy runs along these lines:

"The mobility of people, their capacity, willingness and readiness to move with their skills from one member State to another — is to be regarded as a valuable asset for a truly competitive European economy".

If this may be applied to the member states of the EC, it should not be difficult to stretch the point in favour of the Central Europeans.

(b) *Sensitive Industries.* One question that worries the EC members is whether their products of textiles, footwear, coal and steel would lose out to the low cost products of Central Europe. At present, trade in these products is restricted by the "Europe Agreements".

But this objection by the EC is not economically so sound. It will be of mutual benefit if the EC-members stop producing these goods and import them since they are produced more cheaply by the Central Europeans. Of course, the transitional process may be painful, as the westerners have to deploy their resources in more productive lines.

But the EC apprehends that such gains may not be reaped in certain "sensitive industries" which deserve special attention. A good part of the export growth can be attributed to the new private companies dealing in high technology goods like computer components and pharmaceuticals. This is because the region enjoys the greatest comparative advantage in the sphere of skilled and highly educated workforce that is the cheapest in the world.

It seems that it is rightly argued that the EC may be "worrying about nothing", because "international trade in computers is often conducted between branches of the same firm. Intra-firm trade tends to generate less friction than ordinary trade between countries."

(c) *Central Europe is not Ready.* The reform process in Eastern/ Central Europe is far from a satisfactory state of completion and has been accompanied by many stresses and strains, often soured by debates, with some twilight zones still remaining.

For example, one commentator, Nigel Harris, (*1993*) has recently described the state of the economy of Eastern Europe in these words:

"Eastern Europe's economic capacities at the moment are so severely limited, it is difficult to see when they would be capable of serious competition; for example, the cumulative debt of $115 billion in 1989 ($82 bn. without Russia) required servicing with 35 per cent of export revenue. The internal markets are disorganised and chaotic; the slump in output and employment extraordinary....The capital needs are enormous."

One may rightly raise the question whether it is possible for Eastern Europe, with such an economic condition, to become integrated into the EC at present. It is only after some order and stability is built into the economic system that integration may become feasible and useful.

This conclusion may not be valid for Central Europe, though its economic performance is not yet very remarkable. It is true that in 1989, the three countries we have mentioned were almost at the same level of affluence as Greece or Portugal. Thereafter their economies have shrunk by one-third. To retrieve their former affluence, they will have to grow at 10 per cent a year for the next three years. By that time Greece and Portugal will stand to gain by large transfers from the EC, so that Central Europeans, if they are to keep pace, will have to grow at more than 10 per cent a year.

But the Central Europeans claim that they are ready for full membership of the EC. They urge that there are already certain favourable conditions which would render the process of integration less difficult, Central Europe and the EC have become pretty close to each other through foreign direct investment, tax harmonisation and suitable modifications in the legal systems. For example, as "The Economist" states :

"All three countries either have or are about to introduce value added taxes.... Poland's banking and company laws are based on EC directives; its government is planning to make its legislation consistent with European law."

The point at issue is whether the Central Europeans can fulfil the "Maastricht criteria" — the guidelines that countries are required to follow so that they can use the future common European currency. One of the Maastricht criteria stipulates that the government's budget deficit has to be 3 per cent of GDP or less. "The Economist" (*1993*) has cited some figures : The Czech Republic's deficit is less, whereas Hungary's and Poland's are smaller than Italy's. Total debt, it is supposed, does not exceed 60 per cent of GDP; as far as inflation is concerned, each performs as well as or better than Southern European economies; in the sphere of interest rates, Poland has failed, but all of them fail by one criterion, viz, devaluation. One can however expect their currencies to appreciate, because each currency is now considered to be undervalued in terms of international purchasing power.

If we are to go by these figures and suppositions, there does not seem to be any strong obstacle standing in the way of the integration process. However, one fundamental question still remains : given the present state of economy in Central Europe, how far will it be feasible at present and in near future to successfully coordinate the macro-economic policies and the policies on internal and external balance of the EC and Central Europe so that the Maastricht criteria may be fulfilled? Ultimately, it is only "political will", as Jacques Delors had pointed out, that will allow the Europeans to find "good compromises, that is to say dynamic compromises" (*Commission of the European Communities, 1992*).

(d) *Institutions.* The EC's institutions are "painstakingly constructed edifices'' which represent every interest. Originally set up with six members, these institutions are considered to be groaning under the weight of 12. If membership were extended to Central Europe, a renegotiation of the function of each EC institution will be required. This may most probably give rise to conflict and raise fundamental questions about the type of federalism to be followed by the EC.

In fact, this poses a serious challenge. But, the first thing to note, the bureaucratic problem is no reason why the Central Europeans should be left out. Instead of harping on the bureaucratic problem, one should take a close look at the central feature of the Maastricht Treaty : i.e. the ''principle of subsidiarity'' which lays down that ''the community should deal only with those matters it is better equipped to deal with than the Member State and the regional and local authorities''.

This implies two things : one, there are certain matters for which joint action is necessary for Europe and to that end the right type of bureaucratic set-up has to be found. A typical example of a community matter is environmental protection.

Secondly, the principle implies that considerable scope for action remains for the individual countries, regions and cultures. This is shown by the importance attached to the regions. The Heads of States had decided to set up a special committee of the regions. It will consist of representatives of regional and local authorities (regions, districts) and have advisory competence. If this can be done for the present Member States, there is no reason why this cannot be extended to new memebrs. If more such advisory bodies at the lower levels are set up (another body that has been set up is the Economic and Social Committee), the bureaucratic problem can be considerably eased.

In this context the EC should always focus its attention on the importance of the central objective of European Union — an objective which has been admirably spelt out in the words of Jacques Delors:

''Europe cannot attain political union — indeed it cannot survive unless it is in control of its economic destiny. That is why we need an organized economic area. By that I mean an area based on three pillars of equal importance : First, competition; second, cooperation between Member States in economic policy and also between firms, whose research efforts we are supporting; third, solidarity between richer and less rich regions and the social dimension of the European venture''.

(e) *Cost.* Inclusion of the Central Europeans would be costly. ''The Economist'' (*1993*) gives a preliminary idea of the costs involved : "Budget transfers from the EC's regional fund (which accounts for about a quarter of the Community budget), plus the cost of supporting their farmers under the common agriculture policy (this accounts for about half of EC spending), would amount to between $6 billion and $10 billion a year that would add 14 to 20 per cent to the EC's current budget".

It is felt that the EC members are likely not to agree to shoulder this extra burden and this may stand in the way of the integration of Central Europe into the EC.

But there have been already certain signs which are encouraging. The EC has already participated actively in multilateral aid programmes. At the 1989 Western Economic Summit in Paris, the European Commission was entrusted to coordinate assistance from the 24 OECD countries, the G-24, to Poland and Hungary and this came to be known as the "Phare" programme ("Poland and Hungary assistance with restructuring the economy"). The EC's own contribution to Phare is substantial. It had contributed ECU 500 million in 1990. The total for 1991 is ECU 795 million with ECU 1 billion earmarked for 1992. The Commission has further extended its coordination as the scope and geographic coverage of the Phare programme has widened to the rest of Central and Eastern Europe. The G-24 has played a vital role in making preparations for the setting up of the European Bank for Reconstruction and Development (EBRD). The EC and its Member States hold a majority of the shares. All these measures strongly suggest that cost cannot be a binding constraint. Ultimately, however, the more important consideration before the EC should be whether the benefits flowing from expansion of membership outweigh the cost. There are two special benefits, as "The Economist" (*1993*) rightly sees it, if membership is extended; firstly, trouble on the Community's Eastern borders may be avoided. Central Europe's current policies (regarding the creation of free market economies and stable democracies) may be sustained by the EC, for it opens up its markets to help the countries grow and also strongly discourages the formation of extremist government. Central Europe may retain stability outside the EC, but its possibilities of doing so are considered to be stronger if they are integrated into the Community.

The second benefit is that extension of membership to Central Europe would enhance European stability to face a mighty Germany. This is particularly relevant when the "Franco-German alliance" which provided stability and support to Europe for fifty years, is almost withering as a result of problems with the Maastricht Treaty and the European exchange rate mechanism. It has been argued that, "If it is true that Germany is manageable only if tied down by regional alliances, then an alliance down its eastern border from Poland to Croatia could play a vital role".

If governments remain stable and economic policies are pursued successfully, Central Europe may well become "one of the world's fastest growing economic regions". Already western firms in Hungary believe that in a few years' time productivity will catch up with or even exceed that attained in Western Europe. It is further believed that even if Hungarian wages rise ten times, Hungary will still enjoy a labour-cost advantage over Western Europe. All these trends indicate that ultimately, as it has been put, "the EC will find itself drawn in willy-nilly".

Impact of the Integration of Europe on India

Some economists believe that, as a result of the integration of Europe and inclusion of Eastern/Central Europe into it, there is a possibility of Europe becoming more inward-looking, building up what is called a 'Fortress Europe'. This may lead, it is feared, to the diversion of European aid flows and foreign direct investment away from less industralised economies (LIEs) like India to Eastern Europe and new trade blocs. It is also felt, as Tisdell (*1993*) has pointed out, that in the sphere of trade, India is in a "vulnerable" position. This is because "in 1988, 24.3 per cent of its exports were to the EC, 18 per cent to U.S.A., 12.8 per cent to U.S.S.R. and 10.6 per cent to Japan," and also because India was "highly dependent for import on the EC (32 per cent), U.S.A. (11.3 per cent) and Japan (9.3 per cent)."

All these fears may be in the final analysis unfounded. A close look at the recent publications of the Delegation of the Commission of the European Communities (New Delhi) reveals that the relationship between India and the EC is a vibrant one promising to grow stronger in future. This will become evident when we note the following facts :

(i) First of all, the Delegation (1991) holds out the hope out that "a tremendous scope exists to increase India's market share — currently 0.8 per cent — in the Community's total imports."

(ii) In the context of the emergence of the "European Single Market", Ambassador and Head of the Delegation (1992) of the Commission of the European Communities, Francine Henrich made a very pertinent point which shows how India can benefit from it :

"The Single Market....would lead to the creation of a market of 345 million consumers; reduced costs owing to minimal border checks and from mutual recognition of testing, abolition of national preferences and reservations in public procurement, and a pooling of R and D skill, talents and cost, which would lead to superior results....The implementation of the Single Market....would benefit Indian business. With common European standards, Indian industry would not have to be bothered by the multiplicity of the requirements of Member States" (*European Community News, 1992*).

(iii) A very significant step in Indo-EEC cooperation was taken in the industrial sphere in 1987. This aimed at, as the Delegation (1991) states very clearly, "assisting in the development of India's industrial structure, in a mutually advantageous manner, thus making its exports more competitive on the EEC and world markets, and its market base more attractive for European technology and products" (*The European Community and India, 1991).* This particular stand of the delegation has not suffered any change even after the possibilities of the integration of Eastern/Central Europe into EC are being explored. In fact Henrich very clearly pointed out that "European experts are assisting Indian industries to diversify its exports in areas such as automobile components, machine tools, medical equipment and shellfish. We are partners in business forum, with offices in Delhi and Bombay, to promote joint ventures and investments." Clarifying it still further, she said, "We have a unique cooperation programme in standardisation, testing and quality which will greatly help would be exporters in the coming years. A venture capital fund called the 'EC Investment Partners', to promote joint ventures between small and medium sized enterprises, has been set up by the EC and will start very soon".

(iv) Intra-EC trade accounts for nearly 61 per cent of the total EC trade today as against 54 per cent six years ago; nevertheless the fact remains that "it is also true that Europe is freer and more open to competition, especially for industrial products from developing countries than either the U.S. or Japan and the growth in Europe's GDP, as a result of the abolition of non-tariff barriers and the opening of public procurement in making the Community a larger market for imports''.

Among other encouraging signs is the role of the Council of the EC Chambers of Commerce founded in India in 1982 to serve as one of the key players in the promotion of Indo-EC industrial and commercial cooperation. The other important event was that fourteen companies from the Member States of the EC took part in India Commission held at New Delhi in 1992. This group participation by the 14 companies from the EC Member States was, according to Rosenbaum, representative of the European Commission, intended to ''show the way we are consolidating and secondly, to show EC's seriousness to assist and participate in the Indian telecom scene''. In view of the liberalisation measures adopted by the Indian Government, India Commission 1992 symbolised an attempt to tap the vast Indian market.

Going by all these facts it is difficult to sustain the view that the integration of Europe will be detrimental to India. The way ahead will certainly not be an easy one, but one can look forward to a promising future.

REFERENCES

Estrin, S. (1991) : 'Yugoslavia: The Case of Self-Managing Market Socialism' *Journal of Economic Prespectives* (henceforth J.E.P), Vol 5, No. 4, Fall.

Collier, I.L., Jr (1991) : 'On the First Year of German Monetary, Economic and Social Union', *J.E.P.*, Vol 5, No. 4, Fall.

Brada, J.C. (1991) : 'The Economic Transition of Czechoslovakia from Plan to Market'. *J.E.P.*, Vol 5, No. 4, Fall.

Jackson, M. (1991) : 'The Rise and Decay of the Socialist Economy in Bulgaria' *J.E.P.*, Vol 5, No. 4, Fall.

Ben-Ner, A and Montias, J.M. (1991) : 'The introduction of Market in a Hypercentralized Economy : The Case of Romania', *J.E.P.*, Vol 5, No. 4, Fall.

Hare, P.G. (1991) : 'Hungary: In Transition to a Market Economy', *J.E.P.*, Vol 5, No. 4, Fall.

Vickers, J and Yarrow, G (1991) : 'Economic Perspectives on Privatization' *J.E.P.*, Vol. 5, No. 4, Fall.

Fischer, S and Gelb, A. (1991) : 'The Process of Socialist Economic Transformation' *J.E.P.*, Vol 5, No. 4, Fall.

Svejnar, J. (1991) : 'Microeconomic issues in the Transition to a Market Economy', *J.E.P.*, Vol 5, No. 4, Fall.

Litwack, J.M. (1991) : 'Legality and Market Reform in Soviet - type Economies', *J.E.P.*, Vol 5, No. 4, Fall.

Murrel, P. (1991) : Symposium on Economic Transition in the Soviet Union and Eastern Europe, *J.E.P.*, Vol 5, No. 4, Fall.

Bardhan, P. and Roemer, J.E. (1992) : 'Market Socialism : A case for Rejuvenation' *J.E.P.*, Vol 6, No. 3, Summer.

Chakravarty, S. (1990) : 'Market Forces and Planning', Bogomolov, O.T. (ed) : *'Market Forces in Planned Economies'* Macmillan, London.

Sadowski, Z.L. (1990) : 'The New Concept of Planning : Interaction with Markets', Bogomolov O.T. (ed) : *op. cit.*

Lin, Cyril (1990) : 'Comment', Bogomolov, O.T. (ed) : *op. cit.*

Narayanswamy, R. (1990) : 'Socialism, Economic Reform and Property Rights', *Economic and Political Weekly,* March 3.

Levy, V. (1981) : 'On estimating efficiency differentials between Public and Private Sectors in a developing economy — Iraq', *Journal of Comparative Economics,* Vol. 5.

Kay, J.A. and Thompson, D.J. (1986) : 'Privatization : A policy in Search of a Rationale' *The Economic Journal,* Vol. 96, March, pp. 18-32.

Vickers, J. and Yarrow, G (1988) : *Privatization : An Economic Analysis,* Cambridge, M.I.T. Press.

Basu, K. (1992) : 'Market, Laws and Governments'. B. Jalan, B. (ed.) *'The Indian Economy'* Viking, India.

'The Economist' (1993) : ''Eastern Europe — Dilemma over EC Membership'' reprinted in *'Business Standard'*, Calcutta, 20 March.

Commission of the European Communities (1992) : 'The Single Market in action', 'Europe : World Partner', 'From Single Market to European Union', 'European Union'.

—— (1992) : ''*European Community News*'' (November-December), New Delhi.

—— (1991) : ''*The European Community and India — Partners in Progress*'', New Delhi.

Tisdell, C. (1993) : ''Economic Transformation, Integration in Europe — Consequences for Asia-Pacific countries, especially India, and including Small Economies'', Paper presented at the International Seminar of the International Institute for Development Studies, Calcutta held in January 1993.

9

Recent Integration and Transformation of European Economies and their Impact on India and other Less Integrated Economies : A Note

SANTIKUMAR GHOSH

From its lowest to its highest forms, integration has been said to progress through the freeing of barriers to trade ('trade integration'), the liberalisation of factor movements ('factor integration'), the harmonisation of national economic policies ('policy integration') and the complete unification of these policies ('total integration').

As the individual European markets were quite fragmented on a national basis because of restrictive trade barriers among the nations, European firms were producing for small-sized markets and thus were unable to achieve economies of scale resulting from high levels of production. By establishing a Customs Union, the European countries hoped to obtain the benefits of a larger European market and at the same time to provide themselves with protection from the competitive pressure of the U.S. firms.

The European Community — consisting of its first coal and steel conglomerate, then the trading and nuclear development associations had not remained a static creation of the Rome Treaty or any other concord. 'Europe 1992' Plan for the 12 nations of the European Community, seeks to reduce all internal tariff and regulatory barriers to trade, harmonize taxes and subsidies, and allow companies operating in Europe to manage their production and trade with freedom. The European Common Market, by way of broadening the frontier — free single market, lowered tariffs, encouraged market integration, and thereby promoted vigorous and effective competition. Internal reallocation of existing resources may have been the most significant aspect of tariff reduction in the EEC. With the completion of the internal market, quotas on imports of textiles and apparel, for instance, earlier negotiated at the country level, will be negotiated at the Community level.

The evaluation of integration in a static framework is likely to be incomplete. The long-run effects of integration may be the more fundamental and more important ones. Viner showed that extending a preferential concession to a partner may well involve replacing imports purchased from the cheapest source with imports from the partner country, in which case trade diversion, rather than trade creation, occurs — resulting in a loss in welfare. As B. Balassa has pointed out, even if the immediate effect of integration is, on balance, trade diverting (and not trade creating), increased income in the Customs Union of Common Market, and other dynamic factors could benefit the world in the long run.

The increases in local production which should follow the setting up of the integration scheme would normally lead to new demand for imports from outside the region, both for intermediate and for consumer goods subsequent to rising income in the integration countries. This new import demand may not benefit the same firms nor the same countries that have been affected adversely by the original shift from extra regional to intra-regional imports and the outsiders to the scheme will have to adapt to the new situation, but the total volume of imports from the outside world would not necessarily fall.

The potential for increased market-based oligopoly by EC firms, and greater bargaining power by both firms and in the EC in economic policy-making is clearly present. There are risks of increased protection and increased use of bargaining power. Some responses to the fears that emerge could themselves create inefficiencies and losses in the international system, for example, through increased regionalisation of trade.

The formation of regional economic bloc may result in a significant trade diversion in agricultural trade. Support has been given to farmers' incomes in developed countries in such a way as to reduce the ability of developing countries to increase their exports. The EEC has provided a decisive measure of protection in the common agricultural policy. The system of price support coupled with a variable import levy and export subsidy has been adopted by EEC.

The high levels of agricultural protection in developed countries are said to be responsible for distorted and destabilised world market for discrimination against farming in developing countries and finally for substantial efficiency losses and environmental stress in the developed countries themselves. The Common Agricultural Policy of the European Community has been especially blamed for such adverse effects on trading partners, domestic consumers, taxpayers and the environment. A movement towards a more rationalised Common Agricultural Policy of the European Community would have to consist in a policy of deregulation and liberalisation.

The EEC is by far the most heavily protected market among the industrialized world. The skillful combination of tariffs and tariff structures with a variety of non-tariff barriers has been turning the EC into a businessman's monopoly. If the EC reacts to its new role and power differently, by formalising its own boundaries and by encouraging a more rule-based international system, the consequences for developing countries could be more favourable offering a more predictable and less protectionist trading system; reducing policy uncertainty could have favourable effects on investment. If there is no deliberate shift to or from protection or use of bargaining power, there will be clearly new types of opportunity from the freer internal movement, and higher incomes, and changes in industrial structure.

During the recent decades, the competitiveness of a number of developing countries in the export of manufactures has increased. The industrial countries have been unwilling and unable to readjust their industrial structure. The EEC has been following its commercial policies in line with other industrial countries. A large number (136 in 1980) of sensitive products (textiles, jute and leather goods as well as hand tools, electronic and other engineering products) exported by developing countries has been subject to tariffs and quotas and of semi-sensitive ones (184 in 1980) subject to ceilings in the EEC General System of Preferences scheme. Quantitative and discretionary limits on imports are bound to affect most adversely the weakest members of the international community, since they have apparently less to offer as a quid pro quo in negotiations geared to the gradual establishment of a managed trading system.

While less developed countries may see integration as a means of initiating industrialisation, more advanced countries certainly see it as a means of protecting industrial development as well as of fostering it further.

The completion of the Single Market programme should provide a significant boost to output and growth over the medium term. The abolition of frontier controls has been applicable to goods, services and capital, as well as to people. Exchange controls went in 1991, with a few exceptions. Efforts are now being made towards forming monetary union.

Limited progress has been made, however, in efforts at 'market integration' in developing countries. First, item-by-item negotiation on tariff reductions encounter considerable difficulties because of the power of special interests. Second, differences in the level of industrial development have made agreements on trade liberalisation difficult. Third, in view of the distortions in relative prices due to protection, it has been difficult to determine the benefits to be derived from integration and there has been a tendency to consider changes in the trade balance as a sign of gains or losses. Developing countries are, however, seeking partnerships with developed countries rather than solely with each other.

The European Community and India are at two different ends of an economic scale. It is no longer the kind of relationship that obtains between a supplier of raw materials and a manufacturer. The two sides have now reached a point where they share other's markets and provide each other with the means of production.

India should be able to usefully exchange experience about Europe's policies on the location of industries, on taxing the cities to feed the villages, and on the intelligent anticipation of the future decline of an apparently flourishing industry, and finally on the participation of people in regional and local government. The example of the European Economic Community is no doubt of relevance and interest to the less integrated economies like India.

Clearly, economic integration is not a way to evade reforms by exporting the problems to the rest of the region. Integration cannot be a substitute for the internal efforts and measures that each country has to take.

Whether a strong and integrated EC is likely to make a substantial contribution to the collective management of important interdependencies in the world economy, is an open question. We know from oligopoly theory that almost anything can happen in such situations.

Integration should not, therefore, be considered as a step towards some sort of new universal economic order. There are indications that the world is increasingly moving towards three trading blocs, centred around the EC, Japan and the United States. Regionalism may well move the world away from free trade.

REFERENCES

Balassa, B. (1961) : 'Towards a Theory of Economic Integration', *Kyklos*, Vol. 14, Fasc. 1.

Viner, J. (1950) : *The Customs Union Issue*, New York.

10

Impact of European Union on Developing Countries with Special Reference to India and Bangladesh

BIPUL MALAKAR and HARIPADA BHATTACHARYA

Introduction

Economic interdependence among the nations emerged as a viable means for furthering economic expansion of all the nations via international trade after the revolution of sea transport. The doctrine of comparative cost advantage mainly based on natural resources became a more effective tool for uniting the world in trade and exchange. Resources and their intrinsic qualities have, however, undergone changes with the advancement of technology.

The application of scientific knowledge in the production of goods and services since the two great wars is continuously becoming intensified. On the other hand, expanding horizon of technology, induced radical changes in the system of global production and exchange. Political process also influences international transaction. In consequence degree and nature of international trade, experienced both quantitative and qualitative changes; foreign direct investment, multinationals and global private enterprises of large size, international transport, communication and information technology started playing key role in accelerating the process of economic interdependence and cultural integration across the world. As a matter of fact, geographical boundaries of nations are increasingly becoming ineffective phenomena. It is thus resolved that sustained economic growth has become more dependent on freedom to engage in global exchange. It has become difficult for any nation to sustain in isolation.

The technological revolution has sharpened the division of the world into two categories — developed and developing (third world) nations. Technological gap between the two groups of countries, is not showing any sign of convergence. Irrespective of the level of development, nations are in general engaged in technological development either by borrowing or by innovation. While the urge for modern technology in the developing world is related with their growth prospects, break through in technology in the fortunate developed world is demanded more for keeping this difference alive rather than for economy of resource use.

One other significant phenomena as observed in the developed part of the world, associated with this emerging technological heterogeneity is the formation of regional trade blocs among neighbouring nations for maximizing gains from international trade. Regional bloc formation may not always be condemned. The UN Economic and Social Commission advocated bloc formation for the prosperity of member countries as the primary objective and optimization of world trade as the secondary one, during the world economic crisis after the Second World War. At least five regional blocs were established in between 1948 to 1960 by the UN Council; most dominant of them is the European Economic Commission. However the commission currently is rather unimportant in comparison to European Union (EU or EEC or EC).

Creation of EC despite the existence of EEC is a matter of great concern and requires deeper probe. A brief historical sketch of EC is given in Section I of the paper. Following the success of EEC or otherwise many regional economic arrangements came into existence with fairly similar objectives. There exist at least 85 such regional arrangements (1993), of which 28 have been considered in GATT.

This zone formation at the background of World Trade Organization (WTO) advocating for transparency in the sphere of international trade and transaction is a matter of significant importance; it has not been deeply probed. Internal arrangements in these groups will no doubt vitiate the primary objective of WTO — uniform code of conduct in the sphere of external transaction for all the nations. It is expected that these (trade blocs) will have an adverse effect on technologically lagging developing countries. Many of them have already opted for or trying hard for integrating with the world economy. The impact of EC and developing world with particular reference to India and Bangladesh is thus analysed in the present paper.

Both India and Bangladesh maintain favouarble trade relation with the EC member countries. About one third of the total exports from India and slightly more from Bangladesh find their ways in the European Common Market. The continuation of this favourable trade link in future will be dependent on composition and configuration of EC primarily and partially on the intra-EC trade. Thus, in Section I, some important characteristics of EC together with functioning are discussed. In Section II, structure and trend of EC trade in the background of changing economic policies in India and Bangladesh — in some sense export-led growth strategy is being favoured in both the nation — is taken up for discussion. The study is concluded with some suggestions in Section III.

I. European Community : A Brief Historical Sketch

In anticipation of the common problems of post-war economic reconstruction, Belgium, Netherlands and Luxembourg (Benelux group) formed a close economic union in 1948. They mutually agreed to dilute trade barriers and encouraged free movement of capital and labour. This may be regarded as a move to revive the loose Belgium-Luxembourg Customs Union formed in 1922. However, the 1948 move again could not be operative due to restrictive trade and commerce policies pursued by the powerful marine states like France, Germany, Spain and England during the time. To some extent geographical factors were also responsible for the failure.

Formation of an European customs union with other nations was thus viewed by Benelux group as a viable alternative relating to the long-term question of developing intra-European trade. The idea readily got support from France and Germany. France, Germany and Italy placed a plan before the Council of Europe to establish a community or a single market for two interrelated industrial intermediaries coal and steel (products) among themselves by removing of all customs duties and other discriminatory practices. In July 1950, (representatives of) Belgium, Luxembourg, Netherlands and Italy met in Paris to give thought to this plan. The conference resulted in the establishment of the European Coal and Steel Community (ECSC); with these six European nations as members, the community came into force from July, 1952.

However, Benelux group of countries failed to derive any noteworthy benefit from the otherwise successful ECSC. The BOP situation in all of these countries was becoming more vulnerable. Thus the demand for extension of cooperation and integration in the field of transport and power production came from these nations. The group suggested (progressive) integration of the economic, financial and social policies among the ECSC member countries. To accommodate the gradually deteriorating balance of payment position of the Benelux group of countries, a treaty was signed in Rome for establishing a 'Common Market' by the representatives of the six ECSC countries. The treaty became effective from January 1, 1958. The common market treaty or the European Economic Community stressed developing a single market for the (manufactured) products of the six member countries without tariff or quantitative restrictions and the common external trade and tariff policies with the non-member countries. It may thus be said that 'The European Economic Community' was born from a treaty on coal and steel, which finally led to formation of 'United Europe'.

The ECSC or the formation of EEC started posing various problems to non-member Western European nations in the sphere of external trade, in particular. They were not unjustifiably concerned regarding the increased adverse effect in the near future of the division that have already been surfaced and the emerging direction of trade in Western Europe. The possibility of disunity in Europe was warned by social scientists and politicians as well. In an endeavour to deal with these issues, a step to form an association between EEC and other European countries was prompted by Organization of European Economic Commission (OEEC) — a UNO body formed in sixties.

The move was a futile one. It did not yield any positive outcome due to rigid attitudes of EEC member states — France and Germany in particular. As a counter-move, European Free Trade Association (EFTA) was immediately created by seven European nations — Sweden, Austria, Denmark, Norway, Portugal, Switzerland and United Kingdom — with the same objective of maximising external trade among member nations. The EFTA became operative from July 1, 1960. However EFTA failed to emerge as a viable trade arrangement or alternative to the EEC, and eventually degenerated. Most of the founder members gradually deserted the organization to join EEC. Presently EFTA have only four regular members, of which Liechtenstein, the nascent East European nation, emerged from non-market socialist bloc.

The dominant characteristics of the EFTA member countries were not conducive for the creation of a barrier free cross country trade area. EFTA is geographically more dispersed compared to EEC. The barrier of physical distance could not be overcome. On the other hand, Austria and Switzerland being neighbouring countries, had little trade with each other. Heterogeneity in the economic structure across the member nations appears to be the prime cause of failure of EFTA arrangement. UK was the most dominant member. It alone accounted for half of the total population of EFTA. Share of UK was more than fifty per cent in both aggregate GDP and in industrial production of EFTA. In consequence intra EFTA trade (about 50 per cent was the share of UK) used to be controlled by the UK. The various problems arising due to skewed nature of economic situation and the level of development among the member countries could not be amicably resolved. For example, the level of economic development in Portugal was substantially low compared to many other members. The economy required special attention to adjust with EFTA. The institutional machinery in the EFTA was not sufficient to cope with the adjustment process required. There was no common agricultural policy which was urgently required for unification and smooth functioning. EFTA emphasises primarily on free trade in industrial goods. This enabled UK to dominate over other member countries. Irony is that, despite EFTA members being more complementary and less competitive with one another, compared to EEC, the counter move failed. However, the causes of failure of EFTA provided the vital guidelines in framing common trade and cooperation platform for EEC.

EFTA has been found to suffer from malfunctioning and was thus unsuccessful. Members failed to agree on harmonizatrion of taxation, social security charges and the like. Britain, Denmark and Ireland withdrew from EFTA and became members of the EEC in 1973. Further enlargement of the Community with inclusion of less developed economies (within EC) Greece, Spain and Portugal gave new impetus to its objectives and strengthened liberal trends in the Western European integration, obviously at the cost of dissolution of EFTA. Austria, Sweden and Finland left the association (EFTA) on 31st December 1994, to become the member of European Union (from 1.1.1995) (*Europa 1995*).

The 15 nation European Union is now an ingenious multi-faceted instrument of power. Over the times, it has acquired a profound significance not only in political development but also in international trade. Some of the important characteristics of EC are discussed in the next section.

II. EEC : Common Market, Common Currency and Trade Preferences

There seems to exist remarkable similarity in the performance measured in terms of GDP growth rate — for all the EEC member countries. During eighties all the countries experienced a set back in their growth rate, except the tiny Luxembourg and U.K. and the decelerating trend continued for the larger number of members during the first half of nineties as well (table 1).

However, improved growth rate of GDP in U.K. may not be indicative of better performance of the economy. The trend could not be sustained (in nineties). The country started facing increased deficit in current account since the second half of the eighties. Thus it may be interpreted as the outcome of acceleration in the GDP growth rate with external help. But such thing can not be said for the tiny Luxembourg, where the balance in current account and GDP have shown positive parallel movement. It may also be observed that in most of the economies acceleration in GDP growth rate have accompanied by improved current account balance in seventies. Deceleration in the rate of growth across countries is obviously a cause of concern to the EEC. The problem of job creation is also common to all the member nations.

However relatively more important reason behind the formation of European Community is the deteriorating BOP situation. The urgency to counteract the challenges posed by the technologically superior Japan and USA in the international as well as in the domestic market was felt by all the members.

EEC as a community failed to compete with cost and quality efficiency with these two countries. This, in turn, has worsened current account balance of some of the economies and more intensely employment situation (table 2). In all countries, the rate of unemployment is increasing, while in sixties unemployment rate was much below 5 per cent in many countries which is considered by many macro-economic experts as full employment level.

At the same time, the fear of being out-competed by newly emerging industrialized countries in the international market obviously guided the members to hasten the process of economic integration. Trade restrictions practiced by developing countries have also been focused by EEC as a threat to their development process. The major policy provision therefore in EEC was to extend (external) market by dismantling trade barriers among member countries (by 1990) i.e. to create a common market by establishing an area without frontiers. This internal market programme of EEC has to be achieved by removing trade barriers within the member countries which in turn would result in increased cooperation and trade among EEC by reducing the economic distance. Operational viability of this Common Market phenomenon requires suppressing of all frontiers disturbing the mobility (free movement) of products and factors of production by progressively approximating the economic policies of the member States. Successful implementation of the programme undoubtedly will make EEC inward looking. This point is however, dissented by EEC on the ground that removal of trade barriers will also be extended to other non-member countries; this again contradicts the EEC provision of preferences to the products of internal members to improve their marketability within EEC. As a matter of fact, EEC accords high levels of protection to some identified items. Over and above, EEC proposal contains discriminatory measures at least for the inflow of agricultrual products. The preferential trade agreement, protection to domestic industries from external competition, over and above assurance of wider market which will help to achieve economies of scale, have been contributory in the formation of common platform by the member countries. Relative weights of the aforementioned factors obviously vary across member countries of the EEC.

Configuration of EEC : The nature of crisis, of course, is not uniform across the member countries. Thus, the reason behind joining EEC may differ from country to country. Some economies with relatively small market size — for example Luxembourg and Finland, may have been attracted by preferential trade agreement while others might be induced by the possibility of greater economies of scale. In what follows, EEC seek to build up a closer relationship between member states in the midst of crisis and, therefore, it appears that economic integration was the only panacea to ease out the economic woes faced by these countries. To realise their cherished dream, it has been contemplated to establish, as noted earlier, a Common Market for the mutual benefit of the member states.

The possible benefits and bargaining capacity of the member countries necessarily depend on several parameters. It seems, resource base, production technology, purchasing power and size of the market are relatively more significant.

If per capita income is any indicator of purchasing power, one notices some spatial imbalance. Denmark, Germany and Luxembourg belonging to highest per capita income (GDP) class are at least four times richer than Portugal or Greece placed at the bottom level of per capita income scale. The disparity is substantially larger with respect to per capita GNP. Ignoring some differences, one may classify Belgium, U.K., Italy, Netherlands, Sweden and France in a homogeneous per capita GDP or GNP class. This group also maintains considerable distance both from high per capita income class and low per capita income group of countries. The impact of this difference in per capita income increases due to difference in population size of individual countries.

TABLE 1

Changes in GDP and Balance on Current Account of EC Member Nations

Country	Annual Average GDP change (p.c)			Balance on current account (p.c.of GDP)		
	71-80	81-90	91-95	71-80	81-90	91-95
Luxembourg	2.6	3.6	3.0	18.1	34.6	27.9
Ireland	4.7	3.8	5.0	–6.1	–4.6	6.5
Finland	3.4	3.1	–1.6	–2.3	–2.3	–1.0
Denmark	2.2	2.0	1.5	–2.9	–2.8	1.9
Austria	3.6	2.1	2.7	–1.1	0.0	–0.1
Sweden	2.0	2.0	–1.1	–0.7	–1.6	–1.1
Portugal	4.7	3.0	1.1	–2.8	–3.6	–1.9
Belgium	3.2	1.9	2.3	–0.1	–0.1	4.6
Greece	4.7	1.5	1.1	–1.6	–4.3	–3.2
Netherlands	2.9	2.0	2.3	1.2	3.2	3.7
Spain	3.5	3.0	2.0	–0.8	–1.1	–1.9
Italy	3.8	2.2	1.2	–0.1	–0.8	1.2
France	3.3	2.4	1.3	0.3	–0.5	0.4
United Kingdom	1.9	2.7	2.0	–0.6	–1.4	–2.3
Germany	2.7	2.2	2.5	0.7	2.6	–1.4

Source : EC commission, EC, various issues.

TABLE 2

Some Basic Indicators of EC Member Nations

Country	Population (in 000) 1994	Per capita GDP (in mil ecu) 1991	Share in[1] EC common market (p.c) 1981	1995	Unemployment[2] rate 1961 to 1970	1981 to 1990
Luxembourg	398 (0.5)	19551	0.13	0.16	0.0	2.5
Ireland	3572 (0.6)	9973	0.63	0.73	5.4	14.7
Finland	50.86 (0.4)	14809	1.68	1.50	2.0	5.4
Denmark	5205 (0.5)	20439	1.92	2.08	1.2	7.4
Austria	8023 (1.1)	18761	2.22	2.79	2.0	3.4
Sweden	8780 (0.7)	17066	3.84	2.60	1.7	2.7
Portugal	9866 (–0.4)	5653	0.93	1.25	2.6	7.0
Belgium	10119 (0.2)	15936	3.22	3.24	2.0	9.7
Greece	10415 (0.8)	5555	1.48	1.31	5.1	6.4
Netherlands	15387 (– –)	15612	4.80	4.70	0.9	8.6
Spain	39223 (0.02)	10926	6.17	6.56	2.5	18.5
Italy	57248 (1.8)	16044	13.67	12.59	4.8	8.3
France	57916 (–0.2)	17009	19.49	18.27	1.8	9.3
United Kingdom	58390 (0.6)	15378	17.10	13.19	1.7	9.8
Germany	81400 (1.0)	19880	22.71	29.06	0.7	6.0

Note : 1. See text 2.p.c. of civilian labour force

Figures in brackets indicate annual growth of population.

Sources: EC Commission, EC, various issues; World Development Report, OUP, 1995.

With respect to population size, some noticeable similarities and dissimilarities may easily be discovered among member countries. One may readily identify two distinguishable different clusters of countries. England, Italy and France, each having population within the narrow range from 57 to 58.5 millions reveal striking similarities; they have some similarity with respect to per capita income. This group of countries is discernibly different from 8 to 10 million population country group consisting of Portugal, Greece, Austria, Sweden and Belgium. This latter group differs from the former one with respect to per capita income as well. Apart from Luxembourg and Ireland, Denmark and Finland are the two countries having small population with 5.1 and 5.2 million respectively. The Netherlands having moderately high level of population around 15.38 million differs from many other members both with respect to population size and per capita income.

The community as a whole is headed by Germany with population of 81.4 million and second highest per capita income ($22,320). Thus, it would not be grossly unjustified to say that Germany with large population and high per capita income (table 1) in the group is likely to emerge as the most dominant partner.

The relative importance of the member countries may be understood from their share in aggregate GDP of EEC, which may be interpreted as their primary share in the integrated common market. From column 4 of table 2, it is amply clear that after Germany, France, U.K. and Italy in that order, are dominant members. These four countries together constitute more than 73 per cent of the EEC's total market both in 1981 and 1995 and the share is about 80 per cent if measured with respect to GNP. Rest of the members, it may be said, are likely to play a passive role in the EEC market. Distribution of market share among the members remained almost stagnant during the 15 year period 1981 to 1995! Changes in the distribution needs to be interpreted with caution. Unification of East and West Germany has influenced the share of Germany favourably. At least fifty per cent of the incremental share of Germany may be attributed to this unification. In this background, stagnancy in the share in Belgium and Luxembourg or increase in Portugal, Austria and Denmark obviously suggest better performance of these economies and increase in their bargaining power in the common market.

However, the degree of benefits will obviously be dependent on nature of trade. Whatsoever Germany may have strong say and likely to play the role of trend setter in total process of economic integration in Europe. The current objections raised in some member states point towards that. It is befitting here to mention the reaction of different member countries regarding Maastricht Treaty. In Denmark the result of referendum went against the treaty while in France, the treaty was saved marginally.

Sucessful operation of EC and its future prospect apart from other things will depend on infrastructural facilities, relatively immobile natural resources including human capital and significantly on availability of funds for investment. This latter aspect — funds for investment — primarily depends on gross national savings. It may be observed that the scarcity of domestic resources is increasing for all the member nations — savings as percentage of GDP is declining in every nation with some exceptions; while during the period 1960 to 1980 this rate was around 25 per cent except in U.K. and Ireland, the average rate after mid-eighties is about 20 per cent (table 4). This declining feature of savings rate will have a telling effect in the process of integration since one of the major objectives of European Union is to encourage cross border movement of capital.It is well known that the movement of capital and technology is in the hands of Transnational Corporation (TNC). The movement however is not independent of technological parameters like labour cost. In what follows, profitability may be regarded as the single-most significant parameters indicating the level of technology. From table 3, it is amply clear that considerable variation persists with respect to both the above mentioned parameters across the Community members.

The spatial distribution of profitablity in EC has become more skewed — inequality measured in terms of the ratio of maximum to minimum profitability has witnessed two-fold increase from 2.32 (during the period 1974 to 1986) to 4.04 in 1995.

However it may be said that measures like dismantling of trade barriers, establishment of 'Common Market' and the attempt to unify currency system for better functioning have endowed the EC with a new opportunity to improve trade connection among members which in turn may be helpful (expected also) in improving balance of payment crisis faced by many member countries.

The inward biased policy package of EEC is however with severe criticisms. It has been pointed out that the successful operation of the EEC strategy, will result in increased intra-EEC trade at the cost of sacrificing the trade link of the member countries with the non-member countries. Thus the trade-off between intra-EEC trade and trade with the countries outside the bloc, will be beneficial to the EEC member but not to the other partners. EC has contested this observation and stated that the increasing quantum of intra-EEC trade and consequent improved cooperation among member countries, hold fake possibility of jeopardizing the trade connection of EEC members with other countries. In what follows, possibly all the EEC members will be able to enhance their bargaining power in the external market by minimizing competition within EEC in future. However, successful operation of this phenomenon is dependent on two important happenings. Member

TABLE 3

Labour Cost and Profitability in European Union

Country	Labour cost (1961-73=100)	Profitability (1961-73=100)	
	1995	1974-1986	1995
Luxembourg	na	54	40
Ireland	82	82	156
Finland	96	73	85
Denmark	112	76	90
Austria	153	81	71
Sweden	74	84	103
Portugal	113	36	62
Belgium	102	67	87
Greece	73	64	71
Netherlands	107	77	88
Spain	109	83	140
Italy	81	67	104
France	88	73	96
United Kingdom	89	77	108
Germany	116	72	91

Sources: EC Commission, EC, various issues; World Development Report, OUP, 1995.

countries need to consolidate their existing trade relations. And the Community should see that the dependence of the members on outside bloc for supply of some essential goods and services is minimized. EC has already made some breakthrough in trade front by establishing 'Common Market'. Operation of the market, if achieved anything, has been successful in building and improving (existing) intra-EEC trade nexus by increasingly substituting trade connection of EC both with industrially advanced countries and developing economies during the last decade. The latter group has suffered relatively more (tables 5A and 5B).

TABLE 4

Gross Domestic Saving in European Union

(per cent of GDP at current market price)

Country	Savings			
	1961-1970	1971-1980	1981-1990	1991-1995
Luxembourg	32.3	42.5	59.5	58.9
Ireland	18.2	19.7	16.0	20.8
Finland	25.3	26.1	23.4	15.1
Denmark	23.0	20.1	15.1	17.2
Austria	27.9	27.4	24.1	24.6
Sweden	25.2	21.1	17.3	13.8
Portugal	26.0	26.8	24.4	26.3
Belgium	23.4	22.3	17.0	22.3
Greece	25.3	32.5	21.4	18.1
Netherlands	27.5	24.4	23.6	24.4
Spain	25.0	24.8	21.0	18.5
Italy	28.1	25.6	21.3	18.8
France	26.5	25.5	20.0	19.6
United Kingdom	19.1	18.5	16.4	13.7
Germany	27.2	23.7	22.8	21.1

Sources : EC Commission, EC, various issues; World Development Report, OUP, 1995.

That intra EEC trade — in both export and import front — has depended during the last decade is evident from tables 5A and 5B. United Kingdom and Denmark being the two exceptions, we observe for all the other countries, concentration of export trade within EEC during the said period was much above fifty per cent of total merchandise trade. Half of the member nations concentrated more than sixty per cent of their export business within the Community. Even Denmark and United Kingdom experienced 2 and 6.5 percentage points increase in their intra-EEC orientation of export basket. During the period countries like Belgium, Luxembourg, Ireland, Netherlands and Portugal have recorded their intra-EC share of exports above 70 per cent in 1988, while in the beginning of the decade only Belgium, Luxembourg and Netherlands had export concentration more than 70 per cent within bloc. It is worthy to mention that relatively less developed Greece, Portugal and Spain have experienced maximum increase in their intra-EEC export. However, none of these countries could balance their external trade. Finally one may observe that EEC as a group still depends on the external world for marketing for more than 40 per cent of its exportable. The impact of intra-EEC trade nexus on economies outside EC may more vividly be understood by exploring the changing pattern of intra-EEC import.

Except Ireland, whose origination of imports changed favourably for the countries outside EC (intra EEC share declined from 75.8 per cent to 71.2 per cent), rest of the countries experienced accelerated growth in their intra-EC origination of import basket. The highest intra-EC origination of import besides Ireland (71.2 per cent) has been acheived by Denmark (70.4 per cent), Portugal (66.4 per cent) and France (65.1 per cent). In case of Germany, France, U.K. and Italy (major countries of the group), intra-EC origination of imports during the period increased by 3.5, 13.7, 7.6 and 15.3 per cent respectively, indicating further consolidation in the intra-EC import trade. The decline in intra-EC share in total imports of Ireland which has attained a very high level does not hold much possibility of influencing intra-EC import origination in an adverse way, increase in the origination of imports within EC for some major members is more important than that of small countries (Luxembourg, Greece, Denmark etc). One can thus, observe an appreciable increase in the intra-EC concentration of import over the period. This growing trade concentration, like 'two person zero-sum-game where one's loss is other's gain', implicitly indicates declining importance of other developed and developing countries for the Community as a group. Developing countries are the worst sufferers in this changed situation.

TABLE 5A

Share in Incremental Export of EEC Countries

(Per cent)

Countries	Total increment in exports in 1988 over 1981 (Unit-ECU)	EEC 1988 over 1981	Developing Countries 1988 over 1981	Developed Countries 1988 over 1981
Belgium*	27973.00 (56.07)	79.37 (62.42)	04.48 (20.80)	16.17 (54.20)
Denmark	8760 (60.30)	53.10 (67.00)	02.24 (09.00)	44.64 (72.37)
France	53439.00 (58.64)	77.80 (87.57)	–1.36 (–30.2)	23.30 (63.80)
Germany	115069.00 (72.88)	60.96 (90.49)	–01.51 –06.23)	40.55 (89.03)
Greece	773 (20.02)	165.67 (75.41)	–77.88 (–48.13)	12.21 (10.36)
Ireland	8803 (125.64)	76.33 (134.51)	02.58 (26.81)	20.43 (166.68)
Italy	40497.00 (59.40)	76.63 (100.05)	–12.69 (–26.09)	38.25 (93.52)
Netherlands	28492.00 (46.28)	79.45 (50.72)	03.38 (13.50)	17.16 (49.96)
Portugal	5261.00 (140.25)	82.19 (204.04)	–00.00 (–3.61)	17.81 (95.42)
Spain	18220.00 (100.32)	74.90 (163.22)	10.30 (31.91)	14.30 (67.91)
U.K.	28038.00 (29.48)	71.84 (48.93)	–04.20 (–5.191)	32.36 (29.36)
EEC	335325.00 (58.71)	71.08 (76.77)	01.46 (–4.13)	30.24 (67.67)

* Belgium includes Luxembourg.

Note : Figures in brackets indicate percentage increase in trade in 1988 over 1981.

Source : Compiled from Eurostat External Trade Statistical Yearbook, 1989. UNSO Contrade Database: DECD; Monthly Statistics of Foreign Trade, April 1990.

TABLE 5B

Share in Incremental Import of EEC Countries

(Per cent)

Countries	Total increment in imports in 1988 over 1981 (Unit-ECU)	EEC 1988 over 1981	Developing Countries 1988 over 1981	Developed Countries 1988 over 1981
Belgium	25125.00 (45.17)	92.53 (69.21)	–06.11 (–16.54)	13.58 (26.79)
Denmark	6461.00 (40.63)	65.51 (57.02)	06.97 (30.24)	27.16 (26.47)
France	48345.00 (44.59)	95.82 (83.13)	–21.43 (–35.15)	24.96 (52.02)
Germany	65107.00 (44.33)	61.19 (54.48)	–04.67 (–10.83)	43.67 (62.03)
Greece	2473.00 (30.84)	99.78 (60.35)	26.97 (–33.02)	26.77 (34.70)
Ireland	3604.00 (37.99)	59.08 (29.61)	(+00.00) (+00.00)	40.91 (81.33)
Italy	34925.00 (42.53)	93.47 (94.21)	–28.39 (–37.04)	34.25 (57.81)
Netherlands	2923.00 (49.97)	77.81 (72.69)	–01.41 (–03.03)	23.30 (49.98)
Portugal	5306.00 (59.67)	102.43 (136.13)	–04.44 (–09.96)	02.01 (04.21)
Spain	19638.00 (68.34)	95.76 (221.85)	–19.98 (–30.14)	23.87 (64.99)
U.K.	70001.00 (73.24)	59.57 104.90	2.04 (8.05)	36.86 (70.63)
EEC	310608.00 (48.62)	77.23 (79.94)	–9.08 (–19.53)	31.60 (56.39)

Note : Same as table 5A

Source : Same as table 5A

However, the acuteness and magnitude of suffering of the developing countries in the post-integration period can better be understood by analysing the distribution of incremental trade among intra-EEC, developed and developing countries. Tables 5A and 5B give a brief account of the distribution of incremental export and import of EEC countries among the three identified groups. From the tables it appears that, apart from Greece and U.K. all the members and EC as a group experienced more than 50 per cent expansion in the export market. Portugal headed the list with 140 per cent growth; Spain and Ireland are the two other countries recording twofold increase in their export market. In consequence or otherwise inflow of importable has also increased for all the countries but by lesser degree. High increment in U.K. may easily be related with her deteriorating external payment situation. However, many other countries are also facing the same crisis. Most discernible feature is that the share of EEC in incremental export and import as well is remarkably high for all the members. That the destination of bulk of incremental export has been confined within EC, clearly portrays a declining trade link of EC with non-member countries. Distribution of incremental import according to its origin is important for the non-member countries. Distribution is extremely skewed in favour of EEC for all the countries. As a matter of fact, all the countries have exhibited a strong preference for getting their import supplied by the bloc itself. The source of this assertion is the observed large discrepancy between the aggregate increment of import and the expansion of import from EC in all the nations except in Ireland. However EC members still depend on the other developed worlds as reflected by the share of this group in incremental imports.

Distribution of incremental import shows that the share of developing countries has been on the decline. The picture of most of EC countries indicate that origination of import from developing countries drastically declined during the periods. Thus developing countries have already started facing problem for sale of their products in EEC. Impact of ECM of developing world is extremely unfavourable. This as well, has long term effect. Growing mutual trade in EC is making developing world an unimportant external trade partner to all the member countries. It seems EC is not interested in further expansion and even retaining their export market in the developing world. In general, share of developing countries in incremental export to EC members is insignificant and for many countries exhibited negative sign as well.

Above exercise clearly points out that for almost all the countries destination of incremental export of EC countries has mostly been confined within EC or to the developed countries (accounts together more than 100 per cent sometimes). Such lopsided distribution of incremental export may easily be understood by observing that export growth for all countries within EEC or in developed world has outpaced the growth of total export for the period while most countries have sacrificed their export market in the third world. Thus, destination of EC exports for developing countries realised a negative growth rate. As a natural corollary, developing countries during the period experienced drastic downward movement in the share of imports origination from EEC indicating trade link for some of the EC members (with developing nations) on the adverse path. This weakening of trade link, obviously has a strong say in the origination of imported EC items from the developing world. Thus developing countries, as a group by losing their export market seem to be the worst hit by the integration mechanism applied by EEC; all the major states — Germany, France, Italy — except U.K. in the group have reduced importing from developing countries. In consequence, in incremental import, within EC and developed countries are 77.23 per cent and 31.60 per cent respectively; share of developing countries, thus showed negative sign (–9.08 per cent); imports from developing countries to EC declined by (–19.53 per cent).

Thus, it becomes amply clear that EEC as a group gradually became more and more inward looking and, therefore, a significant alteration in the EC trade relation is noticed in the current period. This post-integration expansion of intra-EC trade, and the consequent trade nexus though may be attributed to many factors, but most important (of them) and worth mentioning is perhaps increasing self-sufficiency ratio (SSR) of EC with respect to a number of agricultural and related products, for which EC used to be dependent on other developed and developing countries a few years back. SSR and the diversified nature of exports basket of the EC countries jointly explain their declining trade link with developing countries.

Increasing SSR for some selected agricultural and related produces can be understood from table 6. However, EC has yet to attain self-sufficiency for products like sheep meat and goat meat, fruits, vegetables and maize. On the other hand, for a number of products, SSR in EC increased more than what was required to compensate the deficit of the member countries. As a result of growing SSR coupled with further and fuller integration of European Community, the concentration of intra-EC trade would go on unabated in the future. The little opportunities that may exist in post-integration period for other countries in general and developing countries in particular, it is expected may perhaps be riddled with unfavourable terms and conditions that will make the situation more problematic for developing countries. Fears have also been expressed by economists about the unfavourable terms of trade with EC for the developing countries in the post-integration period.

III. Trade Prospect of India and Bangladesh in European Common Market

Partial success of trade bloc in Western Europe or European Union has already started affecting the export market of developing world. However, both India and Bangladesh could increase their export flow to EU in recent period (tables 7A and 7B). But in the long run continuation of this unfavourable trade trend of EU with the third world nations may have depressing effect on India and Bangladesh as well. It is not unexpected also that this phenomenon would stand in the way to derive optimal benefit from the relative abundance of human capital in the developing nations which as the factor of production is gaining importance in the international sphere.

Regional trade knitting in EU is not significant from the angle of capital scarce third world nations only. The underpinning that the prevailing order of international trade might undergo changes in favour of nations with low resource portential once the political and technical barrier of TNC operation in these countries are eased out, has prompted many of them to join WTO. India and Bangladesh are no exception to this general principle — both have became members of World Trade Organisation in order to optimise benefit from the international market. As a sequential step policy changes gained momentum in both of these nations. Such changes are more conveniently termed as 'Economic Reform'. In the name of Economic Reform and/or Structural Adjustment Policy changes have experienced acceleration.

The central theme of recent changes in economic outlook is the external sector of the economy. The main plank of economic reform programme and structural adjustment process, without loss of much generality (may be said to) rest on free market operation to encourage external influence in the every economic sphere. Thus the flow of foreign funds, FDI, TNC, exports and re-exports have become tools of measuring efficacy of policy drift.

In the relatively old and matured India, administrative support and policy changes to encourage export-led growth strategy, has had a modest beginning in eighties. The implicit preference to export sector for achieving higher rate of growth has resulted in liberalization of import flow during the said period. It has turned out to be unsuccessful. However stress on external sector of the economy continued. Thus it may not be wrong to state that 'export-led' growth strategy in India, is no longer in disguise specially after the nation has declared her new policy package in July, 1991.

Remarkably economic reform programme in Bangladesh has also been initiated in second half of 1991. It is not a mere coincidence, that Bangladesh has also changed her strategy in the same direction. There exists a strong opinion that the developing nations are forced to change their preference in favour of export-led growth cne. Or in other words the temptation to follow the path in India could not be postponed any longer, while for Bangladesh it seems the nation is left with no other alternative.

The lack lustre performance of export in Bangladesh is generally attributed to infrastructure facilities, technological backwardness and over and above trade policy. On the other hand, reliance on export front for rapid economic progress led to changes in policies — trade and industry in particular in late 70s as in India. They were only partially successful; thus in 1991, as part of economic reform measure, the trade policy was further modified to boost export.

The growth oriented liberalised trade policy for improving external trade revised in the following direction :

(a) reducing controlling and enhancing facilitating roles of governments on export.

(b) facility of duty free import of capital, machinery, technology and raw materials for installation of any 100 per cent export oriented industry.

(c) full money convertibility for easing import.

(d) introducing export credit guarantee scheme, tax holiday, income tax rebate, duty drawback scheme, duty bond facility, internal back to back L/C, credit cash system for financing export and finally multiple entry visa system for foreign investors and importers for export incentives.

(e) removal of licensing requirements for import as well as reduction in the level of duties for some products and duty free import facility for a number of items.

(f) import control order was withdrawn (favouring import of at least sixty six items).

Liberalization of import flow or the measures to attract foreign investors are all meant for improving export market of the nation. Particular emphasis was on the environment of garment sector, which alone accounts for more than fifty per cent of total export of Bangladesh.

Many of the export-import measures adopted in India are similar with that of Bangladesh. For example, the rupee which was made partially convertible in 1992, is subsequently made full convertible (only in current account) in 1994. The new EX-IM policy in India to facilitate the strategy of export promotion has resorted to (as in Bangladesh) : reduction in the level of duties, removal of licensing requirements for most goods, preferential rate for capital goods import but restriction on import of consumer goods is still continued which however is criticised by a section of economists.

These revisions have been beyond any shade of doubt helpful in boosting the morals of the exporters and in consequence both the economies have experienced favourable upward movement in their total export. However, the major problems faced by exporters of these two nations in terms of cost and quality, will have a telling effect on destination of exports. On the other hand the legacy of colonial heritage still persists in export market of both the nations. Export market of these two nations, is concentrated in Europe. In comparison to India, export trade of Bangladesh is more concentrated with European Community. (see tables 7A and 7B).

In case of India, the effect of changes in outlook (since mid 80s) and subsequent modification and finally radical revision of EX-IM policies with the introduction of new economic direction in 1991 may easily be discovered from the forward movement of external trade. Inflation of trade — inflow and outflow — in absolute values have induced the share in GDP to witness gradual increase; share of export in GDP was below 5 per cent during 1960s and started gradually increasing but it crossed the 10 per cent level only after liberalization — in the first half of nineties. Impact of policy changes is more visible in the import front. It is well known that import flow in India is associated recently with the country's endeavour to overcome technological obsolescence in one hand and on the other to facilitate export and re-export. In consequence, import flow increased above 10 per cent of GDP and current account balance did not improve as expected.

In case of Bangladesh, the influence of liberalised policies may be obscured; because of her size and resource position, external sector is relatively more important in comparison to Indian economy. Nevertheless, type of changes that have occurred is fairly similar with that of India. As a matter of fact in this economy, since 80s share of external trade — export and import taken together — in GDP with some fluctuating trend increased from 20 per cent in early 80s to 28 per cent in early 90s; during the same period corresponding figure for India changed from around 13 to 20 per cent. However, as mentioned before, future expansion of export market or even continuation of present level may pose problem. On the other hand, trade relation of both the nation with European community underwent discernible change.

India's external trade with EU exhibits episodical changes; during seventies the rate of growth (17.85 per cent) of merchandise exports to the union was observed to be higher than her total export growth rate of 15.89 per cent. This is in sharp contrast with the performance of earlier decade (1960-61 to 1969-70) when export to EU grew at less than two per cent while total export growth rate of the nation was marginally below ten per cent. But export flow to EU during eighties experienced a set back; crisis in the domestic front, recession in the world market and scaling down of trade relation of EU with developing countries — all may be held jointly responsible for such happenings. Again, export market has started experiencing favourable change in the Union after the liberalization move in 1991. Such a change may be related to the beneficial effect of rupee convertibility and partly due to other reform measures to encourage exports as mentioned earlier.

TABLE 6

Self-Sufficiency Ratio for Some Selected Agricultural and Related Goods in EEC

(For 1980-1988)

Produces	1980 (EC-9)	1986 (EC-12)	1988 (EC-12)
Beef and Veal	102	106	100
Pigmeat	100	102	104
Sheepmeat and Goatmeat	74	79	82
Fruits	86	87	86
Vegetables	102	108	107
Maize	58	84	96
Sugar	129	129	129
Paultry	107	104	105

Sources : Eurostat, Agricultrual Statistics Yearbook, 1986, EC Commission; The Agricultural Situation in the EC, 1988-89.

More or less, export trade of Bangladesh with EU has exhibited same type of behaviour during 80s — during the period 1983-84 to 1992-93, the compound rate of export flow from Bangladesh to EU (nearly 19 per cent) was at least three percentage points greater than the total export growth of the country. However, unlike India, rates of growth of export of the nation in different time span to EU always was increasing and did not experience any fluctuation in its behaviour. In consequence, export market of the country have increasingly been concentrated in EU, which may not be interpreted as a healthy one. This point is discussed subsequently.

Dependence of Bangladesh on EU for export market is though increasing, import flow from EU to Bangladesh (around ten per cent per annum) during the period 83-84 to 92-93 has grown at a much slower rate than from rest of the world. Available information suggests that growth rates of import from EU is experiencing (an unfavourable) deceleration.

In the import front, Indian experience is marginally different from that of Bangladesh during the post liberalization period. However, it is not astonishing to observe that import flow from EU during sixties is declined by a rate of more than two and half per cent because of her import substitution type industrialization strategy during the early plan period. But during the period 1970-71 to 1984-85, the growth of import flow from Western Europe grew at a higher rate (around twenty per cent) as against of eighteen per cent rate of growth of total import of the country. The relative ranking of rate of import flow from EU and from the rest of the world, during the post liberalisation period again underwent changes — rate of growth of import flow from EU has declined from around 24 per cent during 1970-1980 to 12 per cent.

However, these changes in rates of growth have insignificantly altered the trade connection of India and Bangladesh with EU. EU as a group on an average absorbs 25 per cent of the total export of India and supplier of approximately 30 per cent of total import of the nation. In consequence, India maintains a deficit in her trade balance with EU and the share of EU in her total balance is substantial. Picture of current account balance in case of Bangladesh is completely different. Bangladesh as expected could gradually improve her current account position with the European Union; during the recent past she is able to derive some trade surplus from EU which however is not sufficient to neutralize current account deficit of the economy.

This is because, with some fluctuations, the share of EU in total export of the country has gradually increased from less than twenty per cent in early 80s to around 23 per cent in mid-80s and further to 35 per cent level in early nineties, while the share of EU in total import flow to the economy is declining. Share of EU in the country's total import varied in the range of 13 to 17 per cent during the pre-liberalization period but slumped to 10 per cent level in 1992-93; perhaps internal changes in the country and zone formation in Western Europe jointly explain such a phenomenon.

From the above discussion, it is possible to discover two distinctive features in the trade relation of Bangladesh with EU.

(i) increasing dependence on EU for export market and

(ii) importance of EU as a supplier of foreign product is gradually waning.

Increased dependence on technologically and politically superior EU for export market is obviously not indicative of any favourable trend while it is well known that some of the EU members are competitors of Bangladesh. Will it thus be grossly unjustified to apprehend that the continuation of this trend will pose serious problem unless measures are undertaken to spread the export market of Bangladesh across the globe.

Greater danger seems to lie with the composition of export basket of the economy. Two interrelated causes exist. Export earning of the nation is extremely skewed in favour of garment products. Garment constitutes more than 55 per cent of the total export of the nation. It may also be observed that recent favourable trend in export trade is mostly due to upward swing of garment export. Unfortunately, it has not been possible to extend the market in countries other than Western Europe. This item, as it appears, has experienced improved penetration in European Common Market — share of EU in total garment export is monotonically increasing for the past few years, presently the share is about 85 per cent of total garment export of the nation.

It is difficult to appreciate such a phenomenon. In European Common Market, Asian countries have already been criticised in the sphere of garment trade and EU has already rationed garment import from some Asian countries. It is not unexpected that such type of measures in future will be more intensified in order to accommodate less developed member nations, like Portugal and Greece who also specialise in this labour-intensive product.

TABLE 7A

Trade of India with European Union

(value in current price
Rs. crores, share in pc)

Year	Export		Import		Trade Balance	
	Total	Share of EU	Total	Share of EU	Total	Share of EU
1960-1961	642 (4.21)	36.41	1122 (7.36)	36.17	–480	38.54
1970-1971	1535 (4.15)	18.24	1634 (4.15)	19.58	–99	40.40
1980-1981	6711 (5.48)	21.56	12549	10.25	-5838	20.42
1985-1986	10895 ( )	17.71	19658	26.63	-8763	37.72
1990-1991	32553 (6.81)	27.50	43198 (9.04)	29.35	-10645	35.03
1991-1992	44923 (8.12)	na	51418 (9.30)	na	–6495	..
1992-1993	53688 (8.51)	28.30	63375 (10.06)	30.17	–9687	40.55
1993-1994	69751 (9.64)	26.06	73101 (10.11)	30.04	–3350	112.83
1994-1995Q	82674 (12.64)	26.70	89971 (13.75)	24.83	–7297	3.61

Note : Figures within parentheses indicate per cent of GDP.

Source : Compiled from : Economic Survey (various issues), Govt. of India, New Delhi.

TABLE 7B

Trade of Bangladesh with European Union

(value in current price million Taka share in pc)

Year	Export		Import		Trade Balance	
	Total	Share of EU	Total	Share of EU	Total	Share of EU
1983-1984	20135 (5.66)	26.60	50873 (14.32)	14.28	–30739	–6.21
1984-1985	26225 (6.44)	21.86	68262 (16.77)	13.84	–42037	–8.84
1985-1986	27396 (5.87)	20.69	62929 (13.49)	13.55	–35533	–8.04
1986-1987	33682 (6.24)	25.80	68496 (12.70)	16.44	–34814	–7.39
1987-1988	41161 (6.89)	29.04	91588 (8.63)	16.74	–50427	–6.70
1988-1989	42686 (6.47)	29.03	95075 (14.41)	14.74	–52389	–3.09
1989–1990	51415 (6.97)	31.02	113305 (15.36)	14.93	–61888	–1.55
1990-1991	60272 (7.22)	38.34	111877 (13.40)	14.35	–51605	13.66
1991-1992	74198 (8.18)	34.55	132736 (14.64)	13.48	–58538	13.22
1992-1993	88215 (9.30)	34.18	177710 (18.74)	10.90	–89495	12.00

Note : Figures in parentheses indicate pc share of GDP.

Source : Complied from (1) Bangladesh Export Statistics (various issues), Export promotion Bureau, Ministry of Commerce, Govt. of Bangladesh. (2) Statistical Year Book of Bangladesh (various) issues. Bangladesh Bureau of Statistics, GOB.

REFERENCES

Bagchi, A.K. (1979) : Export-led Growth and Import Substituting Industrialisation; *Economic and Political Weekly,* Annual No.

Baran, P. (1957) : *The Political Economy of Growth,* Monthly Press Review.

Balassa, B. (1978) : Export and Economic Growth, *Journal of Development Economics.*

Ayubar Rahaman Bhuyan and Mohammed Ali Rashid (1993) : *Trade Regime and Industrial Growth : A Case Study of Bangladesh,* ICEG.

Findlay, R : Trade and Development (1984) : Theory and Asian Experience, *Asian Development Review.*

Tayler, W. (1981) : Growth and Export Expansion in Developing Countries. *Journal of Development Economics.*

Khan, A. Matin (1994) : Export Performance of Bangladesh : Structure and trends, 1972/73 to 1990/91.

Parthasarathy, N. (1995) : Regional Economic Groupings, K.R. Gupta (ed.) *World Trade* : Atlantic Publishers, New Delhi.

Malakar, B. and Singh, S.P. (1995) : European Economic Integration: Prospect of Indian Export Oriented Strategy, K.R. Gupta (ed) *op. cit.*

Europa 1995.

Eurostat, Various Issues.

World Bank : *World Development Report,* Various Issues.

EC Commission : *E.C. Commission Reports,* Various Issues.

Govt. of India : *Economic Survey,* Various Issues.

Bangladesh Bureau of Statistics (1994) : *Statistical Year Book of Bangladesh,* Govt. of Bangladesh.

World Bank (1995) : *Bangladesh : Recent Economic Development and Priority Reform Agenda for Rapid Growth.*

11

China's Economic Integration with the Rest of the World

ZHICUN GAO and CLEM TISDELL

Introduction

After 1978, China changed from an inward economic policy to an outward looking one. Together with its economic reforms, China's "Open Door" policy symbolised China's sharp turn towards participation in the world market to speed up its economic growth and technological modernisation. Former Premier Zhao Ziyang in 1981 called on the Chinese people to "abandon once and for all the idea of self-sufficiency", (*Zhao, 1982:47*) Chinese economists and officers began to study the law of comparative advantage and to urge participation in the international division of labour. Zhao himself seemed to embrace these ideas when he explained "by linking our country with the world market, expanding foreign trade, importing advanced technology, utilising foreign capital, and entering into different forms of international economic and technological co-operation, we can use our strong points to make up for our weak points through international exchange on the basis of equality of mutual benefit." China's opening to the outside world was perhaps the most visible of its reforms of the 1980s. China's international trade volume grew dramatically, it attracted tens of billions of dollars of direct foreign investment. In contrast to the pre-reform era, foreign trade grew more rapidly than domestic economy and in some regions of the country became a powerful engine of growth, accelerating not only the speed of domestic development but the pace of structural and technical transformation as well.

Lardy (*1992*) suggested that the reasons for this improvement are as follows : the expansion of foreign trade was obtained by a unified export strategy in which sales on the international market enabled the financing of much needed imports. The growth of exports comes from a new industrial system, that is, from the rapid development of export processing, particularly in South China. Foreign parts and components are brought in, and then exported to world markets. This capitalises on China's comparative advantage in labour-intensive activities and thus contributes to economic growth.

Background to the Strategy

Development economists have long argued that countries pursuing externally-oriented development strategies achieve higher rates of economic growth, both because they attain higher rates of saving and investment and because they have more efficient use of scarce resource (*World Bank, 1987*). Some initial government trade policies were to be used to restructure the industrial sector. The aim of the new trade and industrial policies was to make the industrial sector more efficient and competitive and hence achieve increased production for the domestic market and for export. This restructuring was to be achieved through more reliance on 'new' sectors and foreign investment.

In inward-looking economies, a high degree of protection of domestic industry is usually combined with an overvalued domestic currency and a rigid system of controlling foreign exchange. This provides a mechanism that can in effect tax exports like agricultural products, raw materials, while subsidising those imports that state bureaucrats designate as having a high priority. Under this system, traditional exports are taxed because the official exchange rate, which over values the domestic currency, gives producers of these goods fewer units of domestic currency per dollar's worth of goods sold in the international market. Importers favoured by the state pay a lower price, in terms of domestic currency, than they would with an equilibrium exchange rate. Exchange control is required to wrest foreign exchange receipts from exporters, who do not voluntarily part with foreign currency at such an exchange rate. Similarly, on the demand side, the artificially low price requires government intervention to ration foreign exchange in the face of excess demand (*Lardy, 1992:692-693*).

Before the reforms, China's foreign exchange regime had these features in common with other centrally planned economies. The

Renmibi (domestic currency), was highly overvalued and the Bank of China acted as the agent of the state, exercising a monopoly over the control of foreign exchange on behalf of the planning authorities.

From roughly the mid-1980s onwards, the pace of China's domestic economic reforms accelerated, making it more likely that increased foreign trade would be economically beneficial. China's foreign trade will probably expand considerably in the 1990s and play an even more positive role in contributing to its economic growth.

Policy Instruments in Foreign Trade Reform and New Measures Adopted in Industrial Production to Boost Export

From 1979 onward, the Chinese government implemented a series of measures designed to promote industrial activity in coastline areas and adopted a series of policy instruments to encourage exports. The process can be divided into three stages : (1) experience stage, (2) practice stage, and (3) development stage.

First Stage : *Experience Stage (1979-83)* : In July, 1979, the Import and Export Commission and Foreign Investment Administration Commission were established. These two organisations were responsible for managing, organising and coordinating the relevant ministries' foreign trade. Due to intersection of responsibilities and low efficiency, in March 1982, the Fourth Session of Fifth National People's Congress decided to establish the Ministry of Foreign Economic Relations and Trade to replace the above named two commissions in charge the professional management. In the same year, local agencies were given more autonomy in organising their own trade. Following Guandong and Fujian, the foreign trade of Beijing and eight other provinces was put under dual leadership, in which local governments and sub-companies had more rights than the Ministry to determine their own trade. Following this decentralisation, the export of commodities were divided into three categories : (1) those under ministerial control; (2) local government control; and (3) market adjustment (*Guan, 1991 : 72*). The foreign currency exchange system was also revised to encourage foreign trade. A dual foreign currency exchange system was established by the Bank of China to provide economic advantages to exporters.

Second Stage : *Practice Stage (1983-86)* : In this stage, the reforms to stimulate the exports mainly focused on two fields : the foreign trade system and open coastline areas.

A. Open Coastline Areas : Following the successful creation of four special economic zones, the State Council made the decision in

1984 to open fourteen coastline cities to attract foreign investment, and to establish an Economic Technology Development Area. At the same time, the border trade along 21 thousands kilometres of inland border was broadly encouraged and a series of economic development areas were established in inland areas. Some policies which had been successfully adopted in special economic zones (SEZs) were also used in these areas.

B. Foreign Trade Reform : In September 1984, the State Council officially approved the First Plan for the Foreign Trade Reform designed by the Ministry of Foreign Economic Relation and Trade. The principles in this plan were : first, separation of enterprises from political administration and giving them more autonomy and secondly, the creation of an agency system in foreign trade so as to improve the quality of export goods instead of a system of unified state purchases and foreign sales. (*Guan, 1991 : 212*). From 1985 to 1986, many foreign trade companies were created and approved and all foreign investment companies had the right to import their own used equipment and intermediate materials and export to the international market by themselves. This meant that responsibility for China's foreign trade changed from being a state monopoly to a multiple management system.

Third Stage : *Development Stage (1987-90 and onwards)*

A. Foreign Trade Reform : Early in 1987, the Ministry of Foreign Economic Relations and Trade began to adopt a 'contract' system for exports allowing export earners to retain 45 per cent of their foreign currency earnings. Export subsidies were to be reduced and gradually abolished. The principles in the plan were: "sole responsibility of management for its profits or losses, free operation, strengthen management and organise to bargain abroad." *(Guan 1991 : 74)*. In February, 1988, a new plan was approved to provide fewer restrictions on international trade. Exporters were allowed to retain a higher proportion of foreign currency and currency exchange was further liberalised.

B. Industrial Reform: In 1987, the strategy of "the great international circulation" was advocated by former Party secretary-general Zhao Ziyang. This strategy was intended : first, to take the advantage of abundant rural labour force, develop labour-intensive light industry to increase export production; use the earned currency to import advanced technologies and develop heavy industry further for accumulation; third, develop backward agriculture by use of new equipment produced by heavy industry. The core is to take the advantage of abundant labour force, adopt export-led strategies, pushing the whole coastline area to participate in the international market, and in this way, channel agriculture and heavy industry and push the economy towards modernisation. Zhao Ziyang raised the theory of "the great international circulation" in his declaration that the entire coastal strip would be opened up to foreign investment. Essentially, Zhao's view was that by requesting foreign direct investment (FDI) ventures to "place two heads outside, big import and big export" (processing materials and market outside), China could follow the path of Asian NICs and benefit from the international investment and commodity flows. It also reflected the belief that China's coastline could follow the successful export-led growth strategy of the "four little tigers". In April, 1988, Hainan province was established as a special economic zone and became the biggest special economic zone. After more than one decade of reform, China's system of state monopoly in foreign trade and in export production has changed. A multiple management and ownership system has been created from top to bottom, and export-oriented industry has been established in China's coastline areas.

Policy Instruments in Foreign Trade Reform

Decentralisation of Foreign Trade : "International experience strongly suggests that decentralisation to the enterprise level can be very important in helping realise the potential benefits of increased external economic contacts... Decentralisation of decision-making would make it impossible for the government to predict or control the actions of individual enterprises or the details of external transaction" *(World Bank, 1985a : 99-100)*. Before the economic reform, China's planners determined imports and exports largely via the system of material balances which was used to construct the basic economic plan. They thus co-ordinated the flow of raw materials and intermediate goods among major state enterprises and ensured that production of each good was sufficient to meet both inter-industry demand and final demand for consumption, investment and export. Planners used imports to fill the shortfall between planned demand and domestic production of capital goods where the alternative of scaling back final demand would have meant reducing the level of investment. Exports sufficient to pay for these imports were then identified, starting with goods for which domestic supplies exceeded the quantities of 3,000 individual commodities that were to be produced by the state for export, and the import plan covered more than 90 per cent of all imports *(Sun, 1989 : 53; Lardy, 1992 : 700-701)*.

By the mid-1950s, foreign trade was a complete monopoly of the Chinese Central Government. A handful of specialised foreign trade corporations, some created as early as March 1950, were responsible for implementing the export-import plan. All the foreign trade companies were state-owned and fully responsible for the purchase, transfer, import, export and financial balance under the unified state plan. Trading companies were only executive bodies instead of a "company" responsible to business and to, it present its running report via the Ministry of Foreign Trade in turn responsible to the Ministry of Finance. In 1981, national foreign trade companies responsible to the Ministry of Foreign Economic Relations and Trade accounted for 91 per cent of exports and 87 per cent of total respectively (*World Bank, 1988* : *102-103*).

Reforms in the trade management system in the mid-1980s substantially altered the above situation. The State Council, in a major foreign trade reform document promulgated in September 1984, called for an end of the monopoly power of specialised national foreign trade companies (*Anon, 1986; Lardy, 1992 : 701-702*). This was to be achieved by creating a large number of sub-trading companies with a degree of financial independence. Within two years the Ministry of Foreign Economic Relations and Trade had approved the creation of more than 800 separate import and export corporations. Initially many of these were created by converting the provincial branches of the national foreign trade companies into local companies carrying out trade in the same product lines. However, larger provinces and municipalities established many general trading companies authorised to handle a much broader range of goods. As a result by 1987, the number of companies had increased to more than 2,200, eleven times that prior to the reforms (*Wang 1994 : 107*), and by the end of the 1980s, to about 5,000. This created new problems. China had long enjoyed a high reputation for fulfilment of trade contracts. Some of the newly created companies, however, lacked experience and funding or were not able to acquire domestically the goods they had agreed to export. Non-performance of trade contracts became a matter of growing concern to China's trade partners (*Lubman, 1988 : 557; Lardy, 1992 : 702*). The State Council took steps in May 1988 and in March and November 1989, first to reassert central control over the process of approving the creation of new trading companies and subsequently, to dissolve or merge existing companies found to be inadequate. However, the resulting cutback still left substantial room for competition among these firms.

Just as important as the expansion in the number of trading companies was the reduced operation of the foreign trade plan. The number of planned export commodities fell from 3,000 in the pre-reform era to 112 by 1988 and the share of exports specified in the annual foreign trade plan fell to 45 per cent in the same year. The scope of import planning fell even more rapidly, from more than 90 per cent of total imports at the beginning of the 1980s to 40 per cent by 1988. In the same year, only 17 import commodities fell into the planned category. From the 1985 financial year onwards, the Ministry of Foreign Trade no longer issued a compulsory unified trade plan. Instead it encouraged trading companies to pay more attention on the markets domestically and internationally in importing and exporting. Moreover, from 1985 the foreign trade plan was divided into mandatory and guidance portions. Mandatory plan imports and exports were specified in quantitative terms and were usually the responsibility of the head offices of the national foreign trade companies. In 1988 the mandatory export plan covered 21 specific commodities, only about 20 per cent of China's total exports. Fifteen of these were the sole responsibility of the national foreign trade companies, with the responsibility for the other six shared between national and local foreign trade corporations. The remaining 91 planned export commodities were in the guidance category. On the import side there were nine mandatory plan commodities under the control of the national foreign trade companies and eight guidance plan commodities (*Zhang, 1990 : 7; Lardy, 1992 : 702-703*). The imports and exports in the guidance plan were generally specified in value terms, giving local trading corporations more flexibility. This allowed them to take economic factors into account when determining the price mix of imported and exported products in each category. The presence of more Chinese foreign trade companies provided more information and opportunities to domestic producers and created more competition among them especially in terms of quality. If the quality of products of domestic producers was below the international standard, the foreign corporation companies chose other qualified producers.

Reforms in the Pricing of Traded Goods : Before the reforms, world market prices had little or no effect on the domestic prices of tradeable goods due to highly centralised foreign trade system. It was this that led the World Bank to characterise China's traditional trade regime as an "airlock system" (*World Bank, 1985 : 17, Lardy, 1992 : 703*). Foreign trade corporations purchased goods specified by the plan from domestic producers at officially established prices. Thus producers received the same domestic prices whether goods were sold domestically or in international markets. Moreover, they received none of the foreign exchange income from the sale of their goods abroad nor did they have any direct way of purchasing goods abroad for their own use. Under these circumstances, producers had little economic incentive either to sell on the international market or to expand production of goods for which there was strong international demand. Domestic prices of imported goods also tended to be unrelated to the world market since after 1964 the prices of 80 per cent of China's imports were set at levels comparable to similar domestic goods (*Anon, 1989*). Only when there was no production of a particular commodity or when the volume of domestic production was extremely limited, was the price of an imported good based on the world price.

These procedures substantially distorted decisions because the domestic price of imports diverged from the world price. In some cases, China's domestic industry was highly protected since foreign goods with relatively low production costs had their prices marked up to the level of Chinese goods. The tendency was compounded by liberal adjustment upward from the price of the "comparable" Chinese goods to account for differences in quality. In other cases, some of the imported goods sold close to the price of domestically produced output, which were artificially low, so imports of these products were highly subsidised.

The reforms of the past decade, particularly those of the latter half of the 1980s, transformed the pricing of traded goods. Domestic sale prices of a growing share of imported goods began to be based on the world market prices. By the end of 1989, the administered import list contained only 14 commodities so that the domestic prices of 90 per cent of all China's imports were based on world market prices. In late April 1990, there were only eight administered commodity categories left. And the shrinkage of the list continued with the elimination of sodium tripolyphosphate with effect from January 1991 (*Anon, 1991 : 64*) The domestic prices of well over 90 per cent of all goods imported into China in 1991 were based on world market prices. The old price system, which provided a high degree of protection to some import competing industries or high value of subsidies to domestic users of some imported commodities, had largely faded away (*Lardy, 1992 : 704*).

The initial pace of change in the domestic pricing of export goods appears to have been somewhat slower that for imports. But by the late 1980s, the state used the pre-reform pricing system for only 21 export goods which were either considered necessities or for which there were shortages of supply in the domestic market. These planned exports accounted for only 20 per cent of the value of China's total exports in 1988. In the same year, 55 per cent of total exports fell outside the plan, meaning that producers were not compelled to deliver these to trading corporations at state-fixed prices but could take advantage of the proliferation of competing foreign trade companies to bargain for the most favourable price (*Yang, 1988 : 3*). But over a period of time, with the growing number of trading companies, the degree of competition between them increased, moving domestic prices closer to world market prices. Even producers of the 21 commodities that fell within the export plan could take advantage of this competition by producing quantities of goods above the planned level. Excess production could be sold internationally on a decentralised basis and producers were able to bargain with foreign trade corporations for more favourable domestic prices for that portion of their output (*Lardy, 1992 : 705*).

Thus, the scope of the plan in foreign trade shrank and competition between a growing number of foreign trade corporations increased and the influence of international prices on domestic prices of exports rose. This policy gave domestic producers more opportunities to make contact with foreign businessmen, to gain knowledge of foreign designs and foreign customer requirements, and greater opportunities to sell their products in international markets.

Gradual Abandonment of Exchange Rate and Exchange Control : Just as international prices had only a modest influence on Chinese decisions about import and export of commodities, the price of foreign exchange had little effect on the volume of foreign trade in the pre-reform era. Thus, as in other centrally planned economies, exchange rate policy was largely a passive policy instrument. China's domestic currency was over valued in the pre-reform era and the resulting excess demand for foreign exchange was handled through a rigid system of exchange controls. The domestic currency cost of earning foreign exchange was persistently higher than the official exchange rate, making most exports financially unprofitable which created an anti-export bias (*Kueh and Howe, 1984 : 844-845; Lardy, 1992 : 704-705*). The Ministry of Foreign Trade reallocated the profits that were made by the domestic market to offset or compensate for the losses incurred by other foreign trade corporations on their sale of export goods. In practice this meant that the effective exchange rate varied from corporation to corporation and sometimes even on a product by product basis. This "price equalisation mechanism," was common in centrally planned economies. Compensating for the divergences between domestic and foreign prices, this system undermined the incentive for trading companies to exploit comparative advantage trade opportunities (*Brabant, 1991; Lardy, 1992 : 706*).

Reforms of the exchange rate and relaxation of exchange control were among the most dramatic changes in China during the last decade. As shown in table 1, the Chinese authorities devalued the currency from a rate that averaged 1.6 Yuan per US dollar in the late 1970s to an average of 5.3 Yuan in 1991, and in 1994 to $1=8.71 Yuan.

TABLE 1

China's Official Exchange Rate 1978-1994

Year	Yuan per US $	Year	Yuan per US $
1978	1.68	1987	3.72
1979	1.55	1988	3.72
1980	1.50	1989	3.76
1981	1.71	1990	4.78
1982	1.89	1991	5.33
1983	1.98	1992	5.52
1984	2.33	1993	5.71
1985	2.94	1994	8.71
1986	3.45		

Source : Based on *China Financial Statistics* 1952-1987, *State Statistical Abstract* 1990, *China Statistic Yearbook* 1992, 1994, *People's Daily* February 18, 1995)

After the middle of 1980s, China instituted a dual exchange rate policy. This was an intermediate step between a unified exchange rate to a flexible exchange rate. Changes in the official exchange rate appear to have had only a limited effect on trade in the first half of the 1980s for two reasons. First, since the reform of traded goods pricing was just beginning, the exchange rate had little effect either on the domestic currency earnings of most export producers or on the prices paid by most consumers of imports. Secondly, changes in the official exchange rate did not really affect the foreign trade corporations. They received financial subsidies to cover domestic currency losses from foreign trade transaction. From 1985, changes in the exchange rate had a greater effect on trade. This was partly because in the pricing of traded goods meant that exchange rate adjustments had a direct effect on the domestic prices of an increasing number of imports and exports. In addition, the value of China's currency fell significantly in the second half of the 1980s (*Lardy, 1992 : 707*). This policy generated more competition for export goods in world market. From January 1, 1994, China officially abandoned the dual exchange rate system, and adopted a unified flexible exchange rate which is based on the real value of Yuan to foreign currency. The exchange rate between the US dollar and the Yuan fell sharply from $1=Y5.72 in December 31, 1993 to $1=Y8.71 in January 1, 1994.

The three reforms in foreign trade system analysed briefly above created the conditions in which decentralised trade based on economic incentives could flourish. This is evident in the kinds of enterprises that became the most successful exporters by the late 1980s. Particularly significant is the growing share of China's exports produced by rural township and village enterprises and joint venture enterprises.

New Measures for Promoting Export-Oriented Industry

China has recognised that some innovative export promotion measures adopted by other successful developing countries earn additional foreign exchange, provide new jobs, introduce modern technology and improve the quality of products. Thus, since 1979, China has become more flexible and imaginative in adopting new measures to promote trade and attract foreign capital. From 1979, the Chinese government instituted its outward-oriented economic development strategy : "open the coastline areas first, then develop inland areas gradually." (*Zhao 1982*) In line with this strategy, the country was divided into four economic areas : first, special economic zones; second, coastline open cities; third, coastline economic export zones and fourth, any inland area. The coastline areas include the Yangtze River Delta, the Pearl River Delta, Minnan Delta, Shandong Peninsula and Liaodong Peninsula. These areas cover 0.5 million square kilometres of land and have a population of 200 million. Some deep water ports are located along China's 1,800 kilometre long coastline. One quarter of the gross value of total industry (with relatively advanced technologies and equipment) is concentrated in the areas.

From 1979 onwards, the State Council gradually approved new measures to increase export production so as to earn foreign currency earning, to attract foreign investment bringing with it advanced technologies and equipment and to improve efficiency. In 1987, following the success of the opening of the coastline areas, the plan of "the great international circulation" was generated and advocated. Measures were adopted to encourage the coastal economy to access international markets and to generate export-led growth. The main measures adopted were : export processing, cooperation, use of joint ventures and the compensation trade.

Export Processing : Under this arrangement, foreign firms supply raw materials, semi-finished goods, packaging materials and components, while the Chinese enterprises process or assemble products according to foreign contractors designs, specifications and quality requirements. All the products are passed on to the foreign contractors or their agents, and the Chinese enterprises receive a processing fee. Most of the machinery and equipment used are Chinese made, unless specific machinery and equipment are not available in China, in which case they can be imported and the cost is deducted from the processing fee. Imported materials, components are exempted from duties and taxes, but the volume of these imports has to be in proportion to the appropriate amount of final products. None of these products of imports may be sold in domestic markets. At present, the processing fee for garments, textiles, yarn, and cloth-making enterprises are cheaper than the corresponding cost in Hong Kong and Macao, because wage rates are lower in China. The Chinese firms engaging in export processing of these articles are profitable (*World Bank, 1983 : 433*).

By the middle of 1980, 18 provincial, big city and autonomous regional governments had begun export processing. There were about 6,300 export processing projects, largely operated by medium sized and small plants. 70 per cent of the projects were with Hong Kong, Macao, 20 per cent with Japan, and 10 per cent with other counties. From July 1978 to the end of July 1980, China received a total of $60 million in export processing fees and, this figure increased to $100 million by the end of 1980. Between mid-1978 and mid-1980, China imported about $96 million of equipment for export processing. The advantages of processing for export are obvious. First, the arrangement provides more stable sources of supply of material inputs than domestic sources. Second, export processing operations earn foreign exchange, create employment and utilise excess industrial capacity. Thirdly, they allow Chinese enterprises to become familiar with foreign markets and modern ideas, as well as helping to introduce modern equipment. Due to the lower prices of labour and land than the NICs, and the shortage of supply of some raw materials for export production, export processing will remain important in China's industrial development.

Compensation Trade: Under this mode of trade, China provides the factory building and labour, while foreign firms supply capital, equipment, technology, training, designs, sometimes management or supervision and selected products agreed upon by both sides. In the case of indirect compensation, imported beer-brewing equipment, for instance, can be paid for by starch or wheat germ rather than by beer, if the latter is in oversupply on foreign markets. The beer so saved is sold on the domestic market, where beer is in short supply. However, indirect compensation trade agreements are rare, as they involve rather complicated negotiations and there are difficulties in reaching agreements. Once all the payments are made, the equipment becomes entirely Chinese owned.

From mid-1979 to mid-1980, agreements involving about 330 compensation trade projects were signed with medium-sized and small industries, 60 per cent of the projects were with Hong Kong, Macao and Taiwan, and 34 per cent with Japan. In terms of project value, however, Japan accounted for 47 per cent and Hong Kong and Macao only 41 per cent. By industry, textile, garment and silk fabric enterprises accounted for one half, other light industries for one fourth, and firms producing chemicals, metal and minerals, machinery and food made up the remainder. In most cases, it takes 2-3 years to pay for the equipment imported, and for some relatively large projects, 7-8 years (*World Bank, 1983 : 434*).

Compensation trade has an advantage for the host country over direct foreign investment in that equipment ownership and management are all in the hands of the recipient country. The main financial advantage of this form of trade is that it allows machinery and equipment to be imported without cash payments in foreign exchange; thus it helps the importing country in maintaining a trade balance. However, it also entails many difficult problems. As the Chinese side was unfamiliar with international market and technical standards, they did not know what kind of equipment was appropriate to China's needs. Exports under medium sized and small compensation trade contracts have been minimal and involved only about 20-30 product lines.

All export processing and compensation trade projects of over $1 million in the provinces and small municipalities and of over $3 million in the three large municipalities are subject to the approval of the Import and Export Commission, those below the above ceilings can be approved by the local government. However, the prime responsibility for negotiation and implementation rests with the relevant Ministries (*World Bank, 1983 : 435*).

Cooperative Production: This type of arrangement falls halfway between compensation trade and joint ventures. It involves a form of technology transfer whereby a foreign firm helps a Chinese enterprise to set up a factory and produce an item under licence, by giving extensive technical assistance in stages. In the early stages, the Chinese enterprise imports a large proportion of parts and components and completes the final assembly in its own factory. Gradually, the Chinese enterprise takes over more complex parts of the manufacturing process, until after several years it can complete the manufacture of the product entirely or mostly from its own materials and components. Normally, a Chinese ministry imports equipment and technology to construct a new assembly line or a new workshop in an existing plant over an extended period, either free or at a discount, a share of the output generated by the facilities built or modernised with foreign assistance. Negotiation of these contracts can be very complicated, as they involve such issues as control of quality of the resulting products, costs and prices of the products and equipment, payment guarantees, and insurance of the equipment. No equity investment by the foreign partner is involved, as the facilities are entirely Chinese owned. Cooperative production appears to be motivated by the idea that greater acquisition of foreign technology and more foreign exchange saving can be achieved in this way than by importing complete plants. The first co-production agreement came about through China's inability to produce sophisticated equipment under licence. Many of China's cooperative production contracts are for large projects, sometime involving construction of a new production plant. Among the more important contracts already signed are one involving toy manufacturing ($50 million) and one for two petrochemical factories with a company in the Germany ($21 million).

Joint Ventures : A joint ventures law came into effect on July 14, 1979, to attract direct foreign investment in Chinese enterprises. In addition, a new institution was created to promote foreign investment through joint venture arrangements. In general, the share of foreign investment should be no less than 25 per cent but no maximum limit for foreign capital is stipulated. In practice, however, the Chinese share of the equity capital has been 59 per cent or more in ventures already approved. After-tax profits are shared by the Chinese unit and the foreign firm according to their respective capital shares. Profits may be remitted outside China. The chairman of the board of a joint venture must be Chinese, with the position of general manager to rotate between Chinese and foreign candidates, even if the share of foreign capital is less than 50 per cent. Initially, a foreigner is normally appointed, and a Chinese candidate is the deputy manager, so that the Chinese staff can learn modern methods of management (*World Bank, 1983 : 437*).

Following the current readjustment policy, priority is being given to joint ventures that (a) modernise or restructure existing industries using a relatively small amount of capital, but achieving high yields quickly, as well as generating additional foreign exchange, (b) develop energy resources and install energy-saving devices, (c) construct critical infrastructure facilities to remove production bottlenecks, and (d) develop remote, backward areas. Up to the end of 1980, seventeen joint ventures had been approved, most of them in tourism and the light and handicraft industries. These included hotel, an airline food-catering service, woollen textiles, watch faces, rattan furniture, artificial flowers, elevators and wine. Most of the foreign investors are overseas Chinese, acting on their own or with other foreign investors. Many of these joint ventures are investments to expand or modernise existing Chinese plants. By the end of 1992, the total foreign capital in China is about US $97 billion (*People's Daily, March 2, 1994*). About seventy joint ventures have been negotiated. Feasibility studies have been completed and initial memoranda signed with US companies for offshore oil exploration, coal mining and precision instruments manufacturing, with companies in Germany for automobile assembly and parts manufacturing, and the electronics industry, with Japanese companies for automobile assembly and light industries, with UK companies for float glass manufacturing and with France for nuclear power generation.

Preferential Treatment in the Special Economic Zones (SEZ) : In South China, three special economic zones were established in Guangdong initially. Later four coastal special economic zones and fourteen coastline development areas were established and were granted preferential treatment. Foreign or overseas Chinese investors are encouraged. Foreign investors are allowed to run their own enterprises in these zones, employing foreign personnel for technical and administrative work. In the special zones, land-levelling projects and work to provide various public utilities (water supply, drainage, power, roads, wharves, communication and warehouses) are undertaken by the local authorities. Bank and insurance facilities are also provided. Other special privileges granted in the 1980s to enterprises in the special zones included the following :

(A) While land remained the property of China, foreign investors were given favourable consideration in matters such as land rent, the size of the plot, and the length of tenure.

(B) The rate of corporate insurance tax is 15 per cent, which is half the rate in other parts of China. Firms that reinvest their profits in the special zones for five years or more may apply for exemption of income tax on profits from such reinvestment.

(C) Import duties are waived for machinery, spare parts, raw materials, vehicles, and other means of production for enterprises in the special zones. Needed consumer goods are subject to the full or a lower import duty, or they may be exempted. Enterprises in the special zones are encouraged to use Chinese-made machinery, raw materials and other goods. Preferential prices are offered on the basis of China's export prices for similar commodities, with settlement in foreign exchange.

(D) Legitimate after-tax profits of investors, and salaries and other earnings (after paying personal income tax) of foreign workers and staff members may be remitted outside China. On the termination of the business, foreign investors may, after meeting their debts, remit their remaining assets outside China.

(E) Wages and labour protection regulation for local workers differ little from those in the general foreign investment law, except that wages are not fixed as a proportion of wages in similar state enterprises (*World Bank, 1983 : 440*).

Products of enterprises in the special zones are to be sold on the international market. If an enterprise wants to sell its products on the domestic market, it must have the approval of the local authority and pay customs duties.

The Role of Foreign Investment

Foreign investment has been encouraged and has played a positive role since China began its industrial promotion efforts following its economic reforms. After the Third Plenary Session of the Chinese Communist Party, the Central Committee in 1978 adopted the "Open-Door" policy and a new phase began in China's absorption of foreign investment. On July 30, 1979, the 10th session of the Standing Committee of the Fifth National People's Congress established the Foreign Investment Control Committee. The main duty of the Committee is to work out, in consultation with various relevant department, the policy and law on the absorption of foreign investment, to formulate regulation on joint ventures, to examine and approve the agreement and contracts, and to coordinate the use of foreign funds by various department and location.

Foreign investment in China has grown steadily since the policy of opening up its economy started in 1979; the building of infrastructure, the setting up of laws and regulations, the streamlining of the approval system, and improving of the investment environment. During the period from 1979 to now, foreign investment has occurred in many fields. Foreign investment was halted for a short time after the 1989 Tian Anmen Square incident, but surged forward again in 1991. In 1993, the foreign capital inflow by signed contract and agreement rose to US $ 110.85 billion and the actually used foreign capital inflow reached US $ 25.76 billion. In past six years, following the new strategy, China also began to invest in foreign countries. By the end of 1993, China's investment abroad had reached US $ 5.16 billion (*People's Daily, March 17, 1994*). Foreign investment has become an important source for China's overall strategy of development and includes foreign capital, technology transfer and transfer of management and entrepreneurial skills, and marketing techniques. (*Cf. Tisdell, 1993, Ch. 3 and Ch. 4*).

The single largest source of investment (table 2) is Hong Kong and together with Macao and Taiwan, accounts for 70 per cent of total foreign direct investment (FDI) in China. As most overseas Chinese have advantages of location and language, they tend to be major investors in China. U.S. is in the second position, followed by Japan. Singapore and Germany are in the fourth and fifth position respectively and investment from South Korea has increased rapidly.

Table 3 shows the sector distribution of FDI in 1991. By sector, investment in industry accounted for 47.53 per cent of all foreign direct investment. Industry is located in the first position. Foreign investment in individual industries includes US $ 860 million in textiles,

TABLE 2

Foreign Capital Actually Used in China by Source (1979-89)

Country (Region)	No. of Contracts	Contracted Value (US $ billions)	Percentage
Hong Kong, Taiwan and Macao	13421	17874	70.8
United States	647	2394	8.5
Japan	649	1313	4.7
Singapore	239	530	1.9
Germany	55	333	1.1
Spain	2	111	0.7
Canada	55	162	0.6
United Kingdom	54	160	0.6
Netherlands	14	156	0.6
France	50	147	0.5
Australia	51	119	0.4
Austria	5	92	0.3
Switzerland	17	91	0.3
Thailand	71	90	0.3
Philippines	72	87	0.3
Italy	34	83	0.2
Kuwait	2	50	0.2

Source : Based on *The Statistical Yearbook of the Chinese Foreign Economy and Trade* (1979-1990).

TABLE 3

Sectoral Distribution of Foreign Direct Investment (FDI) in China (1991)

Sector	No. of Contracts	Percentage	Contract Value (US $ billions)	Percentage
Industry	10560	66.01	133.88	47.53
Communication	471	2.94	3.89	1.38
Ore and Coal	2	0.01	0.002	0.00
Physical and Welfare	48	0.30	0.87	0.31
Commercial	977	6.11	15.1	5.36
Finance and Insurance	6	0.04	0.75	0.27
Science and Technology	51	0.32	0.15	0.05
Agriculture and Fishing	853	5.33	9.06	3.22
Construction	474	2.96	4.82	1.71
Culture and Broadcast	60	0.38	1.35	0.48
Real Estate	1388	8.68	79.85	28.35
Others	1107	6.92	31.93	11.34
Total	15997	100.00	281.652	100.00

Source : *The Statistical Yearbook of Chinese Foreign Economy and Trade,* 1991.

US $ 770 million in electronic and communication equipment, followed by machinery, electrical equipment and chemicals. In the manufacturing sector, there was a general increase in large scale foreign investment in basic industries such as automobiles, communications, and inferrous metals in line with China's industrial policy. FDI in China is still in its initial stages with most of the investment being concentrated in coastal areas.

From the middle of the 1980s, Sanzi enterprises (enterprises funded to some extent by foreign investment) began to play an important role in China's foreign trade. Their share of exports rose from 0.15 per cent in 1981 to 27.5 per cent in 1993 (table 4). Thus the growth in exports of foreign investment enterprises has been faster than that of domestic enterprises, and has accelerated China's export of industrial products. However, one also notes from table 4 a large *trade deficit* in the international trade of Sanzi enterprises. They have also shown a very high propensity to import.

TABLE 4

The Value and Share of Foreign Trade of Sanzi Enterprises, China

	Export		Import		Foreign Trade Total	
	US $ billion	Percentage	US $ billion	Percentage	US $ billion	Percentage
1981	0.03	0.15	0.11	0.50	0.14	0.33
1982	0.05	0.24	0.28	1.43	0.33	0.79
1983	0.33	1.49	0.29	1.35	0.62	1.42
1984	0.07	0.26	0.40	1.46	0.47	0.87
1985	0.30	1.08	2.06	4.89	2.36	3.39
1986	0.58	1.88	2.43	5.66	3.01	4.08
1987	1.21	3.06	3.12	7.22	4.33	5.24
1988	2.46	5.17	5.75	10.40	8.20	7.98
1989	4.92	9.35	8.80	14.90	13.71	12.28
1990	7.81	12.58	12.31	23.07	20.12	17.43
1991	12.47	16.75	16.91	26.50	29.00	21.33
1992	17.36	20.42	26.38	32.73	43.73	26.42
1993	25.24	27.50	41.83	40.24	67.07	34.27

Source : *Custom Statistics* 1993, *Statistical Yearbook of Foreign Trade,* 1993.

Recent Trade Performance of China (1980-91)

Increased Exports and Production

After China's trade strategy changed, its volume of international trade increased greatly. Table 5 sets out the trade data published by two different agencies — The Ministry of Foreign Economic Relations and Trade and The General Customs Administration. The Customs data include on the import side the value of imports of and components used in processing activities. The data also include the value of machinery brought into China under compensation trade contracts and export data include all the exports produced using this machinery.

TABLE 5

China's Foreign Trade Growth 1980-1991

	Average Annual Growth Rate (%)
China's trade :	
Ministry data	9.2
Customs data	12.3
Comparison items :	
China's growth of gross national product	8.8
World trade growth	5.5

Note : Gross rates of trade based on constant price data, growth rate of output based on "comparable price".

Source : *China Statistical Abstract,* 1991; General Agreement on Tariffs and Trade, *International Trade* 1989-1990; (Geneva GATT, 1990) *The New York Times,* 18 March 1992, Statistical Report on Chinese Social and Economic Development in 1991, *People's Daily,* 29 February 1992.

Because the net foreign exchange earnings from processing activities are a relatively low share of the total of China's processed export, the Customs data overstate the growth of China's foreign trade. However, as the trade data of most developing countries include processing activities such as compensation trade on gross basis so the Customs data are probably the preferred source when comparing the growth of China's foreign trade with other countries. In 1993, China's foreign trade reached a record US $ 195.72 billion. Its imports jumped to US $ 103.95 billion and exports rose to US $ 91.77 billion (table 6).

China's Foreign trade grew more rapidly than world trade. As shown in table 5, between 1980 and 1991 the average annual rate of growth of China's trade was more than 9 per cent according to Foreign Ministry data and over 12 per cent according to the Customs data. By comparison the rate of growth of the world trade between 1980 and 1991 was 5.5 per cent annum. Thus China's share of world trade, though small, expanded rapidly. In the period 1979-89, China's trade ranking increased more than any other country in the world (*Lardy, 1992 : 694-695*).

TABLE 6

China's Foreign Trade 1978-93

(US $ billions)

	Foreign Ministry Data			Customs Data		
	Total	Imports	Exports	Total	Imports	Exports
1978	20.6	10.9	9.7	—	—	—
1979	29.3	15.7	13.7	—	—	—
1980	37.8	19.6	18.3	38.1	20.0	18.1
1981	40.4	19.5	20.9	44.0	22.0	22.0
1982	29.3	17.5	21.9	41.6	19.3	22.3
1983	40.7	18.5	22.2	43.6	21.4	22.2
1984	49.8	25.4	24.4	53.6	27.4	26.1
1985	60.3	34.3	25.9	69.6	42.3	27.4
1986	60.1	33.1	27.0	73.9	42.9	30.9
1987	68.1	33.4	34.7	82.7	43.2	29.4
1988	80.5	39.9	40.6	102.8	55.3	47.5
1989	82.6	39.2	43.4	111.7	52.5	59.1
1990	84.1	32.4	51.7	115.4	53.4	62.1
1991	99.5	38.5	60.9	135.6	63.8	71.8
1992	—	—	—	165.5	80.6	84.9
1993	—	—	—	195.7	104.0	91.8

Source : Foreign Ministry data : *Almanac of China's Foreign Economic Relations and Trade* 1989; Customs data : *China Statistics Yearbook*, 1992, 1994.

The Changing Pattern of China's Export Structure

The sources of China's trade growth have changed significantly over the past forty years. The surge in the value of exports in the early 1980s came largely from decisions of the state at the central level. A major source was increasing exports of petroleum, one of the key products identified by Deng Xiaoping in 1975 as having the potential to finance China's outward-looking economic development. Between 1977 to 1985 China's exports of crude oil and petroleum products grew from 12 to 36 million metric tons and the value of petroleum exports rose by almost US $ 6 billion. Thus a single product category accounted for one-third of China's incremental export earnings.

Changing from the Primary Export to Manufacturing Export : After the mid-1980s, the share of primary commodities in Chinese exports fell continuously and the share of manufactured goods rose from half in 1985 to over eighty-two per cent by 1993 (table 7). Part of this can be accounted for by the decline in the price of petroleum on world markets in the second half of the 1980s. However, it was also due to the rapid growth of exports of textiles and other light manufactured goods, which reached an all time high by the late 1980s. These goods are more heterogeneous than primary commodities and marketing them in large quantities on international markets requires a sophisticated understanding of consumer tastes, quality standards and

TABLE 7

The Commodity Composition of Chinese Exports 1980-93

(percentage)

	Primary Products	Manufactured Products
1980	50.2	49.8
1981	46.6	53.4
1982	45.0	55.0
1983	43.3	56.7
1984	45.7	54.3
1985	50.5	49.5
1986	36.4	63.6
1987	33.6	66.4
1988	30.4	69.6
1989	28.6	71.4
1990	25.6	74.4
1991	22.5	77.5
1992	20.0	80.0
1993	18.2	81.8

Note : Primary products exports include five categories : foodstuff, beverages and tobacco, non-food raw materials mineral, and fuel, and animal and vegetable oils and fats.

Source : Based on *China Statistical Abstract*, 1983, 1985, 1986, 1987, 1988, 1990, 1991, 1992, 1994, People Daily January 31, 1992.

so on. Moreover, the production of textiles and other light manufactured goods tend to be much more labour-intensive than the production of primary goods, suggesting that composition of China's exports was shifting to reflect China's underlying comparative advantage in labour-intensive products.

Changing from Capital-Intensive Production to Labour-Intensive Production : Table 8 provides the data on the five export categories that experienced the largest absolute increases in China's exports. These expanded by US $ 12 billion and accounted for more than 40 per cent of China's export expansion. The ratio of capital to labour in production in four of these five categories was substantially below the mean of all categories. Thirdly, by contrast, in the first half of the 1980s there appears to have been little 'correction' between relative capital intensity in production and export growth. As already noted, exports of very capital-intensive primary products such as crude oil and refined petroleum products grew rapidly. But so did exports of textiles and apparel. The difference in the second half of the decade is that exports from capital-intensive sectors that had generated significant growth of exports in the first half of the decade shrank in relative and sometimes in absolute terms. In addition, crude oil and refined petroleum products, chemical fibres, railway equipment and ships registered sharp drops in exports (*Lardy, 1992 : 699-700*).

TABLE 8

Capital Intensity of Industries Accounting for the Largest Increments in China's Exports 1985-90

	SITC Trade Category Description	Change in Exports 1985-90 (US $ billions)	Assets per Worker (Yuan)
D 84	Apparel	4.31	5,222
D 65	Textile yarn and fabrics	3.49	8,621
D 89	Miscellaneous manufactures	1.47	6,832
D 76	Telecommunications and sound recording and reproducing equipment	1.41	20,277
D 85	Footwear	1.36	6,178
Mean of all export categories		0.45	13,991

Note : Assets include both fixed capital (valued at original prices) and working capital.

Sources : General Administration of Customs of the People's Republic of China, *Chinese Customs Statistics*, 1991, Lardy 1992 : 699.

From table 9, we can see that the ratio of China's foreign trade to its GNP increased rapidly from 1979 to 1991 and it had reached 36 per cent in 1993; this ratio is even higher than some developed large economies. During the same period, the growth rate of GNP reached an average of 8.9 per cent and industry growth reached an average annual growth rate of 10 per cent. The growth of foreign trade was more rapid than growth of GNP.

TABLE 9

China's Foreign Trade and Export 1979-91

(billion Yuan)

		Foreign Trade		Share of GNP	
Year	GNP	Import + Exports	Exports	Exports + Imports	Exports
1979	399.8	45.6	21.2	12	6
1980	447.0	57.0	27.1	14	7
1981	477.3	73.5	36.8	17	9
1982	519.3	77.1	41.4	16	9
1983	580.9	86.0	43.8	16	9
1984	696.2	120.1	58.1	19	10
1985	855.8	206.6	80.9	25	10
1986	969.6	258.0	108.2	27	12
1987	1130.1	308.4	147.0	28	14
1988	1406.8	382.2	176.7	29	14
1989	1599.3	415.6	195.6	27	13
1990	1769.5	556.0	298.6	32	18
1991	2023.6	722.6	382.7	37	20
1992	2437.9	912.0	467.6	37	19
1993	3134.2	1127.1	528.5	36	17

Source : Based on *Statistical Yearbook of China,* 1992, 1994.

Direction of Trade

Over the period of 1985-91, the bulk of China's foreign trade was directed to four major trading partners, namely Hong Kong, Japan, United States and Europe (tables 10 and 11). However, significant changes have occurred in the proportions accounted for by these partners to total Chinese trade. In 1985, Hong Kong bought 26 per cent of its

TABLE 10

China's Foreign Trade with Selected Countries and Regions

(US $ billion)

	Exports			Imports		
	1985	1988	1991	1985	1988	1991
Total	27.35	47.52	71.91	42.90	55.28	63.79
Hong Kong	7.20	18.27	32.13	4.97	11.97	17.46
Japan	6.11	7.90	9.01	15.04	11.04	10.03
Europe	4.51	8.35	9.40	9.75	13.49	12.70
USA	2.34	3.38	6.19	5.09	6.67	8.01

Source : *Statistical Yearbook of China*, 1992

TABLE 11

China's Foreign Trade with Selected Countries and Regions

(percentage)

	Exports			Imports		
	1985	1988	1991	1985	1988	1991
Total	100	100	100	100	100	100
Hong Kong	26	38	45	12	22	27
Japan	22	17	14	36	20	16
Europe	16	18	13	23	24	20
USA	9	7	9	12	12	13

Source : *Statistical Yearbook of China*, 1992.

merchandise goods from China. This ratio rose to 45 per cent in 1991. The proportion of annual exports to Japan fell from 22 per cent in 1985 to 14 per cent in 1991. Exports in percentage terms to EEC countries have shown a gradual downward trend but at consistently modest rates. Proportionate trade with the U.S. is almost stationary. With regard to the origins of China's imports, Hong Kong and Japan again ranked high vis-a-vis other trading partners. Over the review period, Hong Kong's export to China increased from 12 per cent in

1985 to 27 per cent in 1991, and Japan's share decreased from 36 per cent in 1985 to 16 per cent in 1991. So China had a trade surplus with Hong Kong and kept a trade balance with Japan. The share of goods bought from the EEC countries hovered around 23 per cent to 20 per cent of total import, with U.S. remaining at around 12 per cent to 13 per cent in the same period. Generally speaking, China's foreign trade was concentrated on Hong Kong, Japan, the European Union and the U.S. Its trading with developing countries was in relative terms very limited.

Concluding Comments

Since China adopted its open door policy in 1978, it has made considerable progress in increasing the degree of integration of its economy with the rest of the world. Its foreign trade to GDP ratio is now higher than that for many developed countries. However, it has been suggested that China's GDP may be higher than officially estimated. Nevertheless, there can be no doubt about the increasing importance of foreign trade, of technology transfer, of foreign investment and so on in the development of China's economy. China's exports, for example, seem to have moved in favour of industries in which it has a comparative advantage based on its factor proportions, that is in favour of industries with a high labour-capital ratio e.g. textiles. Since 1980, there has been a major change in the composition of China's exports away from primary products and in favour of manufactures. Foreign investment is closely correlated with China's increased foreign trade but it is also associated with a trade deficit for firms in China involving foreign investment (Sanzi firms). The reasons and significance of this would be worthy of further study. While China's reforms and the increased openness of the Chinese economy to international trade have increased business competition within China, a number of significant regional and institutional constraints to business competition remain within China (*Jia and Tisdell, 1994*).

REFERENCES

Anon, (1986) : *Notice Concerning the Report of Opinions of Reforming the Foreign State System,* Chinese Banking Publishing House, Bank of China.

Anon, (1989) : *Contemporary China Commodity Price,* Social Sciences Publishing House.

Anon, (1990) : *The National Work of Rectifying Foreign Trade Corporation is almost Completed,* International Business Press, 21 March.

Anon, (1991) : "Regulation concerning price issues", *Price Theory and Practice,* No. 1.

Brabant, Josef M. Van, (1991) : *The Planned Economies and International Economic Organisations*, Cambridge University Press, Cambridge.

Feder, Gershon, (1983) : ''On exports and economic growth'', *Journal of Development Economics*, Nos. 1-2.

GATT, (1988) : ''China's foreign trade region'', note by the Secretariat, Working Party on China's Status as a Contracting Party, General Agreement on Tariffs and Trade, Geneva.

Guan Bai, (1991) : *An Introduction to Export-Oriented Economy*, China Foreign Economic Relation and Trade Press, Beijing.

Jai, L. and Tisdell, C.A., (1994) : ''Trade and Resource Transfers within China : Economic Efficiency and Regional Inequality Consequences'', *Discussion Paper 94.4*, School of Applied and International Economics, Massey University.

Kueh, Y.Y. and Howe, Christopher, (1984) : ''China's international trade : policy and organisational change and their place in the 'economic readjustment'' ', *China Quarterly*, No. 100, December.

Kueh, Y.Y., (1992) : ''Foreign Investment and Economic Change in China'', *China Quarterly*, No. 131, September.

Lardy, Nicholas R., (1992) : ''China's Foreign Trade'', *China Quarterly*.

——, (1992) : *Foreign Trade and Economic Reform in China* 1978-1990, Cambridge University Press.

Lubman, Stanley, (1988) : ''Investment and export contracts in the People's Republic of China'', *Brigham Young University Law Review*, No. 3.

Sun, Weixin, (1989) : ''A Review of forecast of the reforms of the foreign trade system'', *Planned Economy Research*, No. 8.

Tisdell, C.A., (1993) : *Economic Development in the Context of China*, Macmillan, London.

Wang, Zhaoxi, (1994) : *The Principle of China's Foreign Trade*, Foreign Trade Education Press, Beijing.

World Bank, (1983) : *China : Socialist Economic Development (Volume II)* , A World Bank Country Study, The World Bank, Washington D.C.

——, (1985a) : *China : Long-Term Issues and Options : The Report of Mission sent to China*, The John Hopkins University Press, Baltimore.

——, (1985b) : *China Long-Term Issues and Options*, The World Bank, Washington.

——, (1987) : *1987 World Development Report*, Oxford University Press, New York.

——, (1988) : *China : External Trade and Capital*, The World Bank, Washington, D.C.

Yang Peixin, (1988) : ''Reform the foreign exchange system to stimulate foreign trade'', *World Economic Herald*, 28 March.

Zhang Yuqing and Wang Hejun, (1990), ''China's laws and regulations on foreign trade management'', *Intertrade*, March.

Zhao Ziyuang, (1982) : *China's Economy and Development Principle*, Foreign Language Press, Beijing.

12

Economic Adjustment and International Trade: A Policy Dilemma for Fiji

BIMAN C. PRASAD and CLEM TISDELL

Introduction

The objective of this paper is two fold, first to provide an overview of the problems and prospects of the changing economic policies in Fiji and second to review Fiji's international trading position in relation to its new economic policies. Fiji is a small island state and to the outside world, it is the hub of the South Pacific. It had a peaceful transition to full political independence with a democratic constitution in 1970 and until 1987 the two major ethnic communities, the Indian Fijians and the Melanesian Fijians had a relatively peaceful co-existence. However, after the two military coups and the imposition in May 1987 of a racially weighted constitution favouring the Melanesian Fijians, the political situation changed remarkably with continual friction between the two major communities. The 1990 constitution instituted a bicameral parliament consisting of an elected House of Representatives of 70 members (lower house) and an appointed upper house (Senate) with 34 members. The 1990 constitution guaranteed Melanesian Fijians of a majority in the House of Representatives. The 1990 constitution is currently a major point of contention amongst the two major races. Many economic commentators on Fiji have pointed out the political instability created as a result of the 1990 constitution is a major impediment to economic growth and development. The 1990 constitution is currently under review.

Fiji is comprised of 320 islands and has a land area of approximately 18,272 square kilometres and a sea area of 1,290,000 square kilometres. Its population is approximately 750,000 and grew at an average rate of about 2 per cent annually during the 1980s and is expected to be much lower in the 1990s. Native Melanesian Fijians comprise an estimated 49 per cent (an increase of 3 per cent since the 1986 census) of the population and are mostly engaged in subsistence agriculture and public sector employment. Indian Fijians who compromised 49 per cent of the population at the 1986 census now make up an estimated 46 per cent of the population. This decline has largely been attributed to Indian Fijian migration after the political upheavals of 1987. Indian Fijians are engaged in sugar cultivation and a small percentage are involved in trading. The rest of the population includes Chinese, Europeans and other Pacific Islanders. The bulk of the Europeans and the Chinese are engaged in pure commercial activities. People of Indian origin migrated to Fiji under British colonial rule soon after 1874 when Britain took over the administration of the Fiji Islands. They were mostly engaged in the production of sugar and continue to be a vital part of the industry today. An estimated 65 per cent of Fiji's population still resides in rural areas, but rural-urban migration is increasing.

The Fijian economy is heavily dependent upon international trade and finance and its production from natural resource-base accounts for almost 60 per cent of its domestic exports (*Thistlethwait and Votaw, 1992*). Economically Fiji is probably the most advanced economy in the South Pacific (*Browne and Scott, 1989*). Amongst Melanesian countries, Fiji ranks at the top according to the recent Human Development Index for these countries (*UNDP, 1994*). While UNDP's Human Development Index provides a relatively holistic approach to measuring living standards it does not take account of such variables as poverty, environmental degradation and social and political matters such as human rights and justice in a country. For instance the GDP per capita does not reflect income distribution and does not indicate the extent of poverty. Furthermore, some advocates of the Human Development Index believe that economic growth will ultimately lead to an improved income distribution. The so called "trickle down effect" of economic growth has proven to be absent in many developing countries where income distribution has actually deteriorated despite rapid economic growth, even though there are few exceptions such as South Korea which achieved rapid growth with equity (*Gillis, et al., 1987*).

Economic Structure of Fiji

Structurally, Fiji is predominantly an agricultural country. Agriculture accounts for about 20 per cent of GDP and absorbs about

TABLE 1

The Human Development Index (HDI) for Selected Pacific Island Countries, 1994

Country	Life Expectancy at Birth	Adult Literacy Rate (15+)	Mean Years of Schooling	Educational Attainment	GDP Per Capita (US $)	HDI
Fiji	63.1	87	6.8	2.08	1991	0.652
Samoa	63.1	98	9.1	2.83	722	0.578
Vanuatu	62.8	64	4.0	0.75	1020	0.424
Solomon Islands	60.7	23	2.8	0.09	529	0.191
PNG	49.6	52	2.1	0.00	999	0.138

Source : UNDP 1994.

44 per cent of the economically active population (*Cole and Hughes, 1988*). The importance of this sector however in terms of the policy formulation of the government has continued to decline since the mid-1980s and this decline accelerated after the two military coups of 1987. The policy emphasis of the Fijian Government is now directly on the manufacturing sector and designed to promote industrialisation at the expense of agriculture. Sugarcane farming still dominates the agriculture sector and contributes about 7 per cent of the GDP, while the processing of cane by the Fiji Sugar Corporation contributes about 4 per cent of GDP (*Browne and Scott, 1989*). The continuing importance of the sugar industry however, can not be guaranteed as under GATT, trade liberalisation of the agricultural sector is scheduled. Current price levels for Fijian sugar may not be maintained. Other low cost sugar producing countries such as Thailand and Australia and some of the bigger and not necessarily efficient producers such as Brazil may cause Fiji's prices to decline. Fiji's sugar is currently sold to the European Union under the Lome Convention and the US markets but this preferential arrangement may not be sustained (*Grynberg, 1993*). Despite the likely decline in the sugar prices, the industry will remain the backbone of the economy for the foreseeable future. Sugarcane farming is still the dominant rural farming activity and a source of employment for some 20,000 cane-cutters and the only source of income for these households. For a further 4000 employment is provided by the publicly owned Fiji Sugar Corporation of which the government is

the major shareholder (*Bureau of Statistics, 1989*). Despite its importance to the economy and as a source of income for the rural population, government commitment to the industry has declined. This is reflected in public expenditure for the development of the industry. For example, in the 1994 budget the government reduced its expenditure for the sugar industry (*Budget Estimates 1994, 1993*.) The government's blueprint for the future direction of economic policy states that it will continue to assist cane farmers in restructuring the industry and in switching to alternative crops.

Another agricultural crop of importance is copra which has been highly subsidised to maintain the incomes of the copra farmers, mostly Melanesian Fijians. Rice (which is grown as the secondary crop to sugarcane mostly by Indian Fijians) saw increasing levels of production to achieve the objective of self-sufficiency in rice which reached about 66 per cent in 1989. The objective of self-sufficiency in rice production was designed to promote rural development and to improve the incomes of the rural and smallholder farmers. Rice is still the staple food for more than half the population of Fiji, even though there is a shift in the consumption pattern of the population as result of the deregulation of the product market and the availability of a range of food products through imports and a general reduction of subsistence activity as the drive towards market economy continues. Other non-agricultural primary production includes forestry and fishing, which together account for 10 per cent of GDP. Of the non agricultural primary industries, fisheries have the greatest potential for further development. However, the development of the non-agricultural sectors such as mining, forestry and fisheries in most Pacific Islands including Fiji are directly dependent on foreign investment (*McKee and Tisdell, 1990*). For example the Fijian gold mining company is fully foreign owned and foreign investments in the timber companies and the only fish cannery is significant. McKee and Tisdell further point out that the benefits of foreign investment in the non-agricultural sector may be very small and the harmful environmental and social consequences may outweigh the benefits such as employment.

Following pressures for structural adjustment, Fiji like many other small developing countries embarked on a process of industrialisation and began exploring the possibilities for manufacturing a wide range of products. However, its industrial sector continues to be dominated by food-processing and by basic processing. It includes manufacture of sugar, coconut oil production, fish-canning, flour-milling and manufacture of biscuits, beer, soft drinks and cigarettes. Saw milling and cement manufacture is also significant. The manufacturing sector contributes about 11 per cent of GDP and the industrial sector as a whole accounts for about 20 per cent of GDP. Tables 2-4 provide aggregate data describing Fiji's economy and are derived from Economic Intelligence Unit (*1995*).

TABLE 2

Macro-economic Indicators for Fiji, 1993

	1990	1991	1992	1993	1994
GDP at current prices F $m	2045	2176	2377	2540	n\a
Real GDP growth %	6.7	0.6	2.1	4.5	4.0
Consumer Price Inflation %	8.1	6.5	4.9	5.2	n\a
Population m	0.73	0.74	0.75	0.76	0.77
Exports fob US $ m	469.6	427.4	417.1	422.5	n\a
Imports fob US $m	644.6	549.5	539.5	653.5	n\a
Current Account US $ m	-33.9	21.8	31.9	-13.0	n\a
Reserves excluding gold US $ m	260.8	271.4	316.9	269.5	n\a
Total External Debt US $m	412.7	360.4	338.6	330.1	n\a
Debt-Service Ratio %	11.3	11.9	9.5	6.0	n\a
Exchange rate (av)	1.481	1.476	1.503	1.542	n\a

F $: US $ April 21, 1995

F $1. 372 : US $1

TABLE 3

Sources of Fiji's Gross Domestic Product, 1993

	% of total
Agriculture, forestry and Fishing	19.6
Manufacturing	10.5
Transport and Communications	10.2
Trade and Tourism	22.8
Services and others	36.9
GDP at factor cost	100.0

TABLE 4

Components of Fiji's GDP, 1993

	% of total
Private Consumption	66.5
Government Consumption	20.2
Gross Investment	13.5
Change in stocks/statistical discrepancy	2.2
Export of goods and services	56.1
Imports of goods and services	–58.5
GDP at market prices	100.0

Structural Adjustment Policies : International/Global Dimensions

After the Second World War many developing countries gained political independence and moved towards a strategy for growth and development that was driven by nationalistic sentiments and self-sufficiency. Industrialisation therefore became the main objective of economic policies in most developing countries particularly in the larger ones. Prebish (*1950*) and Singer (*1950*) advocated protectionist policies for industrialisation (the infant industry argument for tariff protection) and many Latin American countries actively pursued these policies and this model was adopted by many smaller developing countries including Fiji in the South Pacific.

While import substitution policies provided opportunities for developing countries to industrialise and become self-sufficient in food production, problems both domestic and global began to emerge. Todaro (*1994*) for instance identifies the following problems : (1) infant industries remained inefficient as a result of continued protection, (2) multinational firms have been the main beneficiaries of the import substitution policies rather than local and indigenous entrepreneurs, (3) the setting up of capital-intensive industries with high level of import requirements had exacerbated balance of payments problems, (4) overvaluation of exchange rates has occurred thus making exports, particularly primary exports, very expensive and thereby affecting exports. With these undesirable outcomes and other international shocks such as the oil crises of the early seventies and early eighties the economic situation of many of these countries was made untenable. Many developing countries in Latin America for example experienced economic difficulties involving balance of payments deficits, reduced levels of exports, high levels of unemployment and other social problems that accompany declining levels of economic activity. These problems led to the rethinking of the import substitution policies pursued by these countries. While on one hand there was ample evidence that the import substitution policies produced undesirable effects, on the other hand there was growing evidence from the East Asian "gang of four" that export substitution or export promotion policies produced desired results (*Ranis, 1989*). This evidence from the East Asian "gang of four" provided the impetus for the change in domestic economic policies of debtor countries and also major structural changes. The wisdom of generalising the East Asian model however, has been debated by economists. Cline (*1989*) for example points out the East Asian model can not be generalised as the world economic conditions have changed drastically.

The influence of the IMF and the World Bank in a newly assumed role became important. The World Bank after the Second World War was principally concerned with reviving the economies destroyed during the Second World War and the IMF was to oversee the balance of payment situation of the countries and to provide temporary financial facilities to solve their deficit problems. However, partly due to deteriorating economic conditions the IMF and the World Bank changed their roles (*Todaro, 1994*). The overwhelming policy direction of both the IMF and the World Bank is currently directed towards the creation of free markets and free international trade economy. The promotion of Structural Adjustment Policies (SAP) is the main thrust of both the World Bank's and the IMF's role in the economies of the developing countries. In fact IMF loans and most of the World Bank loans are conditional upon the commitment of the government of the developing country involved to pursue SAP.

The structural adjustment policies advocated by the IMF and supported by the World Bank involve the following (*Instituto del Tercer Mundo, 1992*) :

reduction of public expenditure and privatisation of public service programmes such as Health and Education; promotion of domestic savings and private foreign investment; liberalisation of the economy; deregulation of the product, factor and financial markets; export promotion through incentives such as tax holidays; promotion of private foreign investment; elimination of subsidies and grants; reduction of real incomes through de-indexation of salaries; fiscal reform which includes the introduction of indirect forms of taxation such VAT; registration of small scale farmers and those in engaged in the informal sector and withdrawal of state management of social programmes.

Most developing countries invariably adopt many of these policies under the IMF/World Bank conditionality. There is however increasing concern on the impact of these policies particularly on the poor sections of the society including women and children and more recently on the conservation and management of the environment. More generally in a critical analysis of three World Bank studies (*1988, 1990 & 1991*) on the impact of SAP's, Woodward (*1992*) claims that there is no clear and incontrovertible evidence that structural adjustment helps to increase economic growth during the adjustment period. He further states that there is only a small group of high income countries which provide the evidence of economic growth with adjustment and that these countries are not representative of the bulk of the countries undertaking structural adjustment programmes. Singer, Hatti and Tandon (*1991*) also point out that IMF and World Bank package of policy reforms have produced mixed results. They also point out that the main issue with respect to SAPs is how the poor can be protected during periods of adjustment and how SAPs can be designed in a way that allows integration of the poor into the productive economy and also to design adjustment strategy with a human face. In terms of the impact of SAP on the environment, Tisdell (*1994*) points out there is no clear evidence that economic growth as a result of macroeconomic adjustment will lead to the improvement in the conservation and management of environment. In fact he suggests that economic policies need to be specifically targeted to conservation of natural resources and that we can not rely on macro and microeconomic policies such as those espoused by the IMF and World Bank. More radical critics of the IMF and World Bank led Structural Adjustment Policies such as George (*1992*) have stressed that SAPs have cured nothing, and that they have caused untold human suffering and widespread environmental destruction.

Gerster (*1991*) argues that economic reforms are urgently needed in LDCs and the corresponding reform demands of the IMF and the World Bank are justified. However, he points out that the reforms should be instituted flexibly and that reforms in the South should be accompanied by reforms in the North to produce desired results. He raises the following questions about the approach of the IMF/World

Bank. It is worth highlighting these as some will be considered in relation to SAPs in Fiji later in this contribution.

* Is the implementation of the structural adjustment programme by rescheduling and debt reduction as long term as possible?
* Do the LDCs have the possibility to cushion possible export revenue losses through compensatory financing?
* Whether other bilateral or multilateral project and programme financing are cut so that only shift of funds is created and not an increase in volume. From its absorption capacity, is the LDC in a position to master structural adjustment programme. What role is allotted to foreign trade and payments in the adjustment programmes?
* Has the country already had therapies with structural adjustment and with what success compared to specific goals?
* Is a general liberalisation of trade taking place and is integration into the world market promising in view of its product range?
* Who bears the burden of export promotion and who benefits from export promotion?
* Who gains from import liberalisation if it is a component of structural adjustment?
* What effects had devaluation of local currency on the poor classes?
* Are there indications that desired climate through favouring adjustment can attract new foreign investment?
* What restructuring does the adjustment programme provide in other areas of expenditure, e.g health, education and food subsidies?
* At whose expense is the reform of the system of fees and taxes?
* What changes are brought by privatisation of state units for the poor people?
* Does the adjustment programme raise hopes among population or it provokes fears for the future?
* Does the adjustment programme contain measures which ease the access of the poor to more productive inputs e.g land, water?

Nature of Structural Adjustment Policies in Fiji

The genesis of the restructuring process in the Fijian economy can be traced back to the early eighties when the economy was showing signs of a serious decline. High levels of unemployment, declining real incomes of sugarcane growers was halved and the income disparities between workers became more visible (*Smith, et al., 1988*). In 1984, the government also imposed a wage freeze and the tripartite forum which included representatives of the government, employers and workers was abolished as a first step towards labour market deregulation. Since 1984 the Government of Fiji has adopted further industrialisation initiatives and adopted an export-oriented development strategy. For example the objectives of the Development Plan Nine which many believe reflected the real beginning of the IMF and the World Bank influence on the Fiji economy and adoption of the structural adjustment policies were stated as follows: (a) Create a dynamic, growth-oriented industrial structure, (b) expand output, particularly of goods for export markets, (c) increase efficiency and competitiveness of this sector (export) through: (i) setting up appropriate mechanisms to enhance quality and standards: (ii) increasing productivity, (iii) further development of management and technological capability; (iv) support for research and development, and (v) providing performance related incentives; (d) facilitate and encourage vigorous private sector investment activity and (e) create more skill-intensive jobs to fully utilise Fiji's relatively well educated labour force. (*Central Planning Office, 1985:96*).

The policies adopted since the early eighties and particularly after 1984 attracted considerable opposition from most sections of the population particularly from the powerful trade unions and the middle class. In fact the formation of the Fiji Labour Party was triggered by the wage freeze of the 1984, the increasing levels of unemployment, declining levels of income and inflation. It should be noted that the Labour Party subsequently won the general election in 1987 but was ousted by a military coup after only a month in office.

Development Plan Nine however, was basically made redundant after the two military coups. In fact the objectives of Development Plan Nine were intended for slowly restructuring the economy. However, the economic disaster that was created by the coups called for radical and alternative strategies for growth and in particular industrial growth. Immediately after the coups and as a result of massive decline in economic activity, the military government adopted short term measures such as devaluing Fiji's currency, and imposed strict exchange controls and salary cuts for government workers. This opportunity was seized on by the World Bank and the IMF to promote its structural adjustment policies. The manufacturing sector was targeted as the primary sector for growth. An export-oriented manufacturing policy has essentially become the panacea for solving all the economic ills of Fiji and the current government is strongly guided by this view in its policymaking.

While the manufacturing of sugar continues to be the principal manufacturing industry, attempts are being made to diversify Fiji's manufacturing base. In particular, industry is being promoted by huge incentives such as a 13-year tax holiday being granted to new investors. The government has also announced the setting up of tax free zones in 1996 to further promote the manufacturing of garments. Since the promotion of the industry, garment exports have increased to F$ 131 million compared with less than F$ 1 million in 1985 (*Treadgold, 1992*). There are however, a number of issues that needs discussion in relation to the garment industry. First is the issue of the import content of the industry. Fiji does not produce cloth and so the raw materials have to be imported and it is therefore important to look at the import content of the industry. Employment is another issue, one of the incentives for investors to move their operations offshore and particularly to Fiji is the availability of cheap labour.

The review of Fiji's economic performance during the early nineties highlights the following significant problems (*IMF, 1995*): (i) A relatively sluggish growth of real GDP per capita during the period 1990-1994, that is, an average of 1.6 per cent per year, (ii) an overall deficit in its budget; and (iii) a deteriorating external current balance.

The poor past performance of Fiji's economy has been attributed to many factors such as high levels of government regulations, lack of incentives for investment, lack of skilled manpower and the general approach to economic policies which emphasised import substitution rather than export-oriented growth. However, since 1984, and more so since the military coups of 1987, a marked shift in economic policies have taken place. After the first National Economic Summit which was held in 1989 but boycotted by the trade union movement, the government identified the following policy objectives to promote its export-oriented strategy for growth, a strategy which clearly fits in to the IMF and World Bank framework of structural adjustment policies:

trade liberalisation, constraint on the growth of government expenditure, reform of the taxation system (move away from the direct to indirect forms of taxation), deregulation of the product and the factor markets, increasing Melanesian Fijian participation in the business sector, and re-orientation of sectoral policies.

Despite this shift in policy Fiji's economic growth has remained sluggish. There is no doubt that the political uncertainty is having an adverse impact on the level of investment both foreign and domestic and hence is affecting the overall performance of the economy. Furthermore institutions or property rights to land and institutional arrangements in relation to this seem to be another impediment to Fiji's development. Nearly all land is vested in perpetuity in the hands of Melanesian Fijians and the renting of it by Indian Fijians is tightly controlled by the Native Lands Trust Board. The rights of Indians to land use is under a cloud of uncertainty. At a recent conference of the Fiji Institute of Accountants, the president of the Fiji Chamber of Commerce highlighted the following:

> Fiji is perceived by economists to be a very fragile and vulnerable nation because of its undeveloped financial markets and over reliance on foreign trade. Coupled with high cost of funds, Fiji's economic future remains bleak. Another important hindrance to the economy is the issue of property rights where institutional arrangements rather than the market forces dictate the use of native land which forms 83 per cent of available land in Fiji. Disputes leading to conflicts between owners of resources and investors have often led to conflicts which continue to be detrimental to the business climate in Fiji . This is particularly a common problem in the tourism industry. (*Fiji Business Week, 1995 : 6*).

The scope of this contribution however, does not cover the issue of property rights even though it is an important and one which should not be ignored in any analysis of the Fijian economy.

Structural Adjustment Policies and Economic Performance : Its Impact on the Poor

As stated earlier, critical analysis of three World Bank studies by Woodward (*1992*) show that there is no clear evidence that SAPs achieve desired economic growth and associated desirable impacts on the whole economy. The evidence on the success of the SAPs is mixed to say the least. This part of the contribution will discuss the impact of each of the policies on the performance of the economy and on the poor of the society.

Trade Liberalisation : As part of the overall strategy for promoting export, trade liberalisation or deregulation is one of the cornerstones of Fiji's current economic policies. The objective this policy is to turn Fiji into an efficient open economy. The economic logic behind trade liberalisation derives from the fact that trade protection or import substitution policies tend to breed inefficiency both in manufacturing sector and the primary sector. The steps in trade liberalisation in Fiji involve the replacement of import licences with low tariffs. The process began in 1989 with government progressively replacing licences with high tariffs but is progressively lowering the level of tariff.

In 1994, a study on the impact of trade liberalisation policies on the economy was conducted for the government (*Lighfoot, 1994*). While there is increasing cynicism about government sponsored studies, it is still useful to highlight its findings. As expected the report concluded that trade liberalisation has had a positive impact on Fiji. The following were its conclusions:

The replacement of import licences with tariffs has increased the range available to the consumer and the staged reduction in tariffs rates has reduced retail prices.

The indications are that business is adjusting remarkably well to the changing trading conditions. The number of new business stars is growing at around 5 per cent per annum, average business profitability is increasing and there is little evidence of failure.

The fears that the changes in policy would lead to serious unemployment are proving unfounded. After over a decade of virtually static growth, employment rose sharply in 1989-90 and continues to grow, albeit at a declining rate.

The economy's international competitiveness improved markedly after the devaluations of 1987 and the 1989 mini budget. The replacement of the majority of import licences with tariffs in 1989, combined with the subsequent tariff rate reductions, decreased the level of trade restrictiveness in the economy. Some of these gains were subsequently lost in 1992 and 1993, when the pause in trade liberalisation was accompanied by increases in the effective tariff rates.

> The gains being achieved by the trade liberalisation policies are at risk of being compromised by the absence of more widespread reforms to the trading and regulatory environment. The speed of reform of public enterprises and the wider regulatory environment has not matched the pace of implementation of the trade liberalisation policies.
>
> Continuing to implement the trade liberalisation policies will further improve Fiji's international competitiveness. This in turn should improve the welfare of the people of Fiji. (*Lightfoot, 1994 : 1*)

While it is true that the range of goods available to the consumers has increased, there is no guarantee about the quality of goods. In fact the report acknowledges that inferior quality rice and tinned fish were imported to Fiji particularly from South East Asian countries. In fact it is feared that Fiji could become the "dumping ground" for cheap quality imports. For example the recent sale of the Australian owned company, "Morris Hedstrom" a major retail outlet in Fiji, to a Malaysian company has led to increasing levels of imports from Malaysia.

The report generally shows that prices of consumer goods imported decreased after trade deregulation. Imported rice and tinned fish are obvious examples. This can not be disputed and it is possible that prices can further decline as tariff rates are reduced progressively. For the rice industry, however, the issue is not the declining price levels for consumers but declining levels of productivity and income for the farmers. About 70-80 thousand people depend directly on this industry for their livelihood and most them are semi-subsistence farmers. The majority of the farms are small; the average size of a farm for example is between 3-4 hectares. In 1989, Fiji was about 66 per cent self-sufficient in rice. As a result of increased import of rice, the domestic price of rice declined and this has led to declining levels of value of productivity and hence the income levels of farmers. Therefore, the income distribution aspect needs to be addressed. Table 5 shows the production levels since the rice industry was deregulated.

Tisdell and Fairbairn (*1985*) point out that a development path for small economies specialising in international trade and production by exporting non-subsistence goods is much more risky if this specialisation leads to dependence on imported subsistence goods. They also recommend that small economies should encourage technical progress in the subsistence sector to generate surplus and to allow the economy

TABLE 5

Rice Production in Fiji

	1989	1990	1991	1992	1993
Rice Production (000 tonnes)	31.8	26.9	29.0	22.5	23.1
Rice Imports (000 tonnes)	19.3	22.7	26.0	26.5	33.9
Total Supply (000 tonnes)	51.1	49.6	55.0	49.0	57.0
Rice Import value (Value in $ m)	7.2	11.8	9.1	12.0	12.4
Self-Efficiency (Per cent)	66	54	52	46	43

Source : Based on Ministry of Agriculture, Fisheries and Forests, 1992 and 1993 *Annual Reports*

to benefit from trade in the long run. In Fiji recent policy to date is contrary to this view. For example government has continued to promote the export of non-subsistence goods such as cocoa, ginger and clothing. It has also continued to withdraw support from the subsistence or semi-subsistence sectors such as the rice and dairy industry.

The report on trade liberalisation acknowledges that it is difficult to say whether trade liberalisation has actually enhanced or constrained employment. However, the argument that resources including labour released during the adjustment period particularly after deregulation will be absorbed by the growth of the urban-based manufacturing sector, cannot be sustained in Fiji at the present time. The argument assumes that labour will be able to adjust to the new demands of the manufacturing sector in terms of skill and knowledge requirement. The government report clearly acknowledges that this is not happening and that there is no policy prescription to re-skill the workers and in fact the burden of re-skilling and adjustment is on the employers and the individuals. The impact of trade liberalisation on the poor and those in poverty in another issue that deserves attention. The government has not done much in terms of the alleviation of impoverishment of displaced workers even though an honest attempt was made to address this problem with a formation of a poverty alleviation task force in 1991. This task force was later disbanded after bureaucratic and political bungling.

Any effective study however of the impact of trade liberalisation can not be conclusive as there are many exogenous factors which have nothing to do with the process of trade liberalisation, that determine the final impact on the economy. For Fiji, factors such as international economic environment, the political climate and more importantly the issue of property rights can not be ignored. In fact the greatest regulatory challenge to the current economic policy is the property rights issue in land (*Treadgold 1992*).

Reduction in Government Expenditure : The reduction in the size of the government and taxation reform are major components of SAPs in Fiji. The objective often stated in government policy papers (*Government of Fiji, 1993*) is that of bringing prices and incomes in line with those determined by market forces. The government has attempted both to reduce the size of government and reform the taxation system together. Generally in the case of reduction in the size of government the following policies have been put in place : reductions in public sector wages and employment, reductions in public investment, removal and reduction of subsidies particularly to rice and dairy farmers and increases in public enterprise prices.

Wages policy in Fiji has not only affected public sector workers but more significantly those in the non-public sector. The economic objective of the current wages policy is designed to also achieve international competitiveness. The root of the current wages policy can be traced back to government's 1985 budget when a wage freeze was imposed. This was in line with the IMF view that wages in Fiji were excessive by about 15 per cent in relation to Fiji's international competitiveness. While the wage freeze may not have been of serious concern in relation to poverty as many public sector workers already receive wages that are above poverty line, there could be a direct effect on the welfare as a result of real wage reduction. In fact Woodward (*1992*) points out that there are indirect effects of reductions in employment and wage that is usually not taken into serious considerations by IMF studies. Table 6 shows the trends in real wages in Fiji since 1975.

In terms of the 1975 prices, real wages declined in Fiji from 1978 onwards and the overall real wage rate was only 74 per cent that in 1975. Workers in the manufacturing sector also suffered in terms of welfare as their purchasing power was only 66 per cent of what it was 15 years prior to 1990. As a result of declining real wages, the welfare

TABLE 6

Trends in Real Wage Rates and Salaries

Year	MWR	OWR	CPI (base 1975)	RM	ROR	NAS	RS (Prices: 1975)
1975	6.19	5.97	100.0	6.19	5.97	3058	3058
1976	6.64	6.68	106.4	6.24	6.28	3450	3241
1977	6.87	7.11	120.9	5.68	5.88	3900	3225
1978	8.10	7.89	127.9	6.33	6.17	4279	3345
1979	8.48	8.48	134.6	6.30	6.30	4716	3504
1980	9.52	9.28	154.1	6.18	6.02	5084	3299
1981	10.56	10.16	171.3	6.16	5.93	5572	3252
1982	11.20	10.96	183.3	6.11	5.98	6192	3378
1983	11.92	11.68	195.7	6.09	5.97	6579	3362
1984	12.00	11.84	206.1	5.82	5.75	7055	3424
1985	12.16	12.00	215.1	5.65	5.58	7577	3523
1986	11.84	12.00	219.0	5.41	5.48	7818	3571
1987	12.32	12.64	231.4	5.32	5.46	7524	3251
1988	12.56	12.96	258.7	4.85	5.01	7043	2722
1989	11.36	12.64	274.7	4.14	4.60	8055	2933
1990	11.44	13.36	300.7	3.81	4.44	9342	3107

Notes : MWR = Manufacturing Wage Rate, OWR = Overall Wage Rate, CPI = Consumer Price Index, RM = Real Manufacturing Wage Rate, ROR= Real Overall Wage Rate, NAS = Nominal Annual Salary, RS = Real Salary.

Source : Based on *Annual Employment Surveys, Current Economic Statistics,* Fiji and Chand *et al*, 1993).

of the workers both in the public sector and the private sector has worsened.

Another possible impact of the reduction in employment in the public as well as in the formal private sector is an increase in the labour supply in the informal urban sector. There is no quantitative study on the level of increase in the supply of labour in the informal sector. However, on the basis of other indicators such as increasing crime levels and squatter settlements the increase seems to be substantial. The declining levels of economic activity and the continued displacement of labourers from the primary sector such as the dairy and rice industry made a definite addition to the urban informal sector. Towards the late eighties urban poverty was recognised as a major problem of increasing urbanisation. For example it was reported that in 1986 one out of every eight people living in Suva (Fiji's capital city) was a squatter (*Bryant, 1993*).

The Fiji government as part of cost cutting measures also began to reduce subsidies to rural farmers and in particular to rice and dairy farmers. The theoretical rationale for this is that some industries have become "sick" or inefficient and were becoming a burden to government finance. It was also believed that continued government support had made these industries complacent and there was no attempt to increase efficiency. In the case of the rice farmers, the bulk of them are small semi-subsistence farmers and the removal of subsidies on fertiliser and the withdrawal of machines from irrigated area has led to increasing levels of cost and declining production and income. Woodward (*1992*) points out that in the case of Sri Lanka and the Philippines, IMF studies acknowledged that there was a negative impact on poor farmers of removing subsidies on fertilisers.

Taxation Reform : The reform of the taxation system is one of the main objectives of the SAPs. The underlying assumption is that tax system before the introduction of SAPs is distorted, narrow based and administratively complex. As a result of this, it inhibits incentives for production and the low level of revenue collection contributes to increasing the budget deficit of the government. However, according to Stiglitz (*1988*) there are five characteristics of a "good" tax system and these include, economic efficiency, administrative simplicity, flexibility, political responsibility and fairness and the discussion of the impact of tax reform could be analysed using these criteria.

In Fiji, the reform of the taxation system was based on the following objectives: broadening the tax base, reducing administrative complexity and removing distortions and providing consistent incentives to producers and consumers. The introduction of the 10 per cent Value Added Tax replacing turnover tax and exercise duties on everything except cigarettes, liquor, beer and petrol was intended to achieve the above objectives. This change in the tax system was put in place in July 1992, despite massive opposition from the various sectors of the population. The implementation of the VAT was seen by many Fijians as politically irresponsible. It is generally accepted that income taxes or direct taxes are progressive in nature and do not affect the poor sections of the community as it does not cover the poor in both the rural and urban areas. However, the same cannot be said of a broad-based consumption tax, VAT or any indirect form of taxation. The poor normally spend a large percentage of their income on basic items and if these items are not exempted under the tax system then it will directly affect their ability to buy the same basket of goods. The Fijian government was mindful of the burden the VAT would place on the poor and increased its welfare payments from $ F 2.5 million to $ F 5 million to cushion the effects, (*Kamkamica, 1991*). However according to Chand, et al. (*1992*) VAT has reduced the living standard of not only a majority of wage earners but also those in the informal sector who were not subject to tax before its introduction. According to their calculations, over 70 per cent of Fijians earn less then $ F 5000 per year.

The government predicted that a VAT affected price rise would be only 2.86 per cent. For 1992, it claimed that with the average annual inflation rate of 4.9 per cent the price effect of VAT was 3 per cent. Independent calculations however show that price increases to be 6.8 per cent for the Greater Suva area in 1992. Any tax reform system should take into consideration the issue of fairness, that is it ought to be fair in its treatment of the poor section of the community which is the group that normally suffer whenever a broad based or indirect form of taxation is introduced. Clearly in a country where 70 per cent of the wage earners earn less than the income tax threshold and where there is a large informal sector, the introduction of the VAT type tax would cause severe hardship, particularly if there are no exemptions and no well developed welfare payment systems.

International Trade, Problems and Prospects

The efforts towards trade liberalisation in Fiji fits into the overall programme of SAPs and the increasing globalisation of economies. The theoretical underpinning of free trade derives from the Ricardian and Hecksher-Ohlin theory of comparative advantage. The underlying rationale for free trade is that it would lead to improvement in the welfare of the participating countries. As discussed before the impact of trade liberalisation on the performance of the Fijian economy since 1987 is not encouraging. The argument that welfare will improve as a result of free trade can not always be sustained as there are countries which may actually become worse of during the transition or adjustment period.

After the military coup of 1987, the government took steps to diversify its trading relationship. It began to strengthen its diplomatic and economic relationships with many of the South East Asian nations such as Singapore, Malaysia, Indonesia, Taiwan and South Korea. This is not surprising as many of the South East Asian nations were very sympathetic to the regime after the coup. Its traditional and immediate trading partners, Australia and New Zealand, however seem to have been critical of the military coups and subsequent governments.

While export to these East Asian markets at least in the foreseeable future may not be substantial, there is possibility for some investment from East Asian countries particularly when some of the firms in these countries are moving offshore due to increasing costs. Export to its traditional partners such as Australia, UK, USA and New Zealand will continue to provide the bulk of Fiji's export revenue. Exports to Australia still account for 22.7 per cent of Fiji's total exports. Tables 7-9 (based on *Economic Intelligence Unit, 1995*) provide data on Fiji's exports.and imports.

Another concern to Fiji is the impact of increasing globalisation of trade as a result of General Agreement on Tariffs and Trade (GATT). Fiji currently enjoys a preferential position under two agreements, SPARTECA and the Lome Convention. Of these two agreements the Lome Convention is by far the most important as under this agreement bulk of Fiji's sugar is sold above the world market price to the European Community. SPARTECA is a non-reciprocal trade agreement under which Australia and New Zealand provide duty free and unrestricted

TABLE 7

Principal Exports of Fiji, 1993

Principal Exports	US$ m
Sugar	150
Garments	84
Gold	43
Timber	20
Fish	27
Re-exports	67
Total including others	499

TABLE 8

Principal Imports of Fiji, 1993

Principal Imports	US$ m
Machinery	199
Manufactured goods	163
Food	108
Mineral Fuels	86
Total including others	720

TABLE 9

Main Destinations of Fiji's Exports and Imports, 1993

Main Destination of Exports	% of total	Main Origins of Imports	% of total
Australia	22.7	Australia	32.8
UK	20.7	New Zealand	19.2
USA	10.5	Japan	11.0
Japan	7.4	USA	7.6
New Zealand	5.1	Singapore	5.6
China	2.1	China	3.4

access to South Pacific Forum island member nations. Fiji has taken advantage of this agreement over the years but has not been able to negotiate further concessions or increase its exports substantially.

The Lome Convention came into force on April 1st, 1976 and provides for cooperation between the EEC and a large number of developing countries in Africa, Carribean and Pacific (*Brinkhorst, 1977*). The Sugar Protocol which is legally part of the Lome Convention is the most important. It is attached to the Lome Convention as Protocol Eight of Lome IV Convention but it has terms and conditions that are exceptional and reflect the almost unique position held by the sugar-producing African, Carribean and Pacific (ACP) countries in 1974 (*Grynberg, 1993*).

Grynberg also points out that while the Sugar Protocol has served Fiji well in the past in terms of guaranteed price, there are increasing fears that this favourable position may be eroded in future. The basis for this sort of fear is not unfounded as the European Union is now producing more beet sugar then ever and by 1989 its exports accounted for 28 per cent of world exports to the free market. With the GATT in place and the massive production under the Common Sugar Policy, there will be increasing pressure on the EU to re-evaluate its preferential treatment of the sugar exports of the ACP countries in future.

Concluding Comments

The arguments for the changes in economic policies in Fiji and indeed the adoption of SAPs can not be refuted in its entirety. On the contrary, some structural reforms have been necessary and had to be undertaken. The first problem with the adoption of the SAPs in Fiji has been its generalisation on the basis of what the IMF and the World Bank had achieved in other developing countries. While there is no clear evidence on the positive impact of the changes in the economic policies so far, there is increasing evidence that the rural and the urban poor or those in the informal sector may have suffered. The introduction of the VAT led to a general increase in price levels in Fiji and affected the poor most. It has been established that over 70 per cent of workers who earn less then $F 5,000 have been adversely affected by the introduction the VAT.

What needs to be taken into consideration is the unique conditions prevailing in Fiji such as the land tenure issue and a large subsistence economy before any generalisation on the positive impact of SAPs is made. The radical shift in the emphasis of the government's policy away from the agricultural sector causes further hardship to the already poor and subsistence farmers. This also leads to an increasing exodus of people from the rural areas to urban centres in search of wage employment in the manufacturing sector putting pressure on the already fragile urban infrastructure.

Fiji's current strategy for economic growth and development should also be analysed in the context of the institutional structures that it has in place. For Fiji, the single most important institutional impediment to meaningful reforms is the rigidity of the land market. Unless reform is undertaken in this area success of the current economy policy in Fiji could be under serious threat.

REFERENCES

Brinkhorst, L.J. (1977) : "Lome and Further." A.M. Frans and A.V. Geusau (eds), *The Lome Convention and a New International Economic Order,* AW Sijthoff International, Netherlands.

Browne, C. and Scott D.A. (1989) : *Economic Development in Seven South Pacific Island Countries,* International Monetary Fund, Washington, D.C.

Bryant, J.J. (1993) : *Urban Poverty and the Environment in the South Pacific,* University of New England, Australia.

Bureau of Statistics, (1993) : *Current Economic Statistics;* Government of Fiji, Suva.

——, Various Years, *Annual Employment Survey,* Government of Fiji, Suva.

Central Planning Office, (1980) : *Fiji's Ninth Development Plan 1981-1985,* Government of Fiji, Suva.

Chand, G., Prasad, B.C., Reddy, M. and Chand, A. (1993) : *The Woes of Structural Adjustment Policies : The 1994 Fiji Government Budget,* Fiji Institute of Applied Studies, Research Report Series No. 3, Suva.

Chand, G and Reddy, M. (1992) : *The Impact of VAT on Consumer Prices Index in Fiji,* Fiji Institute of Applied Studies, Suva.

Cline, W.R. (1982) : "Can the East Asian Model be Generalised?", *World Development,* Vol. 10, 81-90.

Cole, R. and Hughes, H. (1988): *The Fiji Economy, May 1987 : Problems and Prospects,* National Centre for Development Studies, Australian National University, Canberra.

Economic Intellegence Unit Limited, (1995) : *EIU Country Report 2nd Quarter 1995 : Fiji,* EIU, London

Fairbairn, T.I. and C.A. Tisdell, (1994) : *Applicability and use of Natural Resource Accounting and Environmental Economics in Small Islands Developing States,* A Technical Paper Prepared for SPREP, Western Samoa.

Fiji Business Week, (1995) : Vol. 1 No. 24, June 29-July 5, Suva.

George, S, (1992) : *The Debt Boomerang : How Third World Debt Harms Us All,* Pluto Press, London.

Gerster, R. (1991) : "Basic Development Policy Questions on Structural Adjustment Programmes : Adjustment as if People Mattered." H. Singer, N. Hatti and R. Tandon (eds), *Adjustment and Liberalisation in the Third World,* Indus Publishing Company, New Delhi.

Gillis, M, Perkins, D.H, Roemer, M. and Snodgrass, R.D. (1987) : *Economics of Development,* W.W. Norton and Company, London.

Government of Fiji (1993) : *Opportunities for Growth, Policies and Strategies for Fiji in the Medium Term,* Government Printing Press, Suva.

Grynberg, R. (1993) : "Trade Liberalisation in the Post-Cold War Era : Implications for the Fiji Sugar Industry." *Journal of Pacific Studies,* School of Social and Economic Development, USP, Suva.

Instituto del Tercer Mundo, (1992) : *Third World Guide 1993/1994,* Montivideo, Uruguay.

IMF, (1995) : *The IMF Survey,* January 23, IMF, Washington.

Kamkamica, J.N. (1991) : *Address by the Minister of Finance and Economic Planning to Fiji National Economic Summit.*

Lightfoot, C. (1994) : *Fiji: Trade Liberalisation Study,* United Nation's Economic and Social Committee for Asia and the Pacific, Vanuatu.

McKee, D.L. and Tisdell, C. (1990) : *Developmental Issues in Small Island Economies,* Praeger Publishers, New York.

Ministry of Finance and Economic Planning, (1993) : *Fiji Budget Estimates*; Parliament of Fiji, Suva.

Parliament of Fiji, (1992) : *Ministry of Agriculture, Fisheries and Forests, Annual Report,* Government Printing Press, Suva.

——, (1993) : *Ministry of Agriculture, Fisheries and Forests, Annual Report,* Government Printing Press, Suva.

Ranis, G. (1989) : "Debt, Adjustment and Development". H. Singer and Sharma (eds), *Economic Development and World Debt,* Macmillan Press, London.

Singer H.W, Hatti, N. and Tandon, R. (eds) (1991) : *Adjustment and Liberalisation in the Third World,* Indus Publishing Company, New Delhi.

Stiglitz J.E. (1988) : *Economics of the Public Sector*, W.W. Norton Company, London.

Thistlethwait, R. and Votaw, G. (1992) : *Environment and Development : A Pacific Island Perspective,* Asian Development Bank, Philippines.

Tisdell, C. (1994) : "Conservation, protected areas and the global economic system : how debt trade, exchange rates, inflation and macroeconomic policy affect biological diversity." *Biodiversity and Conservation* 3, 419-436.

—— and Fairbairn, T.I.J. (1985) : "Subsistence Economies and Unsustainable Development and Trade : Some Simple Theory." Fairbairn, T.I.J. *Island Economies,* Institute of Pacific Studies, Suva.

Todaro, M.P. (1994) : *Economic Development,* Longman Publishing, New York.

Treadgold, M. (1992) : *The Economy of Fiji: Performance, Management and Prospects,* Australian Government Publishing Service, Canberra.

UNDP, (1994) : *Pacific Human Development Report : Putting People First,* UNDP, Suva.

Woodward, D. (1992) : *Debt Adjustment and Poverty in Developing Countries : National and International Dimensions of Debt and Adjustment in Developing Countries,* Volume I, Pinter Publishers, London.

——, (1992) : *Debt Adjustment and Poverty in Developing Countries : The Impact of Debt and Adjustment at the Household Level in Developing Countries,* Volume II, Pinter Publishers, London.

13

Economic Integration, Trade and Development : Concluding Observations

RAJ KUMAR SEN

Economic integration among several countries specially as trading blocs has been considered beneficial by many in spite of the present trend towards globalisation. Both economic and political factors have worked towards forming such blocs and such formations are also in conformity with the provision of the WTO. Though, some trading and regional blocs like SAARC are in existence in name only, important blocs like EU, ASEAN, APEC and NAFTA have been effective in accelerating the economic development of their member countries since their formation. In particular, in any analysis[1] of economic integration, the performance of the EU and the impact of its activities on its members and non-member countries have been areas of interesting analysis since late 1950s. In this context, the economic relation between India and the EU attracted the attention of analysts in India and outside experts since the inception of planning mechanism in India for rapid economic development. India being both non-EU member and a non-member of any important bloc has worried to suffer from the trade diversion effects of the EU while the EU members expected an increase in their welfare in terms of net trade creation effects, growth in real income and employment etc. On the other hand, Australia, earlier in a similar position like India, took the intiative to form APEC group of trading blocs feeling the difficulties of remaining alone in the current trend towards regional blocs.

On the theoretical and other issues relating to economic integration it is noted[2] that our dynamic and interdependent economic world is generating considerable uncertainty about the economic future for Asian-Pacific countries including India. Some major concerns are the likely impact of (1) the single European Market, including its possible extension for additional European countries; (2) the future of countries formerly a part of or associated with the Soviet Union and (3) the North American Free Trade Association (NAFTA). Concerns exist in relation to (a) restricted trade possibilities for the Asia-Pacific area, (b) reduced levels of inflow of foreign direct investment to them and (c) reduced levels of foreign aid to less developed countries in the Asia-Pacific region. There is a possibility of Europe becoming more inward-looking and concerned with politically stabilising and providing economic support to members of Confederation of Independent States and Eastern Europe. This is likely to divert European aid funds away from LDCs and will possibly result in increasing trade concessions for Eastern European countries at the expense of Asian-Pacific LDCs. Furthermore, foreign direct investment may be diverted from Asian-Pacific countries to new free trade blocs. Economies of scale within these blocs and gains in efficiency by extension of the size of markets could further reinforce economic centre-periphery tendencies. However, some argue that rising incomes within the trade blocs might generate increased demand for imports, for example from Asian-Pacific countries.

As far as trade is concerned, India is in a vulnerable position from at least one point of view. In 1988, 24.3 per cent of its exports were to the EC and it was also highly dependent on the EC for imports (32 per cent). India has strong trade links with Europe and USA but much weaker links with East Asia. Thus, developments in Europe and North America could be expected to have a substantial direct impact on Indian trade. However, a bright spot may be that India in percentage terms only depends to a relatively minor degree on foreign trade as a contributor to its GDP. In 1989, for example, India's exports amounted to less than 6.2 per cent of its GDP and its imports to 8.4 per cent of its GDP. Thus, India is relatively self-sufficient from an economic point of view — much more so than is China. It seems that India could maintain much the same economic position as is now even if its trade was somewhat reduced. The Indian socio-economic system seems as though it can survive almost as an autarchic entity. However, most of India's current imports are vital for it to maintain its modern sector.

In contrast small island economies in the Asia-Pacific region are much more vulnerable economically. Most are highly dependent on foreign trade and/or on foreign aid to maintain their incomes. Many have been assisted by the Lomé Convention to retain continuing access for their exports to Europe and to receive aid funds. There is a view, however, that trade and aid support for small nations under Lomé IV is unlikely to increase but most likely will remain stationary or decline in real terms marginally as the EC struggles to respond to the economic recession and the economic problems of East Europe and the former Soviet Union. Economic difficulties for small island nations seem likely to increase.

The formation of new regional trade groupings in the Asia-Pacific Region have been touted as a counter to European Economic Integration and possibly NAFTA. Strong economic interdependencies now exist in the Pacific Basin, particularly in East Asia. Whether these will be sufficient to form a basis for closer economic integration in the region remains to be seen. Australia has promoted the Asia-Pacific Economic Cooperation (APEC) group as a means to fostering greater economic cooperation in the region and as a forum for encouraging an open and free global trading system. A number of Indian economists have also suggested that India might do well to cultivate a closer economic association with East Asia. But for India to do this will not be easy given its existing pattern of trade.

Turning to APEC and its implications[3], it may be mentioned that there is uncertainty about the magnitude of the benefits to be enjoyed by Australia from an APEC free trade zone. This is primarily because of the considerable disparities that currently exist between countries in terms of their various stages of development which makes it very difficult to ensure a complete free trade area by 2020. The consequences of the free trade proposals on the areas like income distribution, environment etc, are yet to be fully realised by the APEC countries. The economic theory of customs union which helped to mobilise support in favour of the EU and NAFTA needs modification for APEC in spite of difference of opinions emerging from economic dogmatism which tends to ignore the theories of List, Myrdal and others. The implications of APEC for India is still buried in its future shape and successes. Of course India's interest can be best served if ultimately India can join the group as a member. Generally speaking, for large countries like India and China, APEC may lead to problem for sustainable development by placing more demands on the natural environment, adding to pollution and accelerating loss of biodiversity. This is quite realistic as individual countries will try to by-pass environmental regulations for the sake of retaining their shares in the international trade.

Like APEC, the concept of Indian Ocean Grouping[4] (IOG) has strong and significant potential as the process of internationalisation is taking place in some of the major Indian Ocean economies. The common features of transformation aimed in this process include : "Ensuring macro-economic stability through fiscal and monetary policies, currency devaluation to ensure realistic exchange rates, investor-friendly policies to attract flow of capital and technology, elimination of non-tariff barriers, general reduction in tariff rates and removal of exchange controls to gain outward orientation and achieving greater efficiency in resource allocation through privatisation, deregulation of prices and marketing of industrial and agricultural products". This is observed in varying degrees at different times in countries like India, Australia, South Africa, Sri Lanka, Bangladesh, Singapore and other countries in the ASEAN region, Indonesia, Thailand, Malaysia etc. The empirical results indicate that the amount of intra-industry trade taking place within IOG is at a low level but that the share of intra-industry trade in total trade between individual countries within IOG has been increasing. These countries, unlike APEC, contain far greater economic diversity and constitute a sub-region which is most populous outside China.

In this context is has been also suggested[5] that regional economic zones are usually formed to counter the protectionism and adversarial trade — degenerated forms of free trade. The three such zones viz. the EEC, NAFTA and the Japan-centred Pacific Rim region — popularly known as the Triad — are formed on the abiding principle of reciprocity. But there cannot be reciprocity unless there is equality and to be equally strong, large economies like India must also form regional economic bloc with China, Russia or any other neighbour. This regionalisation must also be effected soon — before the already formed blocs with their might and main overpower India and other economies. The trio — India, China and Russia — if formed as a regional economic bloc, can be quite formidable in terms of land mass, resources, population and economic power. It would be a fitting reply to the recent integration and transformation of the European economies as well as to such other regional blocs.

However, the relationship between India and EEC has attracted the maximum attention of the researchers in the context of discussion on European economic integration. Thus, focussing on some of the issues in the matter of India's export[6] of capital goods to the EEC, it has been noted that, between 1950 and 1970 the growth in the economy of the EEC countries was around 5 percent per annum. The next two decades witnessed much lower growth but prospects in the 1990s suggest an upturn. The erstwhile communist ruled East Germany will need an increased public investment and expenditure programme. End of cold war and armament expenditure will make possible re-orientation of scientists and technologists hitherto engaged in defence related activities to growth induced sectors. Some areas in the EC offer much scope for modernisation programme.

India's export of capital goods to developed countries including EEC vis-a-vis that of her competitors, although impressive and in recent years moving up, have not been that good as some of her competitors viz. South Korea, Hong Kong and Brazil. Exports of other developing countries to these markets are increasing at a faster rate.

A large measure of protection and import substitution policies helped India in creation of a good industrial base. One negative aspect of import substitution policies was however its ad hoc and flexible nature which prompted large scale industries to prematurely diversify into new areas to take advantage of ad hoc productwise policy of protection. In some sectors, *e.g.* in machine tools, Indian industry failed to take advantage of economies of scale and as such of export market. Besides, skewed income distribution at home resulting restricted demand for good quality products, was another attributing factor for losing competitive edge in international market.

India's liberalisation policy has to be supplemented by an overall positive attitude at the ideological level in general and at the trade union level in particular. Liberalisation should not imply merely freedom from government regulation in savings-investment decisions, nor so to undertake economic activity in response to profit potentiality. To be effective, it also calls for an outward oriented trade policies. And for this some measure of positive intervention by government in helping the Indian industries to gain a competitive edge in international market vis-a-vis her competitors should not be ruled out.

Another area of continued interest is the Maastricht Treaty — which has played the most important role in European economic integration — and its impact[7] on India and other low income economies. It has been observed that since the inception of the Indo-EU trade, India's balance of trade was unfavourable to India and it increased cumulatively. The impact of the EU on India's foreign trade depends on trade creation and trade diversion effects as a consequence of tariff and non-tariff barriers. Opinions differ about the likely impact from India's point of view. Empirically it is difficult to accept the hypothesis that the European integration will adversely affect India's trade to EU.

Moreover, the impact will vary from one product to another. For many other developing economies, the net effect is positive though small in magnitude. The Maastricht Treaty may also lead to a positive impact on the flow of FDI to such countries following the reforms through liberalisation.

The concern of the impact of an integrated Europe in the perspective of the transformation[8] of East European economies on developing economies is another important area of deliberation. Specifically, we are to consider the case of countries like Poland, Hungary and others, where the transformation process has been the most rapid and pervasive and who have also shown their eagerness to join the EC. The point of issue is whether these countries can fulfil the Maastricht criteria so that they can use the common European currency. So far as the impact of integration of such economies with the EU on India is concerned it is expected that in spite of the possibility of Europe becoming more in-ward-looking leading to diversion of aid flows and FDI away from LIEs like India to Eastern Europe, the existing level of Indo-EEC cooperation has not suffered any change. The event India Comm' 92 may be symbolic of a promising future in this area considering the interest of the EU to tap the vast and growing Indian market.

Of course, the evaluation of integration in a static framework is likely to be incomplete.[9] The long-run effects of integration may be the more fundamental and more important ones. Even if the immediate effect of the integration is on balance, trade diverting (and not trade creating), increased income in the customs union or common market and other dynamic factors could benefit the world in the long-run. During the recent decades, the competitiveness of a number of developing countries including India in the export of manufactures has increased. The industrial countries have been unwilling and unable to readjust their industrial structure. The EEC has been following its commercial policies in line with other industrial countries and it is by far the most heavily protected market among the industrialized world. The skilful combination of tariffs and tariff structures with a variety of non-tariff barriers has been turning the EC into a businessman's monopoly.

A large number of sensitive products (textiles, jute and leather goods as well as hand tools, electronic and other engineering products) exported by developing countries has been subject to tariffs and quotas and of 'semi-sensitive' ones subject to ceilings in the EEC General

System of Preferences scheme. Quantitative and discretionary limits on imports are bound to affect most adversely the weakest members of the international community, since they have apparently less to offer as a *quid pro quo* in negotiations geared to the gradual establishment of a managed trading system.

The European Community and India are at two different ends of an economic scale. It is no longer the kind of relationship that obtains between a supplier of raw materials and a manufacturer. The two sides have now reached a point where they share each other's markets and provide each other with the means of production. India should be able to usefully exchange experience about Europe's policies on the location of industries, on taxing the cities to feed the villages, and on the intelligent anticipation of the future decline of an apparently flourishing industry, and finally on the participation of people in regional and local government. The example of the European Economic Community in utilizing the availability of larger resources from the central organisation and, at the same time, in correcting any difficulties which have come about by the creation of a larger free trade area and customs union within the Community is no doubt of relevance and interest to the less integrated economies like India.

Focussing on trade prospects[10] of India and her neighbours like Bangladesh in ECM it can be said that the initial success of trade bloc in Western Europe has already started affecting the export market of such and other developing countries. Though, India and Bangladesh could increase their export flow to EU in recent period, the trend is otherwise if we consider the third world nations as a whole. A continuation of this unfavourable trend may prevent such countries to derive optimal benefit from their relative abundance of human capital which is gradually becoming important in the international market. For Bangladesh, two distinctive features in the trade relation with EU can be identified viz, an increasing dependence on EU for export market and a declining importance of EU as a supplier of foreign products. The continuation of these features may pose serious problems for Bangladesh in the near future unless measures are taken to spread her export market throughout the world. Moreover the skewed composition of export basket of Bangladesh in favour of garments in her trade with EU is another area of her weakness in this sphere.

We may now shift our discussion to some other countries and the relationship between economic adjustment and trade in the context of economic integration. China's economic integration[11] with the rest of the world is one of the important economic events in recent times. Since 1978, when China started to open her economy, she has made considerable progress in increasing her integration with other countries of the North in particular. This has led to a change in the composition of her exports in favour of industries with a high labour-capital ratio and from primary products to manufactures. Increased foreign investment and openness to international trade have, also increased business competition within China.

Illustrating the case for a small economy like Fiji[12] — an island state in South Pacific — in respect of her changing economic policies and international trading position, it is observed that for Fiji her political instability in recent period has been a major impediment to her economic growth and development. The peculiar position of this country shows the inadequacy of the general application of the structural adjustment programme to all developing countries. For instance, the institutional rigidity of the Fijian land market, the existence of a large subsistence economy and similar other factors led to hardship to the poor farmers and put pressure on inadequate urban infrastructure resulted from an increasing exodus from the rural areas to urban centres.

Finally, to look into the future integration programmes and prospects of the EU in particular and its relation with India, we find the following count down schedule to Euro: (a) In 1998, the government of the member countries to decide which member states will be the first to take part in the single currency on the basis of the covergence criteria and in the light of economic data for 1997; (b) As soon as possible after that, the date will set for introduction of Euro notes and coins, (c) Before 1.1.99, the European Council to adopt legislation on the key for capital subscription, collection of statistical information, minimum reserves, constitution of the European Central Bank etc; (d) On 1.1.99, the Council to fix irrevocably the conversion rates of currencies of participating countries both among themselves and against the Euro; (e) During 1.1.1999 to 1.1.2002, European System of Central Banks (ESCB) and public authorities in member states to monitor change-over developments in the banking and finance sectors; (f) From 1.1.2002, ESCB will gradually put Euro notes into circulation and withdraw national banknotes. The changeover to Euro will be complete by 1.7.2002 at the latest in all the participating member states. No doubt the logistics behind the transition effort is staggering but it is not impossible and everything is proceeding according to schedule.

When it will be complete, travellers to Europe will find that exchange margins and commission fees accross different countries do not eat up large chunks of value. From an Indian trader's point of view, a single European currency would be for more stable than any single currency.

It is true that the future EU may sound like a mean trade bloc but India is crucial to the EU in the post Cold War period. It is correctly predicted by many that India will be one of the poles of the future multipolar world. With growing trade relationship with India, most countries are looking at political and strategic link-ups too. In the trade front, in 1993, the value of trade stood at Rs. 47, 3813 million and the EU and India have granted each other the most favoured nation status. The EU has a host of cooperation agreements including those for energy cooperation exchanges programme in management and telecommunication training. Among the non-trade roles of the EU in India, the most important ones are those for modernisation of Indian testing laboratories, setting up of a National Accreditation Scheme to international norms and sponsoring of a European Business Information Centre and a Technology Information Centre in India. Among other non-trade area of common interest of both India and EU, we find one involving cooperation between municipalities of these two regions. The EU is also funding developmental projects in maritime transport. It has also a host of rural development projects focussing on environmental rehabilitation, agro-industry development and assistance for primary education.

Economic integration, trade and development are thus closely and probably positively interrelated in spite of the teething troubles experienced by a disintegrated world.

REFERENCES

1. Roy, K.C. and Tisdell, C.A. : Economic Integration, Regional Blocs and Non-Members in World Trade and Development : Issues and implications.
2. Tisdell, Clem : Economic Transformation and Integration in Europe — Consequences for Asian-Pacific Countries.
3. Chai, Joseph, C.H., Roy, Kartik, Tisdell, Clem : APEC and its Implications.
4. Kalirajan, K.P. and Shand, R.T. : Indian Ocean Grouping : An Emerging Reality?
5. Debnath, J.C. : The Challenge of the Triad and the Indian Response : A Note.
6. Guha Thakurata, S.N. : India's Export Possibilities of Capital Goods in the EEC.
7. Bhowmik, Debesh : Problems and Prospects of Maastricht Treaty : Its Impact on India and other LIEs.

8. Bhattacharya, Supriyo : Transformation of Eastern Europe and the Problems and Prospects of its Integration into the EEC.

9. Ghosh, Santikumar : Recent Integration and Transformation of European Economies and their Impact on India and other less Integrated Economies : A Note.

10. Malakar, Bipul and Bhattacharya, Haripada : Impact of European Union on Developing Countries with Special References to India and Bangladesh.

11. Gao, Zhicun and Tisdell, Clem : China's Economic Integration with the rest of the World.

12. Prasad, Biman C. and Tisdell, Clem : Economic Adjustment and International Trade : A Policy Dilemma for Fiji.

* All articles mentioned under References are from the Volume : Sen, Raj Kumar, Roy, K.C. and Tisdell, Clem (eds.) (1997) : *World Trade and Development : Economic Integration, Regional Blocs and Non-Members*, Atlantic Publishers and Distributors, New Delhi.

Appendix

Rapporteur's Report on the session "Recent Integration and Transformation of European Economies and their impact on India and other LIEs"

SUJIT KUMAR GHOSH

In all eight papers were presented for discussion in the IIDS First International Seminar on 'Recent Integration and Transformation of European Economies and their impact on India and other LIEs'. The authors of these papers were Dr. S.N. Guha Thakurta, Dr. J.C. Debnath, Dr. K.K. Mukherjee, Dr. Santikumar Ghosh, Prof. Rakhal Datta, Dr. Amalendu Guha, Mr. Debesh Bhowmik and Prof. Supriyo Bhattacharyya. Dr. S.N. Guha Thakurta brought into sharp focus, on the basis of a sound statistical base, the importance of India's trade relation with EEC. In his observation, most of the EEC registered significantly high growth rates, and this rate slowed down during the 1980s plagued by recessionary trend. For India, during 1965-82 the pattern of foreign trade had undergone sea changes with a fall in the export of primary commodities and rise in the export of manufactured goods. In India over the recent past, yawning trade gap loomed large before our eyes, Prof. Guha Thakurta also added that the full potential of protection and import substitution of the earlier period within the domestic economy could not be fully exploited. Moreover growth of export in many cases was found to be limited by the overwhelming competiting domestic demand. In regard to India's relation with EEC, Prof. Guha Thakurta reflected on the need for adhoc protection or income-generating export for which in particular, we have yet a long way to go.

Dr. K.K. Mukherjee's paper brought to the fore basic problems smack of close similarities. In Kenya, like other Sub-Saharan countries, extremely high population growth rate (even of the order of 3.5 per cent per annum), acute inequality of distribution, large scale rural urban migration eventuating in a situation close to high level unemployment equilibrium trap in the urban areas, external debt crisis, etc., have been causing much concern. Hence, a disquieting trend is that foreign investments are on the decline for such domestic economic crisis and internal insecurity. This must have paved the path of privatization and deregulation giving the economy a direction towards a pure market economy. At the same time, of course, it is heartening to note that consequent upon increased flow of tourist traffic in Kenya the economy holds out a larger income prospect.

Prof. Santikumar Ghosh in his paper came to reflect on economic integration of different forms and order, starting from lower to higher order. For example, he cited the cases of trade integration, factor integration marked by liberal factor movement, policy integration and so on. In Prof. Ghosh's opinion, EEC presents a case of trade liberalisation and enlargement of European markets would go in for economies of scale, security against American supremacy, harmonisation of tax and tariff issues, etc. It is also a clear case of integration through internal tariff removal. Such market and trade integrations, as Prof. Ghosh apprehends, is fraught with the danger of oligopoly growth in international economic scenario and the less integrated LDCs with weak bargaining power, obviously stand to lose vis-a-vis heavily protected market of EEC. This manifestly brings home the significance of quota negotiation at community level, not at country level. Prof. Ghosh has rightly pointed out that regionalisation runs counter to a desirable world order and what we need today is world welfare to trade-oriented policy and a coveted type of partnership between the integrating and the non-integrating countries

In the opinion of Prof. J.C. Debnath, India, Russia and China, these three Asian giants, can well form a strong Asian economic bloc which can be a good countervailing force vis-a-vis EEC.

Prof. Rakhal Datta reflected on varying degrees of economic integration, characterised as (i) economic union; (ii) customs union which inexorably leads to common market, to monetary union, and ultimately to total political economic integration; (iii) free trade areas; (iv) sectoral or partial integration; and (v) preferential application of quantitative restrictions. Prof. Datta, regarding the response of the developing countries reacting upon European economic integration, has pointed towards the development strategies of these countries, followed so far; and he has also underlined the importance of evolving a proper strategy for export diversification. Prof. Datta has also added that regional blocs have become the order of the day, but the SAARC has so far been a non-starter in economic sphere. In his view, it is time for intensifying and strengthening of mutuality of economic interests on the part of the South Asian economies and a liberal world trading system with liberal national trade policies within must create an atmosphere congenial for the growth of these economies.

Dr. Amalendu Guha's paper was presented by Dr. Raj Kumar Sen in his absence. In this paper, Dr. Guha pinpointed two counter distinctive trends with contrasting points of departure as to be experimented by Europe today; these are (i) for Western European countries from disintegration to integration and (ii) for East European countries from integration to disintegration. In his view, it is difficult to avoid the future danger of verticality in economic, political and ecological relationships between the integrated and disintegrated parts of Europe.

Sri Debesh Bhowmik expressed his opinion that Maastricht Treaty would hurt Indo-EEC trade, if the single EC would adopt more restrictive trade policies (India having the trade share with EEC amounting to 27 per cent of total export share and 30 per cent of total import share). In terms of percentage distribution of exports, France dominates Africa and Germany dominates Asia. There is now a crying need in Asia to pose a counter challenge to the dominating trading block in Europe.

Prof. Supriyo Bhattacharyya aptly focussed on the work of Adolph and Lowe, two eminent German economists, distinguishing planning as form of 'instrumental interference' from planning by command or dictated. In his discussion, Prof. Bhattacharyya pointed to the failure of command type planning in the East European economies, while at the same time maintaining the importance of planning in the sense of instrumental interference. His paper has demonstrated the significance of deriving the macro-targets-cum-objective and the major action directives from a properly formulated plan, whereas its micro analogues would be implemented through markets as a co-ordinating system. Hence, he dilated upon the 'allocative' and 'creative' functions of markets. His paper has uniquely interpreted the rationale of synchronising planning and market forces in the context of strengthening the economic position of India vis-a-vis the recent integration and transformation of European economies.

The presentations of papers followed by interesting deliberations by the participants.

Index

IIDS AND RELATED PUBLICATIONS

1. Economic Development of Poor Countries : Experiences, Obstacles and Sustainability in Global Perspective. Rs. 100/-, USD 15/-
2. From Diamond to Platinum : IEA Presidential Addresses (1977-91) Rs. 400/-, USD 30/- (Rs. 100/- for IIDS & IEA Members)
3. Development, Management and Administration : A Third World Perspective. Rs. 200/-, USD 20/-
4. Trade, Technology and Development Rs. 200/-, AUS 20/-
5. Development and Future Studies : India and the Third World. Rs. 100/-, AUS 10/-
6. Economic Reform, Liberalization and Trade in the Asia-Pacific Region. Rs. 300/-, USD 30/-
7. Fiscal Management and Fiscal Discipline in India in Recent Years Rs. 100/-, USD 15/-
8. Sustainable Development : Policy and Practice Rs. 350/-, USD 35/-

9-10. Environment and Sustainable Agricultural Development Vols. I and II Rs. 250/-, USD 25/- (each Volume)

11. Sustainable Economic Development and Environment, India and other Low Income Economies Rs. 295/-, USD 25.95
12. Economic Development and Change : South Asia and the Third World Rs. 375/-, USD 35/-
13. Economics of Small Island Nations Rs. 400/-, USD 40/-
14. Liberalisation, Adjustment and Reforms in India Rs. 200/-, USD 20/-

(N.B. : FIFTY PER CENT DISCOUNT FOR IIDS MEMBERS)

15. Development that Lasts Rs. 450/-, USD 45/- (*forthcoming*)
16. World Trade and Development : Economic Integration, Regional Blocks and Non-members Rs. 375/-, USD 35/-

17. Market Capitalism and New Forms of Socialism : The Emerging Scenario.
18. Poverty, Inequality and Policies in India.
19. Poverty and its Alleviation in SAARC
20. Tourism and Economic Development.